The Pearl

The Author

Patricia M. Kean is Lecturer
in English Language and
Literature at Lady Margaret
Hall, Oxford, and Lecturer in
the University of Oxford.
She is a member of the
Council of the Early English
Text Society.

The Pearl

AN INTERPRETATION

P. *Patricia* M. KEAN

LONDON
ROUTLEDGE & KEGAN PAUL

First published 1967
by Routledge & Kegan Paul Limited
Broadway House, 68-74 Carter Lane
London, E.C.4

Printed in Great Britain
by Richard Clay (The Chaucer Press) Ltd
Bungay, Suffolk

© *P. M. Kean 1967*

CONTENTS

v

NOTE ON THE TREATMENT OF LATIN QUOTATIONS

These are followed by an English translation except in the case of citations from Alchemical writers. These are, as a rule, of such a technical kind that I have thought it best merely to offer the version of an expert in the subject. References to the originals will be found in the notes.

ABBREVIATIONS

E.E.T.S. *Early English Text Society* (E.S. = Extra Series)

J.E.G.Ph. *Journal of English and Germanic Philology*

M.E.D. *Middle English Dictionary*, ed. S. M. Kuhn and J. Reidy.

M. Aev. *Medium Aevum*

M.L.N. *Modern Language Notes*

M.L.R. *Modern Language Review*

M.P. *Modern Philology*

O.E.D. *The Oxford English Dictionary*

P.G. J.-P. Migne, *Patrologiae Cursus Completus* . . . Series Graeca

P.L. J.-P. Migne, *Patrologiae Cursus Completus* . . . Series Latina

P.M.L.A. *Publications of the Modern Language Association of America*

R.E.S. *Review of English Studies* (N.S. = New Series)

PREFACE

MY AIM in this book has been to try to show how an English poet of the late fourteenth century, writing on a devotional theme, set about his work. I have tried to indicate the kind of material he had to draw on, and to show how he organized it in his poem. My answer to the question of what the resulting work is about, will, I hope, emerge from the book as a whole. I have not been anxious to revive in its original form the old controversy as to whether the poem is an allegory or an elegy. Much of what was formerly written on this subject, valuable as it was for the development of our understanding of the poem, seems out of focus now, in the light of a clearer knowledge of the poem's background. Full references to this earlier controversy will be found in the bibliography of E. V. Gordon's edition of *Pearl*, to which, in common with all students of the poem, I am constantly and deeply indebted. My other debts are, I hope, sufficiently admitted below, but I have tried to spare the reader too frequent notations of agreement or disagreement with others on minor points. I am, nevertheless, well aware that I owe much to my predecessors both for the stimulation of new and rewarding ideas and for the occasional clarion call to disagreement and rebuttal. I also have to thank many people for suggestions and corrections, especially Miss E. G. W. Mackenzie for her constant help; Mr. J. A. Burrow for his constructive suggestions; Fr. E. J. Stormon, S.J., for help with III, i, 'Less and More', and for permission to print the substance of an unpublished note on *partermynable;* Mrs. D. R. Sutherland and Miss Valerie Barnes for help on special points. I owe a great debt of a different kind to the late Dorothy Everett. She first introduced me to the *Pearl* twenty-five years ago. I do not know whether she would have agreed with the interpretation that I have arrived at here, but I know how much

vii

it owes to those early discussions. I have also, through the kindness of her literary executor, Dr. M. W. Porter, had access to all her notes on the poem and to an unpublished translation. My use of this material is acknowledged in its proper place. My thanks are also due to the Delegates of the Clarendon Press for permission to quote in all cases from E. V. Gordon's edition of *Pearl*; and to Mrs. Nicolete Gray for permission to use the translation of the *Divina Commedia* by Laurence Binyon, published by Macmillan and Co., and to John Murray Ltd. for permission to quote from Herbert Musurillo's translation of Gregory of Nyssa, in *From Glory to Glory*.

The *Pearl* is, textually, a difficult poem, but, here too, I have tried to cut down on detail which would have clogged the argument, and have only annotated difficult passages when it seemed essential to do so. The various editions, especially that of E. V. Gordon, provide full discussions of such difficulties, the justification for the interpretation followed here, and an account of divergent views.

A considerable part of this book is concerned with the imagery and symbolism of the *Pearl* and, in my effort to put a modern reader in a position to understand the poet's intentions as fully as possible, I have made an attempt to trace out what I should like to call the 'semantics' of the individual images and motifs—that is, to explain how certain ideas came to attach themselves to certain figures, and how groups of images tended to form into clusters, and, in the process, to influence and modify one another. In doing this I am aware that I am often in danger of writing in too general a way—of explaining the history of the image at the expense of its particular appearance in the poem. It seemed, however, best to take a reasonably wide sweep in order to give the reader the kind of background of feelings and associations which the original audience must have had; although it is not, of course, always possible to be certain how much could have been known to any given individual at any given moment. Nevertheless, it seems to me that the style of Christian writing in the Middle Ages was, in spite of much surface variation, so essentially homogeneous, and so continuous in its development, that works which were, perhaps, quite unknown to a particular writer, may still have left their mark on the tradition he uses. For this reason I have not hesitated to cite writers—St. Ephraem the Syrian is a case in point—who show the tradition as it was formulated early in the Christian period, and who, although they were not known to later Western writers, show ideas and associations which, demonstrably, were known. It often happens, too, that intermediate links are not forthcoming. In such cases it seems to me useful to cite late works—and I have drawn particularly on the English poets of the seventeenth-century metaphysical school. The fact that they so often provide apt illustrations of ideas and metaphors used by Middle English poets can be accounted for in two ways. First, there is the undoubted continuity of English poetry to be taken into account, due to the fact that fourteenth- and fifteenth-century works were kept in circulation and also, I think, to the contents of some of the poetic miscellanies of the sixteenth century. Secondly, the poets of the seventeenth century used Early Christian and patristic sources freely, and were therefore independently using much of the same material as the earlier poets. This fact at least attests to the vitality and continued importance of the imagery; and the contrast between its treatment by poets of the seventeenth and of the fourteenth centuries may help the modern reader to approach and understand the *Pearl*.

I have designed the book to follow the poem as closely as possible, through its four parts—the proem; the dream and its setting; the instruction and revelation which are the purpose of the dream; and the author's final coda. This has involved a certain amount of overlapping, especially between the chapters on the imagery of the proem and the symbolism of the main body of the poem. Nevertheless, it seemed to me that the gain in clarity by following the poet's own structural lines, outweighed the inconvenience of occasional repetition, and I must hope that the reader will agree with me.

What strikes me most forcibly when I read the poem is its unique quality, and I must also hope that this has not been obscured by an attempt to relate it to a common medieval tradition. For this reason, I have been more intent to try to indicate its place and special achievement within this common tradition than to talk much of sources. I do not know, in the last resort, whether the poet was deeply read in the works of St. Bernard and in Dante's *Divina Commedia*. I think that the weight of the evidence suggests that he had knowledge of both, but incontrovertible proof does not seem to me to be either possible, or very important. It does seem to me that in spirit and very often in style—taking the word in its widest sense—he is nearer to these two writers than to any others among his predecessors. I have therefore illustrated his ideas by much reference to St. Bernard, and I have re-examined the case for his knowledge of Dante. But I have also tried to do what seems to me more important, to show what was his actual and individual achievement as a writer of English poetry, and to demonstrate that he was the master of a style that was brilliantly adapted to his purpose.

P. M. K.

Oxford, 1966.

Part One
PROEM

I

PURPOSE AND STRUCTURE

I

LIKE THE GREAT MAJORITY of medieval poems the *Pearl* is provided with an opening section which states the themes and lays
down the main lines of the development. Medieval rhetorical
teaching was at its weakest on the subject of structure, but it did
treat of the main divisions of the work, and of these the *exordium*
was the most important.[1] Dorothy Everett has shown how
Chaucer built up his *exordium* in the *Parlement of Foules*, on a
pattern of rhetorical figures.[2] J. A. W. Bennett pointed out how
important the use of a standard literary *topos* also was in its
structure.[3] The *Pearl*-poet, as we shall see, uses the same
methods in his *exordium*: he follows out a plan based on the use
of the figures of rhetoric, and he also builds the opening on
a familiar *topos*.

Like the *Parlement*, *Pearl* is, moreover, a Dream Vision, and
for poetry of this sort the opening section is of special importance; not only has the foundation of the work to be laid in a
general way but a relation must also be established between the
problems of the waking world and the experience, usually a
consolatory one, of the country of the dream. The vision, as a
rule, comes at a crucial moment—when 'Paene caput tristis

---

[1] The poet of *Pearl* shows himself aware of the possibilities of the
art of rhetoric in all his works. Cf. D. Everett, *Essays on Middle English
Literature* (Oxford, 1955), p. 93. For the Latin treatises on the subject,
see E. Faral, *Les Arts Poétiques du xiie et du xiiie Siècle* (Paris, 1923).
For the art of the *exordium*, see E. R. Curtius, *European Literature and
the Latin Middle Ages* (New York, 1953), pp. 85 ff.

[2] Op. cit., pp. 103 ff.

[3] *The Parlement of Foules* (Oxford, 1957), pp. 26 ff. On topics as a
branch of rhetoric, see Curtius, op. cit., pp. 79 ff.

3

merserat hora meum', or, 'Nel mezzo del cammin di nostra vita', when the right way has been left behind.⁴ The poet is assailed by doubts before sleep overtakes him—whether there is clear cause for his grief, or whether his uneasiness, like Chaucer's in the *Parlement of Foules*, is less sharply defined.

The Dream, which will follow lines indicated in the opening, will bring these problems into the foreground, subject them to examination, and suggest consolation, if not a complete solution. Chaucer solved the problem of establishing a suitable basis for an extremely complex structure in the proems of his three vision poems by the use of what Clemen has called a 'highly complex art of allusion and reference,' which can become, for example in the *House of Fame*, even an 'art of the initiates'.⁵ He also uses the art of rhetoric in a particularly subtle way to provide links between one part of a work and another, and to prepare for developments to come.

Chaucer's learned references are comparatively easy to detect. In the proem of the *Parlement of Foules*, for example, he lays a clear trail by using the *Somnium Scipionis* quite overtly as the central prop of the whole system. In the same way the rhetorical structure of the opening lines is clear cut and easy to follow. He is using a familiar *topos*, a paradoxical statement about love which is made the basis of an argument, and which demands elaboration according to the rules of what later writers called 'speche and eloquence'. The poet of *Pearl* is also, I believe, using an accepted *topos*—that of the contrast of earthly and heavenly riches,⁶ but his statement of it is less obvious, and he develops it in a different way, although he, too, draws heavily on the figures of rhetoric. One reason for this is, perhaps, his love of suspension. Throughout his poem he holds back the full meaning of what he has to say, allowing the obvious meaning to

⁴ Boethius, *de Consolatione Philosophiae*, I, m. i, 18. Chaucer translates 'the sorwful houre hadde almoost dreynt myn heved'. Dante, *Inferno*, i, 1.

⁵ *Chaucer's Early Poetry* (London, 1963), p. 67.

⁶ Sister Mary Vincent Hillmann also sees the contrast of earthly and heavenly treasure as a major theme in *Pearl*: see *The Pearl* (New Jersey, 1961), p. xiii. As will appear, I am not otherwise in agreement with her interpretation.

make its impact before he reveals more than a hint of other senses.

Another reason may be that Chaucer works openly under continental influence. He draws deliberately on the technique of French and Italian poetry, and in doing so avoids traditional English forms and stylistic devices. With the poet of *Pearl* the case is quite different. He writes within the typically, and indeed exclusively, English tradition of the alliterative technique of the fourteenth-century revival. In *Pearl*, it is true, the stanza form is of ultimately continental origin, as are all the stanza forms of this type in Middle English, but it is a stanza which was not uncommon in England in the fourteenth century.[7]

The native tradition before the second half of the fourteenth century had not made much use of formal rhetoric, and certainly knew little of it as a structural principle.[8] Nor had it developed the kind of allusion to a common background of knowledge and reading with which Chaucer seems so much at home. An obvious reason for this is that such allusions would have no meaning to the predominantly unlearned audiences of almost everything that was written in English verse before the second half of the fourteenth century. For a romance writer like the poet or translator of *Sir Orfeo*, for example, the classical story is so much straightforward narrative material: it could not occur to him to explore its ramifications into a world of ideas as Chaucer does for the story of Scipio's dream. In the rare cases when audiences may have been more select and better-read we can sometimes detect a difference. The thirteenth-century author of the *Owl and the Nightingale* treats his material with a blend of seriousness and light-heartedness which is not too far from Chaucer's own attitude in the *House of Fame*, and he, too,

[7] For a list of poems in which it is used, see E. V. Gordon, *Pearl* (Oxford, 1953), p. 87, n. 1.

[8] It seems likely that for English poets, up to and including Chaucer, rhetoric was primarily a part of grammar, and was known through school textbooks rather than specialist treatises. Geoffroi de Vinsauf was known to Chaucer, and was often named in the fifteenth century—perhaps because he worked in England. (See J. J. Murphy, 'A New Look at Chaucer and the Rhetoricians', *R.E.S.*, N.S., XV (1964), pp. 1 ff.)

seems to have utilized new ideas and discoveries to give point and zest to his work.[9] On the whole, however, a poet who, though he might be aware of the new models and *newe science*, still preferred to keep to the old forms would be unlikely to bring as much of his technique to the surface of his work as Chaucer was able to do. It is for this reason that it has so long been a matter of dispute whether or not the *Pearl*-poet really drew on Dante, whose influence is so easily traced in Chaucer's work; or just how much use he made of the great French exemplar of later poetry, the *Roman de la Rose*, which Chaucer quotes freely;[10] whether he was acquainted with philosophical writers like Boethius and Alain de Lille, whom Chaucer regularly names. That he was a learned poet cannot now be seriously doubted; but, as H. L. Savage says, 'the author's learning does not strike one on a first perusal. It is not evidenced by an imposing body of quotation and reference . . . One becomes aware of the range and depth of the *Gawain*-poet's reading, not by his own recital of the books he has read, but by recognizing the contribution which a Peter Lombard, a Thomas Aquinas or a John Mandeville has made to the thought he expresses.'[11]

There is another fact, too, which makes the tracks of the *Pearl*-poet at times less easy to follow than those of Chaucer. If he is in a sense old-fashioned in keeping to traditional English forms, there is also a sense in which his material itself is less new than that of some of his contemporaries. He is, even more than Langland, the poet of the Bible. *Patience* and *Purity* actually belong to the genre—possibly an old-fashioned one—of the verse paraphrase.[12] *Pearl* is also in part a paraphrase—the

---

[9] See A. C. Cawley, 'Astrology in the *Owl and the Nightingale*', *M.L.R.*, XLVI (1951), pp. 161 ff.

[10] The reference in *Purity*, 1057, shows that this work was known to him.

[11] *The Gawain-Poet: Studies in His Personality and Background* (Chapel Hill, 1956), pp. 13–14.

[12] On verse paraphrases of the Bible in Middle English, see J. E. Wells, *A Manual of Writings in Middle English* (New Haven, Connecticut, 1926), chapter viii, pp. 297 ff. Psalm versions were always popular and continued to attract serious poets for some centuries, but, as far

description of the New Jerusalem follows the corresponding passages in the Book of Revelations closely. But, more than this, the poem as a whole is built up on a network of biblical quotation and allusion.

That this is so, has never, of course, been doubted. All editors provide copious reference to the Bible in illustration of the text. The proem, however, is sometimes thought of as a primarily secular piece of writing, in deliberate contrast to the technique used later in the poem. It is claimed that it uses the typical motifs of courtly love poetry—presumably with the aim of drawing an unsuspecting reader on so that the more austere matter which follows can take him unawares. The wording of l. 11 with its *luf-daungere* and the description of the garden of spices and herbs has been derived directly from the *Roman de la Rose*. Indeed, the first biblical reference to be pointed out by any editor is that of ll. 31–2, to the grain which dies to live of 1 Cor. 15, 36–8 and John 12, 24–5. It is, clearly, of the utmost importance to decide whether the journey which we are to make with the poet takes its starting-point from the world of the *Roman* or from that of the Bible. I believe that there is, in fact, no change in the material here, and that the proem is as much a tissue of biblical allusions as the later part of the poem. But before examining the details it will be best to make a general survey of the structure of the proem.

---

as biblical translation in general was concerned, after the unambitious versions, mostly in couplet form, of the early Middle English period there seems to have been a gap. Then come the more elaborate renderings of the late fourteenth and fifteenth centuries, some of the most important closely linked to the *Pearl* group. *Pety Job* ('the ix lessons of þe diryge whych Iob made in his tribulacyon'), uses the same twelve-line stanza, and, at times, the same phrases (see Gordon, p. 87). The strophic versions of the Old Testament (Wells, p. 398) and the *Pistill of Susan*, also testify to a strong interest in the North and West Midlands in translation and adaptation of a technically ambitious kind. It seems possible that the *Pearl*-poet was, at least in part, responsible for the revival and transformation of a temporarily outdated form.

The poet uses the first of his twenty sections as a proem to introduce his Vision. He describes the circumstances which led up to it and, even more important, his mental state before he fell asleep. The form he has given his poem, a division, except for one problematical group of six stanzas,[13] into twenty sets of five, means that his proem is unusually brief—in the *Parlement of Foules*, only half the length of *Pearl*, Chaucer devoted 91 lines to the proem. Sixty lines form a brief introduction to a poem of 1,212 lines, and the result is an extreme economy of organization and a condensation of meaning which calls for the greatest attention on the reader's part if he is to appreciate the careful laying down of the lines on which the whole work is to develop. The best way to understand the poet's purpose will be to study the rhetorical structure of his opening. The devices of formal rhetoric were the natural tools of a poet of this period.

The poem opens with an *exclamatio* which gives the *propositio* to be elaborated, in epigrammatic, if not proverbial form:

> Perle, plesaunte to prynces paye
> To clanly clos in golde so clere![14]

Chaucer began the *Parlement* with a descriptive formula cast in a similarly exclamatory form:

> The lyf so short, the craft so long to lerne,
> Th'assay so hard, so sharp the conquerynge,
> The dredful joye, alwey that slit so yerne—[15]

---

[13] Section xv. See Gordon, p. 88.

[14] Osgood (*The Pearl*, Boston, etc., 1906) and Gollancz (*Pearl*, London, 1921), both punctuated these lines as an exclamation. Gordon's comma after *clere* does not seem to me to be an improvement. *Purity* and *Patience* also begin with 'sentences' describing the subject-virtue. All quotation from *Pearl* is based on Gordon's edition, though I have sometimes altered the punctuation.

[15] *Parlement of Foules*, 1–3. All quotations from Chaucer are taken from *The Works of Geoffrey Chaucer*, ed. F. N. Robinson, 2nd edn (Cambridge, Mass., 1957).

and Guillaume de Lorris used a 'sentence' about the nature of dreams to start the *Roman de la Rose*:

> Maintes genz dient que en songes
> N'a se fables non e mençonges.

(Many people say that dreams are nothing but deceitful lies.[16])

That the pearl is a jewel fit for princes, most suitably set in gold, may seem a commonplace. In fact, it is a well-established formula, and it has, therefore, something of the weightiness of a proverb, and something of the proverb's force in clinching an argument. As early as the third century Tertullian could use it in support of an assertion:

> Non es diligentior deo, uti tu quidem Scythicas et Indicas gemmas et rubentis maris grana candentia non plumbo non aere non ferro neque argento quoque oblaquees sed delectissimo et insuper operosissimo de scrobibus auro.

> (Your care for your property is not greater than God's: yet you mount Scythian and Indian gems and the gleaming pearls of the Red Sea, neither in lead nor bronze nor iron, nor even silver, but in choice gold carefully separated from its dross.[17])

Even so, he concludes, God will choose carefully the vessel in which He puts the soul.

In the ninth century Milo of St. Armand used the same formula in verse to make a neat point in combination with the *topos* of affected modesty:

> Margarita micans, praecellens unio gemmas,
> Cum te debuerim ter cocto ornare metallo,
> Sit veniale mihi, quia clausi indoctior aere.

> (Shining Pearl, all gems excelling,
> To you thrice-fired gold is owing—
> Alas, I've only harsher bronze for your enclosing![18])

---

[16] All quotations from the *Roman* are taken from the edition of E. Langlois, *Société des Anciens Textes Français*, 5 vols. (Paris, 1914–24).

[17] *De Resurrectione Carnis*, 7. I quote from the text and translation of E. Evans, *Tertullian's Treatise on the Resurrection* (London, 1960), pp. 22–3.

[18] *De Sobrietate*, II, 44–6, *Monumenta Germaniae Historica: Poetae Latini Aevi Carolini*, III (Berlin, 1896), p. 646.

9

Latin hymn-writers continued to make use of the formula, and it finds its way with or without the association with the king and his crown into other vernacular poetry besides *Pearl*.[19]

The proem, therefore, opens with a conventional formula, an exclamatory *propositio* which would be familiar enough to amount to a 'sentence'. The poet's aim is obvious: such formulae were used because they fitted in with the whole purpose of the *exordium*, which was to put the reader in the right frame of mind—to start his mind working on the desired lines, before he comes to the main body of the work. The point of this particular formula is that it treats of the real pearl, as it exists in the actual world, and thus forms the proper jumping-off point for the elaboration of the *topos* of the contrast of earthly and heavenly treasure.

The extension of a formula into a fully elaborated symbolism of the pearl in the poem as a whole comes later: here the poet speaks—though in terms capable of more than one interpretation—of the actual jewel, and praises in it all the brilliance and beauty of earthly treasure. The paraphrase of the opening lines with which the poem ends brings out the latent ambiguity of his words—but it is an ambiguity only to be understood when we have reached the end, and which should not blur the sharpness of the opening description. The final lines are:

> He gef vus to be his homly hyne
> And precious perle3 vnto his pay,

where the linking phrase with which the stanza opens is 'To pay þe Prince'—of Heaven not of earth—and where the golden setting has been replaced by the sharply contrasted idea of the *homly hyne*—the servants of the household.

Chaucer and Guillaume de Lorris both work their opening formulae into the texture of their poems by a complex sequence of rhetorical figures. Analysis of the first two stanzas of the *Pearl* shows the same surprising dominance of *amplificatio* over narrative.

[19] For examples, see Gordon, note to these lines. For further material, in which symbolical senses are present, see below, II, iii, pp. 161 ff.

Purpose and Structure

The opening *propositio* is followed by a piece of *descriptio*. This, in ll. 5–8 follows the conventional pattern for the description of human beauty. As E. Faral points out, description, in medieval rhetorical theory and practice, never entirely loses its connection with panegyric or denunciation.[20] Its aim is always to persuade—to induce the acceptance of the person or thing described as either good or bad. Here the first two lines of the *descriptio* are intended to persuade the reader to regard the pearl as of special excellence:

> Oute of oryent, I hardyly saye,
> Ne proued I neuer her precios pere.   (3–4)

They are reinforced, through the figure called *expolitio* (repetition of the same idea in different terms), by ll. 7–8:

> Quere-so-euer I jugged gemmeȝ gaye,
> I sette hyr sengeley in synglere.

The next four lines begin the story—with another *exclamatio*—and there is further *expolitio*, since l. 10 repeats and amplifies l. 9:

> Allas! I leste hyr in on erbere;
> Þurȝ gresse to grounde hit fro me yot.
> I dewyne, fordolked of luf-daungere
> Of þat pryuy perle wythouten spot.   (9–12)

The first four lines of the next stanza continue the story, but also introduce a fresh rhetorical device, that of *circumlocutio*: the pearl becomes 'þat wele'—

> Syþen in þat spote hit fro me sprange,
> Ofte haf I wayted, wyschande þat wele,
> Þat wont watȝ whyle deuoyde my wrange
> And heuen my happe and al my hele.   (13–16)

There is more use of *expolitio* in ll. 17–18:

> Þat dotȝ bot þrych my hert þrange,
> My breste in bale bot bolne and bele.

[20] *Les Arts Poétiques*, p. 76.

Lines 19–21 continue the story with, if my punctuation and
interpretation are accepted,[21] yet another *expolitio* in l. 21, which
repeats 19–20:

> ꝫet þoȝt me neuer so swete a sange
> As stylle stounde let to me stele—
> For soþe þer fleten to me fele.

The stanza ends with an *exclamatio* followed by an apostrophe
to the earth, and a final repetition—'iuele . . . perle':

> To þenke hir color so clad in clot!
> O moul, þou marreȝ a myry iuele,
> My priuy perle wythouten spotte.   (22–24)

In these twenty-four lines, in fact, only six or seven carry the
actual narrative—and in estimating the amount of formal
rhetoric contained in them we have taken no account of the
minor figures of speech. It would, however, be a mistake to
imagine that this careful use of the figures of *amplificatio* means
that the poet's aim is simply the rather naïvely expressed one of
Geoffrey de Vinsauf, who bids the writer use every possible
device 'longius ut sit opus'.[22] The *Pearl*-poet devises his amplification to convey to the reader what is more important to him
than the slight narrative frame—the themes and ideas which his
poem is to develop: and, though he uses what is, technically,
amplification to do this, he nevertheless achieves his object with
the greatest economy.

3

The opening *descriptio* is used, first, to introduce the Dreamer
in the first person:[23]

[21] See below, p. 22.

[22] *Poetria Nova*, III, A, 229 (Faral, op. cit., p. 204).

[23] The *Roman de la Rose* also passes from the opening 'sentence' to
the poet's personal comment—'qui ce voudra, por fol m'en teigne'
(14)—and the *Parlement* has the same insistence on the pronouns of
the first person: 'Al this mene *I* by Love, that *my* felynge / Astonyeth
. . .' (4–5). The establishment of the presence of the Dreamer/Poet
is an important function of the *exordium* in poems of this kind.

> Oute of oryent, *I* hardyly saye,
> Ne proued *I* neuer her precios pere.
> So rounde, so reken in vche araye,
> So smal, so smoþe her sydeʒ were,
> Quere-so-euer *I* jugged gemmeʒ gaye,
> *I* sette hyr sengeley in synglere. (3–8)

Secondly, it is with these lines that the suggestion that the pearl stands for a human being as well as a jewel begins to develop. It was already implicit in the use of the feminine pronoun—*hit* is only used when the poet speaks of the fall of the pearl to the ground, when the metaphor depends on the idea of an object which can drop and be lost.[24] The line

> So smal, so smoþe her sydeʒ were,

is equally appropriate to the description of the jewel and of feminine beauty. It is cast in terms conventional for both topics,[25] and the resulting ambiguity helps to hold in suspense the full recognition of the fact that the dropped pearl stands for a human being lost through death. Later the poet paraphrases these lines, just as he later paraphrases the opening ones. The Dreamer sees 'a faunt', 'a mayden of menske', who is described:

> Þat gracios gay wythouten galle,
> So smoþe, so smal, so seme slyʒt,
> Ryseʒ vp in hir araye ryalle,
> A precios pyece in perleʒ pyʒt. (189–92)

It is only at the beginning of the next section (l. 241) that the poet's form of address completes the identification of the maiden with the pearl. His favourite process of suspension is, in fact, gone through in the reverse direction; whereas the jewel

[24] The shift of gender may not, however, be as significant as it would be in modern English. See Gordon, p. 46, note to l. 10.

[25] In the Scottish *Legend to St. Margaret*, 17, the pearl is 'lytel and rond alsa' (cf. Lydgate's *Life of St. Margaret*, 34, 'rounde and smal'). These and other instances are discussed below, pp. 155–8. Examples of *smal* and *smoþe* in descriptions of feminine beauty are also common. Chaucer's line (*Troilus and Criseyde*, III, 1248), 'Hire sydes longe, flesshly, smothe, and white' is very close to Pearl in phrasing, but the adjectives are used for a purely sensual effect with no hint of any other meaning.

hints at the person in the opening, in the later passage it is only gradually that the person is allowed to recall the jewel.

The roundness and smoothness of the pearl emphasizes the fact that it is a perfect sphere—a jewel without facets. It is through this aspect:

> For hit is wemleȝ, clene and clere,
> And endeleȝ rounde,[26] (737–8)

that it is a symbol of perfection. Much the same thing is said of the beryl and the pearl in *Purity*:

> As þe beryl bornyst byhovez be clene,
> Þat is sounde on uche a syde and no sem habes,
> Wythouten maskle oþer mote, as margerye-perle.[27] (554–6)

The pentangle in *Sir Gawain and the Green Knight* is also 'endeleȝ', and it is this fact as much as its five-fold nature which seems to appeal to the poet, and to enable him to treat it, as he does the spherical jewels, as a perfection symbol.[28]

Lines 5–6 of the proem, however, like the opening formula, only hint at the symbolism of the pearl. The poet is careful to

[26] For this aspect of the symbolism of the pearl, see below, pp. 141 ff. *Wemleȝ*, *clene*, and *clere* can all have a moral significance, 'pure', 'free from sin'. They are also all associated with visual effects. *Wem* can mean 'stain', 'tarnish', and *clene* and *clere* can both mean 'brilliant' or 'translucent'. Further, all three can imply freedom from knots or protuberances. All these groups of senses are appropriate to the context, and the poet probably plays on them. (See *O.E.D.*, clean, a. I; II, 4; IV. Clear, a. I; IV; V, 20b. Wem sb. 1; 2; 3.)

[27] R. J. Menner ed., *Yale Studies in English*, LXI (New Haven and London, 1920). All quotations are from this edition. There is the same play on the senses of *clene* here as in the passage from *Pearl*. *Sem* could mean the joining of two surfaces, usually with a ridge or other raised joint. (*O.E.D.*, seam, sb. 1, I, 1.) It can also, like *wem*, mean a scar. Alternatively it could represent the rather rare *seam*, sb. 4, from O.N. *saumr*, a nail, meaning in English a rivet for fastening overlapping edges. Whichever way we explain the word, 'no sem habes' means smooth, in one piece, without joint or protuberance.

[28] *Sir Gawain and the Green Knight*, ed. J. R. R. Tolkien and E. V. Gordon (Oxford, 1936). All quotations are from this edition. For the description of the pentangle, see ll. 625 ff., and for a discussion of its meaning, see J. A. Burrow, *A Reading of* Sir Gawain and the Green Knight (London, 1965), pp. 41 ff.

14

prepare his reader for what is to come, but he never allows his hints to become explicit enough to obscure the purpose of the opening section which is to present the pearl as a real, not a symbolical treasure.

In the last four lines of the stanza the loss of the pearl is described in direct narrative, and the setting of this loss is given by the introduction, in l. 9, of the *erber*, the *locus* of the proem as a whole. It is the place where the Dreamer falls asleep and it is the basis of much of the complex imagery of this section. What kind of a garden this is and what precise significance it has in the structure of the poem is a question to be left for the next chapter. Here, however, it is necessary at least to try to fix the meaning of the word.

The term *erber/herber* was common in the fourteenth and fifteenth centuries and was used in a number of different contexts.[29] It could mean a grassy plot, and also a space where herbs grew, through its association with *herba*, 'grass' and *herbarium*, 'collection of herbs'. These meanings were added to when it was associated, after the pronunciation had, by a normal sound-change altered from (h)*erber* to (h)*arber*, with Latin *arbor*, 'a tree', and Italian *arborata*, 'a bower', a 'shady retreat'. Thus, *The Flower and Leaf*, (about 1400) describes a *herber* as 'shapin . . . rofe and all / As is a pretty parlour', and Chaucer also seems to imply this meaning in *Legend of Good Women*, Prologue B, 97 ff. Since these instances probably precede the change in sound, they may well derive from the common medieval feeling for a garden as a place of retreat. An *erber* could also be an orchard of fruit trees, and this sense is well evidenced for the fourteenth century. It seems likely that it arose not so much through an early linking to *arbor* as because fruit trees are naturally associated with the grass they are planted in. So the word 'orchard' itself derives from Old English *wyrtȝeard*, an enclosure of plants, just as French *verger* was derived from Latin *viridarium*, a green place. The word *erber* therefore brings together the ideas of greenness and grass, of herbs and fruit trees, of shade and a leafy retreat. It

[29] See *O.E.D.* under arbour. *M.E.D.* will deal with this word under herber in a forthcoming volume.

has, too, another association in Middle English which the dictionary has not noted. It is used more than once to suggest the phrase, from the Song of Songs, *hortus conclusus*, in poems addressed to the Virgin. For example, a carol by John Audelay, which makes complicated play with the flower from the root of Jesse has these lines:

> The sede hereof was Godis sond,
> That God himselue sew with his hond;
> In Bedlem in that hole lond
> [In] medis here herbere ther he hir fond;
> This blisful floure
> Sprang neuer bot in Maris boure.[30]

The *erber*, therefore, can have associations in Middle English with the imagery of the Song of Songs. The line that follows in *Pearl* which describes the poet's state of mind as he enters this garden 'I dewyne, fordolked of luf-daungere' has been connected by modern editors with the typical terminology of courtly romance and Love Vision, and in particular with the *Roman de la Rose*. In the *Roman*, Daungier is a character, and stands for the power of love over the Lover exercised to his harm or deprivation. It seems likely that the word *luf-daungere* would carry some overtones from writings of this sort, and there is no doubt that in the world of the *Roman*, lovers are accustomed to pine and that love is often spoken of as wounding. But the line as a whole would be hard to parallel from the *Roman*, whereas it is very close indeed to the phrasing of the Song of Songs 2, 5:

Fulcite me floribus, stipate me malis, quia amore langueo.

(Stay me up with flowers, compass me about with apples: because I languish with love,[31])

---

[30] R. L. Greene, *The Early English Carols* (Oxford, 1935), no. 172, p. 129. Cf. *Hymns to the Virgin and Christ*, ed. F. J. Furnival, *E.E.T.S.*, 24 (1867), p. 6: Heil be þou marie þat art flour of alle, / As roose in eerbir so reed!

[31] Translations of the Vulgate text are in all cases taken from the Douay version.

and 5, 7–8:

Invenerunt me custodes, qui circumeunt civitatem, percusserunt me et vulneraverunt me; tulerunt pallium meum mihi custodes murorum.

Adiuro vos, filiae Ierusalem, si inveneritis dilectum meum ut nuntietis ei, quia amore langueo.

(The keepers that go about the city found me. They struck me and wounded me. The keepers of the walls took away my veil from me.

I adjure you, O daughters of Jerusalem, if you find my beloved, that you tell him that I languish with love.)

'I dewyne, fordolked of luf-daungere' is a good rendering of 'vulneraverunt me . . . quia amore langueo', and if we understand 'luf-daungere' as implying enforced separation from the beloved object,[32] we are close to the Song of Songs 5, 6–8, where the Bride and Bridegroom are in fact separated. To use words which echo the Song of Songs and at the same time have associations with secular love poetry, as *luf-daungere* must have had, would not seem incongruous to a medieval writer.[33] The poet's purpose is not, it is certain, to invoke any clear-cut allegorical interpretation of the Song of Songs. The echoes of it serve, rather, to help to establish the seriousness of his theme—we are warned that his loss will not prove an ordinary or unimportant one—and to prepare the way for other references, as he describes the *erber*. The list of spices[34] recalls the Song of Songs 4, 14:

[32] On the meaning of *daungere* in the literature of Courtoisie, see C. S. Lewis, *The Allegory of Love* (Oxford, 1938), pp. 364 ff. His sense B, the 'power to withold' is the one in question here.

[33] *Quia amore langueo* is used as a refrain in lyrics of divine love, but is left untranslated. In other respects, however, the phrasing of such lyrics is indistinguishable from that of lyrics of secular love. Cf. 'In a tabernacle of a toure', Carleton Brown, *Religious Lyrics of the Fourteenth Century* (Oxford, 1924), no. 132, in which the Virgin complains: 'I longe for loue . . .'; 'I byd, I byde in grete longyng . . .'; 'I loue . . . I pleyne'; 'Loke on þy loue þus languysshyng, / Late vs neuer fro other disseuere.' Although the phrasing is deliberately modelled on the Song of Songs here, as the refrain shows, there is nothing to distinguish it from that of a secular lyric on the sorrows of love.

[34] The list of spices given in *Pearl* in the fourth stanza does not, of

Proem

Nardus et crocus, fistula et cinnamomum cum universis lignis
Libani; myrrha et aloê cum omnibus primis unguentis.

(Spikenard and saffron, sweet cane and cinnamon, with all the
trees of Libanus, myrrh and aloês, with all the chief perfumes.)

Their scent—

> A fayr reflayr ȝet fro hit flot—(46)

is described in terms which are reminiscent of the Song of
Songs 4, 16, 'Let the aromatical spices thereof flow'. This scent
is associated with the sleep which follows in 5, 2 in the Song of
Songs 'I sleep and my heart watcheth'. In *Pearl*:

> Suche odour to my herneȝ schot;
> I slode vpon a slepyng-slaȝte. (58-9)

These allusions help to fix the *erber* as a garden that is in some
way linked to the *hortus conclusus*. But first the Dreamer tells
us how he haunts the place of his loss and of his uncontrollable
grief for something:

> Þat wont watȝ whyle deuoyde my wrange
> And heuen my happe and al my hele. (15-16)

---

course, correspond to those listed in the Song of Songs or in Revelations. The reason for this is, I think, that the biblical spices, for example
spikenard, myrrh, nard, suggest oils and resinous extracts rather than
the growing, flowering plants which the poet requires to carry out the
idea of the seeds growing from the grave. In fact, spice lists of this
type, as Gordon notes (p. 48, note to 43-4), are a commonplace in
vernacular literature. *The Roman de la Rose* has one which has the
clove and ginger in common with *Pearl*. (The Chaucerian version has
clowegelofre (1368), corresponding to *gilofre* in *Pearl*. Gordon is, I
think, wrong in glossing this as the clove-scented pink, which would
not fit the context.) But the Garden of Love of the *Roman* is not the
only context in which the device is found. *Annot and Johon* has it (see
English Lyrics of the Thirteenth Century, Carleton Brown, Oxford,
1932, pp. 136 ff.), with *gromyl, gylofre,* and *gyngyure* in common with
Pearl. Here the herbs have nothing to do with courtly love, but are
used allegorically to describe Annot. The *Pistill of Susan* also has a
long list, with only the peony in common with *Pearl*. Here, the spice-
plants grow in a biblical garden—as the poet observes: Spyces speden
to spryng / In erbers enhaled (103-4).

18

Purpose and Structure

These lines suggest a relationship to the pearl which is un-expected: the jewel is receding farther into the background, and other senses and associations are beginning to develop. We can begin to see the careful building up of a section of the poem on a structure of biblical allusion. In the first stanza the Dreamer has spoken of himself as one with a more than ordinary interest in jewels. He 'judges them', that is 'appraises them', and this prepares us for the Jeweller of later stanzas. The figure of the Jeweller is, of course, to be compared to the Merchant of the parable of the pearl of great price in Matthew 13, 45–6. But, when this parable is directly referred to in ll. 730–5, the Dreamer is advised not to regret the pearl he has lost but to purchase another pearl, which, though it is not the pearl of the proem, is yet still very much his own—the pronoun *þy* is significant:

'I rede þe forsake þe worlde wode
And porchace þy perle maskelles.' (743–4)

The pearl of the proem, therefore, is certainly not the pearl of Matthew 13, nor is the Jeweller the wise merchant of the parable. But there is another part of the Bible in which pearls and jewellers are important—the Book of Revelations, on which the poet draws so heavily later on. Here the pearl is important in the description of the New Jerusalem (21, 21), but it also features, with a different significance, in the description in chapter 18, 11–17, of the destruction of Babylon. Here, too, there are mourning jewellers, and princes who are pleased by treasure. The passage also has links with the imagery of the garden of the Song of Songs.

The whole passage runs:

Et negotiatores terrae flebunt et lugebunt super illam, quoniam merces eorum nemo emet amplius;
  merces auri et argenti et lapidis pretiosi et margaritae et byssi et purpurae et serici et cocci et omne lignum thyinum et omnia vasa eboris et omnia vasa de lapide pretioso et aeramento et ferro et marmore;
  et cinnamomum et odoramentorum et unguenti et turis et vini et olei et similae et tritici et iumentorum et ovium et

equorum et raedarum et mancipiorum et animarum hominum.

Et poma desiderii animae tuae discesserunt a te, et omnia pinguia et praeclara perierunt a te, et amplius illam iam non invenient.

Mercatores horum, qui divites facti sunt, ab ea longe stabunt propter timorem tormentorum eius flentes ac lugentes.

Et dicentes: Vae, vae civitas illa magna, quae amicta erat bysso et purpura et cocco et deaurata erat auro et lapide pretioso et margaritis;

quoniam una hora destitutae sunt tantae divitiae!

(And the merchants of the earth shall weep and mourn over her; for no man shall buy their merchandise any more.

Merchandise of gold and silver, and precious stones, and of pearls, and fine linen and purple, and silk and scarlet, and all thyine wood, and all manner of vessels of ivory, and all manner of vessels of precious stone and of brass and of iron and of marble;

And cinnamon, and odours, and ointment, and frankincense, and wine, and oil, and fine flour, and wheat, and beasts, and sheep, and horses, and chariots, and slaves, and souls of men.

And the fruits of the desire of thy soul are departed from thee; and all fat and goodly things are perished from thee; and they shall find them no more at all.

The merchants of these things, who were made rich, shall stand afar off from her, for fear of her torments, weeping and mourning,

And saying: Alas! alas! that great city, which was clothed with fine linen and purple and scarlet and was gilt with gold and precious stones and pearls.

For in one hour are so great riches come to nought.)

In verse 9, before the merchants are introduced, the kings of the earth 'shall weep and bewail themselves over her'. The pearls of Babylon, too, were pleasant to princes.

Thus, the outline of this section of *Pearl*, and the whole conception of the mourning Jeweller who was held 'lyttel to prayse' and who seemed 'put in a mad porpose' could have been suggested by chapter 18 of Revelations. Verse 12 furnishes the Jeweller himself; verses 14–15 describe his sorrow, deprived of all his former wealth: 'omnia pinguia et praeclara perierunt a te', corresponding fairly closely to ll. 13–18:

Purpose and Structure

> Syþen in þat spote hit fro me sprange,
> Ofte haf I wayted, wyschande þat wele,
> Þat wont watȝ whyle deuoyde my wrange
> And heuen my happe and al my hele.

The resemblance here is of a general kind, but l. 26, 'Þer such rycheȝ to rot is runne' corresponds closely to Rev. 18, 17, 'quoniam una hora destitutae sunt tantae divitiae!' Moreover, the last word of the verse before is *margaritis*. The spices of l. 26 and of the next stanza may have been partly suggested by verse 13, but their main source is, I think, the Song of Songs. The '*poma desiderii animae tuae*' of verse 14 also suggests a link with this book.

This interweaving of allusions to the treasure of Babylon is a further means of developing the theme of earthly and heavenly riches, and, more particularly, of keeping the former in the foreground. This is necessary in a section which, while it lays down the main lines on which the poem is to develop, deals primarily with the Dreamer's unrelieved grief for a material loss. The poet, however, does not depend on any generally accepted system of exegesis here, any more than he does in the case of his allusions to the Song of Songs. It is the overtones produced by the biblical allusions which are important. They lend his poem gravity, and help to support the feeling, which is being induced in a variety of ways in the proem, that his matter will have wide implications. To interpret his use of biblical material in any more precise manner would, it seems to me, be to disrupt the carefully balanced structure of the proem.

4

The beginning of the second stanza emphasizes the violence of the Dreamer's grief. Nevertheless, even at this early stage he feels some intimations of consolation:

> Ȝet þoȝt me neuer so swete a sange
> As stylle stounde let to me stele—
> For soþe þer fleten to me fele.

21

Proem

I do not think, with Gordon, that these lines refer to the poet's own poem.[35] They are, rather, a further hint, to be elaborated later, of the kind of *erber* with which we are dealing; and their full implication will be best discussed in the next chapter. For the moment it is enough to say that the lines are, I believe, a straightforward statement that in this garden the bereaved man hears sweet sounds and voices to which his grief prevents him attending.

In the opening stanza the pearl, which is not only a pearl but has the slenderness of human beauty as well as the round wholeness of the perfect gem, slips through the grass to the ground, as a real jewel might do. In the second, the phrasing is significantly altered so as to make it abundantly clear that it is the grave that receives it

> To þenke hir color so *clad in clot*!
> O moul, thou marreȝ a myry iuele.

Color is a word which can equally well be used of the human complexion and of the lustre of the pearl. The phrase *clad in clot*, or *clay*, and its many variations, is the traditional one to indicate the physical effects of burial in Middle English poetry, and it expresses all the horror of the grave: 'To lie in cold obstruction and to rot' is the direct descendent of the medieval image. The actual phrase 'clad in clay', in fact lived on into the seventeenth century and beyond.[36]

[35] See *Pearl*, p. 47, note to 19–20. Gordon punctuates with a full stop after *stele* and a comma at the end of the next line. The connection with what follows seems strangely loose, however. I would repunctuate as above, and translate: 'And yet I thought I had never heard such a sweet sound as a momentary stillness allowed to steal over me— truly, many (such sounds) reach me.'

[36] See *O.E.D.*, clay, sb. sense 3. The medieval examples of the association with mortality are usually extremely concrete. By the seventeenth century figurative senses prevail, or the clay of the grave is associated with the 'mortal clay', the body as the (confining) habitation of the soul. Cf., e.g., 'Disorder and Frailty', st. 2 (*The Works of Henry Vaughan*, ed. L. C. Martin, 2nd edn (Oxford, 1957), p. 445), 'I threaten heaven, and from my Cell / Of clay, and frailty break, and bud.' Cf. 'The Check', st. 3 (p. 444), where the clay both as the body and the earth which receives all living things is part of 'one large

One or two examples of the many fourteenth-century variations on the theme will stand for all, and establish its close
association with 'death's worst, winding sheets, tombs and
worms, and tumbling to decay':

> Þenke þi lyf is but a breth,
> Þenke þou schalt passen, as mo han past.
> Clottes of clay þi cors schal cleth,
> Þi careyne vn-to wormes cast.[37]

A further twist gives an even more gruesome effect:

> For beo vr mouþ crommed with clay,
> Wormes blake wol vs enbrase—
> Þen is to late, Mon, in good fay,
> To seche to A-Mende of þi trespace.[38]

With this phrase, in fact, the poet has set the world of gleaming
jewels and flowering gardens against the grimness of the
momento mori poems, which flourished throughout the fourteenth century.

Several variations on this uncompromising idea recur in
Pearl. At l. 320:

> Þy corse in clot mot calder keue.

At 857:

> Alþaȝ oure corses in clotteȝ clynge ...

Finally comes the brutally direct statement of ll. 957–8:

> Þat is þe borȝ þat we to pres
> Fro þat oure flesch be layd to rote.

There can, in fact, be no doubt as to the importance in the
poem of the idea of death and dissolution in their most terrible
aspects. No interpretation which does not take account of the
new-made grave of the proem can be seriously considered.

---

[37] Carleton Brown, *Religious Lyrics of the Fourteenth Century*, no.
120, 53–6 (p. 206). From the Vernon Series.

[38] Ibid., no. 95, 113–16 (p. 129), also from the Vernon Series.

---

language, *Death*'. It is possible that for the poet of *Pearl* the clay
already had more than its obvious concrete and merely horrifying significance.

Yet even here the poet, I think, hints at a resolution to come. He has, after all, chosen the pearl to stand for the body which goes down into the grave. If he and his readers were familiar with a tradition preserved for us two centuries later by Bacon, the Dreamer's words at his bitterest moment of grief become a foreshadowing of consolation. Bacon tells us, in the *Silva Silvarum*, 380, 'There hath beene a Tradition, that *Pearle*, and *Corall*, and *Turchois-stone*, that have lost their Colours, may be recovered by *Burying* in the *Earth*.'

5

The next two stanzas centre on the grave which has been so forcibly brought before us in stanza two, but in their method and content they are sharply contrasted, as an analysis of their rhetorical structure will show.

Stanza three begins in ll. 25–6 with a *propositio*—a statement about the grave:

> Þat spot of spyseʒ mot nedeʒ sprede,
> Þer such rycheʒ to rot is runne.

This is twice repeated with variations, in ll. 27–8:

> Blomeʒ blayke and blwe and rede
> Þer schyneʒ ful schyr agayn þe sunne,

and then in ll. 29–30:

> Flor and fryte may not be fede
> Þer hit doun drof in moldeʒ dunne.

The poet, in fact, uses *expolitio* to build up this section. The second half of the stanza in ll. 31–2:

> For vch gresse mot grow of grayneʒ dede;
> No whete were elleʒ to woneʒ wonne,

turns on a *sententia* which transforms the opening proposition, which referred to a particular grave, into a general statement of universal truth. The poet again uses *expolitio* to elaborate this in l. 33:

> Of goud vche goude is ay bygonne.

24

The last three lines of the stanza contain the conclusion, in the form of a *repetitio* which combines the opening proposition with the 'sentence' concerning the dead grain:

> So semly a sede moȝt fayly not,
> Þat spryngande spyceȝ vp ne sponne
> Of þat precios perle wythouten spotte.

The system by which the first and last lines of the stanza are verbally linked means that the end must echo the beginning, but the additional echoes *spyceȝ . . . sprede | spryngande spyceȝ . . . sponne*, and the close juxtaposition of the three images round which the stanza is built, seed, plant, and the pearl as treasure, make the final lines an effective conclusion to a reasoned argument. There is, in fact, no description in this stanza.

Stanza four is built up quite differently. It continues the narrative by giving the *locus* of the action:

> To þat spot þat I in speche expoun
> I entred in þat erber grene.   (37–8)

Lines 39–40 fix the time:

> In Auguste in a hyȝ seysoun,
> Quen corne is coruen wyth crokeȝ kene.

Lines 41–6 provide a *descriptio* of the mound, proceeding in a logical manner from the plants in general to their particularization, and then to their scent:

> On huyle þer perle hit trendeled doun
> Schadowed þis worteȝ ful schyre and schene,
> Gilofre, gyngure and gromylyoun
> And pyonys powdered ay bytwene.
> Ȝif hit watȝ semly on to sene,
> A fayr reflayr ȝet fro hit flot.

Lines 47–8 sum up and repeat the statement of the opening:

> Þer wonys þat worþyly, I wot and wene,
> My precious perle wythouten spot.

There is a good deal of repetition—for example, in ll. 37–8—and circumlocution is used in l. 37 and l. 47. But on the whole this stanza tells the story straightforwardly with such description as is necessary to provide its setting. The fact that the poet uses yet another rhetorical device, that of *concatenatio*, to link the stanzas throughout the poem, means that his stanzas are often built up from a definite opening statement to a conclusion cast in equally definite form. He is ingenious in avoiding the necessity when it does not suit his purpose, but in his closely wrought proem and in the sections of argument and discussion he exploits all the possibilities of a close stanza structure. Stanzas three and four thus add to our ideas about the grave in quite different ways. Stanza three, with a wealth of imagery cast mainly in the form of 'sentence', introduces the idea of growth and transformation. The detailed discussion of this imagery must be left for the moment, but it is important to note that it stands immediately after the harshest statement of the Dreamer's loss in terms of mortality.

The fourth stanza elaborates the description of the *erber* in terms, as we have seen, of the Song of Songs, and prepares us for the final stanza of the proem in which we return to the Dreamer's state of mind, to the actual circumstances in which he fell asleep, and to the nature of the dream which visited him.

Stanza five deals with the Dreamer's emotions in terms which repeat, in different words, stanza two; ll. 50–1:

> For care ful colde þat to me caȝt;
> A deuely dele in my hert denned,

lines 53–4:

> I playned my perle þat þer watȝ spenned
> Wyth fyrce skylleȝ þat faste faȝt;

and l. 56:

> My wreched wylle in wo ay wraȝte,

all repeat ll. 17–18:

> Þat dotȝ bot þrych my hert þrange,
> My breste in bale bot bolne and bele;

26

while ll. 52 and 55:

> Þaȝ resoun sette myseluen saȝt . . .
> Þaȝ kynde of Kryst me comfort kenned,

repeat, in different terms, the basic idea of the comforting sounds of ll. 19–21:

> ȝet þoȝt me neuer so swete a sange
> As stylle stounde let to me stele—
> For soþe þer fleten to me fele.

This part of the stanza is, therefore, an elaborate *expolitio* in which the interweaving of the two themes of mental conflict and the possibility of consolation emphasizes the Dreamer's anguish of mind. In this stanza, instead of the reference to unexplained songs and sweet sounds, the poet is specific on the subject of consolation. It is offered by Reason and by Nature 'of Kryst',[39] and it is the Dreamer's 'wretched will' which is opposed to these two. This statement of the position is quite definite; the poet introduces ideas which the poem is to develop and to which we must duly return.

In the meantime, the conflict brings sleep or rather loss of consciousness. The Dreamer falls into a *slepyng-slaȝte*, 'a dead sleep' or a sleep that brings unconsciousness like a blow.[40] This recalls, for example, Gen. 2, 21: 'Immisit ergo Dominus Deus soporem in Adam' (Then the Lord God cast a deep sleep upon Adam:), and Gen. 15, 12: 'sopor irruit super Abram . . .' (a deep sleep fell upon Abram:), or 1 Kings 26, 12: 'sopor Domini irruerat super eos' (a deep sleep from the Lord was fallen upon them). All these refer to miraculous sleep, associated with revelation, or great events.[41] The unusual *slepyng-slaȝte*,

---

[39] On the meaning of this phrase, see below p. 41.

[40] See *O.E.D.*, Slaught, sb. sense 2. The sense 'stroke' seems to me more probable than 'spell', since *slaught* in a nonfigurative sense means 'slaughter', and the other phrases in which it occurs figuratively are *slaȝtes of sorȝe* (*Patience* 192) 'strokes, onslaught, of sorrow' and *slaght o fire* (*Cursor Mundi*, 17372) 'flash of lightening'.

[41] Adam's sleep during the creation of Eve could be thus interpreted. This is shown in visual art by the typical posture of the visionary— with hand to head. A good example, reproduced as plate 21b in *English*

only used by this poet, may be an attempt to reproduce the phrasing of the Bible in these verses, since *immisit . . . in, irruit super* imply a sudden, deep sleep which overcomes the sleeper through an outside agency.

Lastly, in the few lines which link the first section to the next, the poet uses terms which tell us much about the nature of his dream and show us what we may expect from it. He calls it in l. 62 a *sweuen*, and this *sweuen* is associated in the next line with God's grace. At the end of his poem (l. 1184) he calls his dream a *veray avysyoun*. If, as seems likely, he was following the dream-lore of the most influential of writers on the subject, Macrobius,[42] these terms must correspond to some of the types of dream which Macrobius classifies as veridical. Macrobius considers that three out of the five types of dreams which he distinguishes are true and valuable. These are the *somnium*, the *visio*, and the *oraculum*. The *somnium* hides its meaning under the form of 'figures', that is, it is usually allegorical. The *visio* brings true information about the future; the *oraculum* is a dream in which 'a parent or other holy and grave person' announces openly in sleep what is to come to pass, what is to be done or what is to be avoided.[43] The dream in *Pearl*, like the dream of Scipio to which Macrobius is referring, partakes of the nature of all three. It is a *somnium* of the sub-division *proprium*, that is, it has a personal meaning for the Dreamer under the form in which it is cast, i.e. it brings moral teaching and the resolution of his conflict. It is a *visio* since it gives true information about heaven and the next life; and here the poet is careful to reproduce the information provided by the Vision of John in the Apocalypse, whose truth could not be questioned. It is an *oraculum* since a grave and sanctified figure gives the instruction; and, as we shall see, the reversal of the normal

[42] In the *In Somnium Scipionis*, I, iii.
[43] Ibid. (Lugduni, 1560), p. 20.

Art 1216–1307 by Peter Brieger (Oxford, 1957), comes from a Bible, Cambridge University Library MS. Dd. VIII. 12. A later example which shows the prophetic substance of Adam's dream can be found in a Salzburg miniature of 1481 reproduced in H. Rahner, *Greek Myths and Christian Mystery* (London, 1957), plate I, opposite p. 42.

position so that it is the child who instructs the parent, has a more than accidental significance.

It seems likely, therefore, that the word *sweuen* in l. 62 is intended to correspond to *somnium*. There is precedent for this usage. Chaucer uses both *dreem* and *sweven* for *somnium* in *The House of Fame*.[44] *Avysyoun* certainly corresponds to *visio*. Chaucer uses the same word for the same purpose.[45] Chaucer also uses *oracle* to correspond to *oraculum*, but the *Pearl*-poet does not carry the terminology of dreams farther than the two terms, *sweuen* and *avysyoun*, both so qualified, by the reference to 'Godes grace' and the epithet *veray* that their force is not doubtful.

Apart from naming the kind of dream which he experiences and placing it as a serious and truthful one, the poet is careful to dispose of his Dreamer, body and soul:

> Fro spot my spyryt þer sprang in space;
> My body on balke þer bod; in sweuen
> My goste is gon in Godeʒ grace
> In auenture þer meruayleʒ meuen.[46] (61–4)

By 'spyryt' he may mean 'vital spirit', the substance which animates the body and joins it to the soul. The sleep which

[44] *Dreem* and *sweven* can both have a merely general sense in Middle English. Either can, on the other hand, be used for a veridical dream if the context requires it. Thus, in the *House of Fame*, I, 58, Chaucer speaks of 'every drem' (i.e. of whatever kind), but also calls the particular one he means to relate 'a drem' at l. 62. This becomes 'my sweven' at l. 79. In spite of the implied distinction of, e.g. 'Why this a drem, why that a sweven,' (I, 8) the terminology does not seem to be fixed. C. S. Lewis's excellent short account of dream-lore in *The Discarded Image* (Cambridge, 1964), pp. 63–5 is, therefore, a little astray on this point.

[45] *Avysyoun* seems to be always technical. Chaucer uses 'visions' for Macrobius' *insomnium*, the dream caused by waking preoccupations, at *H.F.*, I, 40, but *avision* (as it l. 48) is always more precise. In *H.F.*, for example, it is linked to Macrobius by a few lines of translation: ll. 48–50 correspond to '(Somnium) . . . quod tegit figuris, et uelat ambagibus, non nisi interpretatione intelligendam significationem rei quae demonstratur. Quod quale sit, non a nobis exponendum est: cum hoc unusquisque ex usu quid sit, agnoscat' (p. 20–1).

[46] My punctuation.

overtakes his Dreamer is so deep and so deathlike that his body is left lying on the ground deprived of its vital spirit, and the soul, the *goste*, is entirely freed. This would suggest a vision of a particularly significant kind. It may be, however, that the poet is thinking of the biblical phrase 'in the spirit'—indeed, he may be imitating St. John's words in Revelations: 'I was in the spirit on the Lord's day' (fui in spiritu in dominica dei, 1, 10). The phrase 'in spirit' is often used in Middle English when a heavenly vision is in question, and in this context 'spirit' came to have an almost technical sense. In this case *spyryt* and *goste* are synonymous.[47]

The proem has thus established that the subject of the poem is a loss described in terms which link treasure to the grave seen in its harshest aspect, and also to a garden with its spices and flowers, scents and sounds. Through the idea of the garden images of growth and regeneration are introduced. Secondly, a conflict is in progress in which Will is ranged against Nature and Reason. Thirdly, through a network of biblical allusions, both the treasure and also the garden itself, are given a deep seriousness, and a significance beyond the ordinary. Fourthly, the links with scripture and the phraseology in which sleep and the onset of the dream is described, increase our conviction that the dream itself will have a significance of the kind which Macrobius called an *altitudo*,[48] and will bring true knowledge of the future.

[47] See *O.E.D.*, spirit, sb. I, 2a, where two medieval examples are given to illustrate the usage, then rare, 'spirit' = 'soul'. For a good short account of the spirit as the vital power, see C. S. Lewis, *The Discarded Image*, pp. 166–9.

[48] 'Est somnium: quia rerum, quae illi enarratae sunt, altitudo, tecta profunditate prudentiae, non potest nobis nisi scientia interpretationis aperiri' (p. 21).

II

THE GARDEN OF LOSS

I

Pearl begins with two examples, placed one after the other, of the most beloved of medieval *topoi*, the description of the ideal landscape, the *locus amoenus* of classical poets, in the form of a garden or of parkland laid out as pleasure-grounds. The *erber* of the opening is a garden pure and simple, planted with spices and herbs. The country of the vision is open country, with the emphasis on trees, and on natural features, rocks and river, though the water appears to be channelled into formal pools.[1]

It is important for the modern reader to realize that although the *topos* of the garden is conventional, it is a convention without rigidity in which, besides the classical, several traditions met and mingled. Gardens and parks, in fact, could take as many forms in art as in nature, and could be used by writers for many different purposes, secular or devotional.[2]

Methods of treatment vary as widely as significance. There is,

[1] Lines 139–40. But this is a difficult passage. See Gordon's note, p. 52.

[2] On the classical origins of the *topos*, see Curtius, *European Literature and the Latin Middle Ages*, pp. 183 ff. The Garden of Love is discussed by C. S. Lewis, *The Allegory of Love*, passim, and by J. A. W. Bennett, *The Parlement of Foules*, especially chapter II. Scriptural gardens are discussed by D. W. Robertson, Jr., in 'The Doctrine of Charity in Mediaeval Literary Gardens', *Speculum*, XXVI (1951), pp. 24 ff. (For some corrections to this article, see *A Preface to Chaucer* (Princeton, 1963), pp. 91 ff.) Much valuable information about the moral garden, especially as an image of the regeneration of the soul, has been collected by L. L. Martz, *The Paradise Within* (New Haven and London, 1964). The gardens of *Pearl* are interestingly dealt with, in '*Pearl* and the Medieval Garden' by R. W. V. Elliot, *Les Langues Modernes*, 45 (1951).

for example, the purely allegorical garden of *Piers Plowman*, B. XVI and C. XIX, where landscape is so subordinate to meaning that we are not required to form any visual impression at all, as

> ... we comen in-to a contree, *Cor-hominis*
> hit hyhte,
> Herber of all pryuytees and of holynesse, (C. XIX, 4–5)

and the allegory is so discontinuous that it is only with difficulty that the modern reader can follow it.[3] At the other end of the scale comes the Garden of Love in Guillaume de Lorris's *Roman de la Rose*, a garden which, apart from a few features like the Rose itself, the hedge, and the fountain, is not allegorical at all. Its flowers and trees, birds and beasts, are elaborated as a beautiful backcloth against which the action is played out by actors who *are* allegorical. Here, in fact, the action, not the setting is the allegory. But this is not the only allegorical kind; it is possible for the setting itself to be cast in allegorical form and to carry the argument of the poem. The allegory of the tree in the *herber* in *Piers Plowman* is of this type. The fruit of this tree does not stay still to be looked at, it develops with the poet's thought, and the changes it undergoes are the action of the poem.

The flowers and spices, seeds and corn sheaves of the opening of *Pearl* are also images capable of carrying the development of the poet's ideas. They are not static features of an imagined place through which we can mentally travel. The rocks and trees, river and flowery banks among which the Dreamer later finds himself are quite different. That landscape is described with incomparable richness of detail. Its woods are all light and colour, sound and movement:

> Holtewodeʒ bryʒt aboute hem bydeʒ
> Of bolleʒ as blwe as ble of Ynde;
> As bornyst syluer þe lef on slydeʒ,
> Þat þike con trylle on vch a tynde.
> Quen glem of glodeʒ agaynʒ hem glydeʒ,
> Wyth schymeryng schene ful schrylle þay schynde. (75–80)

[3] See R. W. Frank, Jr., *Piers Plowman and the Scheme of Salvation* (New Haven, 1957), pp. 86 ff., for an excellent discussion of this passage.

The Garden of Loss

Its rivers can only compare, among the rivers of poetry, with the flashing stream Dante saw in Heaven:

> Swangeande swete þe water con swepe,
> Wyth a rownande rourde raykande aryȝt
> In þe founce þer stonden stoneȝ stepe,
> As glente þurȝ glas þat glowed and glyȝt,
> As stremande sterneȝ, quen stroþe-men slepe,
> Staren in welkyn in wynter nyȝt;
> For vche a pobbel in pole þer pyȝt
> Watȝ emerad, saffer, oþer gemme gente,
> Þat alle þe loȝe lemed of lyȝt,
> So dere watȝ hit adubbement.   (111–20)

In contrast to this country of more than earthly beauty, the garden where the Pearl was lost is described only in its bare essentials, and even these are flattened and muted as far as possible. It is 'þat spot', 'þat erber grene'. The grave is a 'floury flaȝt', or simply 'huyle'. Its flowers are given colours 'blayke and blwe and rede', and its herbs and spices are named, but there is little that can properly be called pictorial, and nothing to make a special appeal to the senses. The gardens of allegory, whatever their kind, are never without sound, and the birdsong of the blissful country is described in loving detail; but the melody of the *erber* is passed over briefly. It breaks into the description of the Dreamer's feelings almost as an irrelevance in ll. 19–21, and, in fact, it is significant not for what it adds to our mental picture of the garden but for its contribution to the development of the poet's thought.[4]

Scent, as well as colour and sound, is a normal feature of the *topos*, and the herbs and flowers of the *erber* are duly scented— 'A fayr reflayr ȝet fro hit flot', 'Suche odour to my herneȝ schot'; but there is none of the sensuous sharpness here of:

> So frech flauoreȝ of fryteȝ were,
> As fode hit con me fayre refete,   (87–8)

and the form of the phrases in the proem has, I have suggested, the deliberate purpose of calling up associations of a different kind through their derivation from the Song of Songs.

[4] See below, pp. 42–6.

The garden of the opening is consistently indicated as an actual place, but, nevertheless, it is not, I believe, intended to stand as a *locus amoenus* in the normal sense, but rather as a frame into which a series of closely interwoven images and scriptural references are fitted, all of which work together to establish and elaborate the theme of mortality and regeneration. The description of the country that lies 'over against Paradise' is straight description. Its imagined marvels stand for nothing but themselves. But the introductory section with its images of treasure, seed, and plant is to be understood in a different way, in terms of the poet's experience of loss and death.

The very march of the verse emphasizes the difference. In the opening section, especially in the third stanza, each image is set in its place with a deliberation which compels and focuses the reader's attention. The swifter rhythm, on the other hand, with which the innumerable glittering facets of the dream landscape are brought into one dazzling whole, induces the same response in us as in the Dreamer before his final vision—'Delyt me drof in yꝫe and ere' (1153). The flowers and spice-plants of the opening work on the mind in another way, and make up for their lack of sensuous vividness by richness of association of a different kind.

Thus, to understand the garden of the proem, a complex series of images has to be separated out. Before this is attempted, however, it will be necessary to look more closely at the *erber* itself and to try to determine—since it seems clear that it is a garden of more than literal significance—just what the poet means to convey by it. It is important here to emphasize that, for all its influence on French and English poetry of the fourteenth century, the Garden of Love as it is described in the *Roman de la Rose* is neither the only nor the earliest model. The beautiful garden with every kind of good plant—fragrant herbs and spices, shady trees and clear fountain—was a motif which was fully developed and lovingly described by generations of writers long before the *Roman* was composed—before, indeed, the courtly love poetry of Western Europe was thought of. As a literary *topos* its popularity, as we have said, owed much to the liking of classical poets for the *locus amoenus*, but the details, and the form it took owed as much to the Bible, and something to Eastern tradition. It is, indeed, one of the many medieval *topoi* in which the art of the Bible and the art of the classical poets met. In the case of the *erber* of *Pearl*, it will be evident, when we consider the use to which the poet puts his Garden, and the themes which he establishes through it, that he is drawing on the tradition as it had been developed by devotional writers.

2

The proem as a whole establishes the theme of treasure and the grave. It deals with the cycle of growth and decay, hints at rebirth in the natural world and, by implication, in the spiritual world as well. The poet, in fact, brings together in his short opening section a number of images and motifs which are linked to the theme of regeneration. The central image in this complex is that of the *erber*, which we have connected with the garden enclosed of the Song of Songs, through the associations of the actual word in Middle English and through the echoes and references in the description to the phrasing of the book itself.

The *hortus conclusus* with its flowers and spices, fountain, trees, and scented breezes is, strictly speaking the exclusive property of the Song of Songs, but it was always linked by patristic and medieval writers to the garden of Genesis, which God planted himself with every good plant, and which was also a place of water, fruit-bearing trees, and refreshing breezes. The two gardens gradually merged together into a single image, a moral allegory of the regeneration of fallen man through which Paradise is regained and the Bride and Bridegroom united. This *topos* was popular from the early Christian centuries onwards. Sometimes one garden is made the basis of the imagery, sometimes the other.

In the *Epistle to Diognetus* (? third century), to give an early example, the garden is Eden:

> If you consider and listen with zeal to these truths you will know what things God bestows on those that love him rightly, who are become 'a Paradise of delight', raising up in themselves a fertile

35

tree with all manner of fruits, and are adorned with divers fruits.[5]

St. Gregory of Nyssa (fourth century) develops the same theme in relation to the garden of the Song of Songs:

> A garden enclosed is my sister, my spouse (Cant. 4, 12). Does anyone lay claim to be the spouse of the Lord, because he is closely united to Him, or His sister, because, in the words of the Gospel, he does His will? Then he must become a flourishing garden, having within himself the beauty of all kinds of trees. There must be the sweet fig, the fruitful olive, the lofty palm, the blossoming vine. He must have no thorn bush or fleabane; these must be replaced by the cypress and the myrtle.[6]

Among later writers William of St. Thierry makes brief use of the *topos*:

> Locaveras in paradiso voluptatis tuae, ut operarer et custodirem illum, operarer bonorum studiorum exercitiis, custodirem ne serpens irreperet. Serpens irrepsit. Evam meam seduxit, et per eam me praevaricatorem constituit. Propter quod expulsus de paradiso bonae conscientiae, exsul factus sum in terra aliena, in regione dissimilitudinis.

> (You have placed me in the paradise of your delights; I was to cultivate and watch over it—to cultivate it by the practise of virtue, to watch over it to prevent the serpent creeping in. But the serpent did creep in; it seduced my Eve, and through her made me a prevaricator, so that, driven out of the paradise of a

[5] XII, 5, 1–4. Quoted from the translation of Kirsopp Lake, *The Apostolic Fathers*, II (Loeb Library, Cambridge, Mass., 1946), pp. 376–7. The date is uncertain, but Harnack argued for the third century.

[6] Quoted from the translation of Herbert Musurillo, *From Glory to Glory: Texts from Gregory of Nyssa* (London, 1962), p. 227. Greek text in *P.G.*, 44, 961. Cf. Origen, *Commentary on the Song of Songs*, III, 8, *P.G.*, 12, 150 f. Gregory of Nyssa and Origen were influential in the West in the later Middle Ages through St. Bernard. See É. Gilson, *La Théologie Mystique de St. Bernard* (Paris, 1947), pp. 28–9. Tree-lists are another case of the merging of classical and biblical tradition. Statius has one, which was certainly influential (*Thebaid*, vi, 98 ff. Cf. J. A. W. Bennett, *The Parlement of Foules*, p. 73); so has Isaiah (41, 49), who was no doubt in the mind of devotional writers who used the device.

good conscience I was exiled in a foreign land, in the region of dissimilitude.[7]

William of St. Thierry is closely paralleled, perhaps imitated, by Langland in the description of the garden of the Tree of Charity. This tree, which bears virtues and good actions as its fruit:

'Groweth in a gardyne,' quod he, 'that god made hym-seluen,'

(i.e. Eden; compare Gen. 2, 8, 'and the Lord God planted a garden', A.V.).

'Amyddes mannes body the more is of that stokke';

(cf. Gen. 2, 9, 'the tree of life also in the midst of paradise, and the tree of knowledge of good and evil')

'Herte hatte the herber that it in groweth,
And *Liberum-Arbitrium* hath the londe to ferme.'

(Gen. 2, 15, 'and the Lord God took man and put him into the paradise of pleasure to dress it and to keep it').[8]

St. Bernard was particularly fond of the *topos*. In the *Sermons on the Song of Songs* he blends the Garden of Eden with that of the Song of Songs, when he writes of:

viri virtutum, tanquam ligna fructifera in horto sponsi et in paradiso Dei.

(Virtuous men who are like fruit-trees in the garden of the Bridegroom, and in the paradise of God.[9])

These examples will be enough to show the early development and popularity of the moral garden, but they are insufficient in themselves to account for the garden of *Pearl*. When, however, we turn to St. Bernard's most elaborate treatment of

[7] *Meditativae Orationes*, ed. M.-M. Davy (Paris, 1934), pp. 102–4.

[8] B. XVI, 13–16. I believe that the allegory owes its *form* to the book of Genesis. I do not think, with D. C. Fowler, *Piers the Plowman, Literary Relations of the A and B Texts* (Seattle, 1961), that it reproduces the content of Genesis, and that this 'act of our drama will therefore be concerned with the Fall of Man' (p. 119).

[9] *In Cant.*, sermo xxiii, 4 (*P.L.*, 183, 885 D). Many more examples could be collected from St. Bernard's works. Cf., e.g., *In Cant.* li, 2; lviii, 8; *de Diligendo Deo* III, 7 ff.

Proem

the *topos* in the *de Conversione ad Clericos*, chapters xii–xiv, we find something which is much nearer. Here is the entry into a garden enclosed; the sense of loss, the conflict and lamentation and the offer of consolation. In chapter xii he writes:

> Inveniet paradisum voluptatis plantatus a Domino; inveniet hortum floridum et amoenissimum; inveniet refrigerii sedem, et dicet: O si audiat vocem meam misera illa voluntas, ut ingrediens videat bona et visitet locum istum!

(She (the soul) will find the paradise of delights planted by the Lord (Gen. 2, 8). She will find the garden, flowering and delightful, she will find a place of refreshment, and she will say, 'O! if this wretched will would only hear my voice so that, entering in she could see these good things, and visit this place.'[10])

This garden is described more fully in chapter xiii:

> Nec vero locum reputes corporalem paradisum hunc voluptatis internae. Non pedibus in hunc hortum, sed affectibus introitur. Nec terrenarum tibi commendatur arborum copia, sed virtutum utique spiritualium jucunda decoraque plantatio. Hortus conclusus, ubi fons signatus in quatuor capita derivatur, et ex una sapientiae vena virtus quadripartita procedit. Splendidissima quoque inibi lilia vernant: et cum flores apparent, etiam vox turturis auditur. Illic nardus sponsae fragrantissimum praestat odorem, et caetera quoque aromata fluunt; austro spirante, aquilone fugato. Ibi media est arbor vitae, malus illa de Cantico, cunctis pretiosior lignis silvarum, cujus et umbra sponsam refrigerat, et ructus dulcis gutturi ejus. Ibi continentiae nitor, et sincerae veritatis intuitus oculos cordis irradiat: auditui quoque dat gaudium et laetitiam dulcissima vox consolatoris interni. Ibi quibusdam spei naribus influit jucundissimus odor agri pleni, cui Dominus benedixit. Ibi avidissime praelibantur incomparabilis deliciae charitatis; et succisis spinis ac vepribus, quibus antea pungebatur, unctione misericordiae perfusus animus in conscientia bona feliciter requiescit.

(Do not imagine that the paradise of inward delights (Gen. 2, 8) is a corporeal place. That Garden is not to be entered with the bodily feet, but with the mental faculties. It is not a multitude of terrestrial trees which is presented to you, but a delightful and beautiful grove of spiritual virtues. It is a garden enclosed (Cant.

[10] *P.L.*, 182, 847A.

38

4, 12) where a sealed fountain (Cant. 4, 12) flows out into four streams (Gen. 2, 10) just as the four virtues flow from the same source of wisdom. There too, the most glorious lilies bloom (Cant. 2, 1–2); and when the flowers appear the voice of the turtle is also heard (Cant. 2, 12). Here the nard of the Bride gives out its most fragrant scent (Cant. 1, 11) and other spices give forth their odours (Cant. 4, 16). The wind blows from the South; the North wind has fled away (Cant. 4, 16). In the midst of the garden grows the tree of Life (Gen. 2, 9), that apple-tree of the Song of Songs, more precious than all the trees of the forest, whose shade refreshes the Bride, and whose fruits are agreeable to her taste (Cant. 2, 3, 5). There the light of continence shines out, and the clear knowledge of truth irradiates the eyes of the heart; to the ear also the sweet voice of the interior Comforter brings joy and gladness. There the pleasant scent which comes from a field in full harvest which the Lord has blessed (Gen. 27, 27) penetrates the nostrils dilated by hope. There the incomparable delights of charity are tasted with avidity. The thorns and thorn bushes which pierced the soul outside have been cut back. The spirit, annointed with the oil of compassion, rests with joy in a good conscience.[11])

The links between this garden and the proem of *Pearl* are numerous. There is the same emphasis on a garden which is connected by textual reference with the Song of Songs, and there is the same rebellious Will. In both comfort, offered, as St. Bernard goes on to say, by Reason, is represented as a voice or sound heard in the garden. In both, too, the scent of spices from the Song of Songs is connected with consolation. We cannot know whether the *Pearl* poet read the *de Conversione*, or whether he drew independently on the traditions which lay behind it. In either case, the use he makes of the material remains very much his own. There is no inherent improbability in the suggestion that he knew St. Bernard's work, since it is likely that no single writer had a greater influence on Middle English devotional literature.[12] Moreover, apart from the details

[11] Ibid., loc. cit., 847C–848A.
[12] See G. L. Prestige, *Fathers and Heretics* (London, 1948), p. 192 ff. For St. Bernard's influence on the English Sermon writers, see G. R. Owst, *Literature and Pulpit in Medieval England* (Index sub Bernard, St.).

just noted, both writers, though their purpose is different, handle the subject matter in a similar way. St. Bernard starts from a consideration of earthly riches and their transitoriness, and from the troubled state of mind which precedes conversion (that is, the act of entering the religious life). He actually speaks of pearls (chapter xiii): 'This is a holy thing; these are pearls'.

The consolation which the garden provides through the comforting voice and the aromatic scents is described several times by St. Bernard. In the passage just quoted he speaks of the 'sweet voice of the interior Comforter' in the same breath as the scent which pleases the nostrils. In chapter xiv he returns to the voices and becomes more explicit:

> In hujus ergo ostio paradisi divini susurri vox auditur, sacratissi-mum secretissimumque consilium, quod absconditum est a sapientibus et prudentibus, parvulis revelatur.

> (Now at the entry to this paradise the sound of a holy whispering makes itself heard, it is counsel of the most sacred and secret kind, which is hidden from the wise and prudent and revealed to the little ones.[13])

Consolation comes through the reason and is passed on by the reason to the will, which is the source of the spirit's uneasy state:

> Cujus sane vocis auditum non sola jam ratio capit, sed gratanter eum communicat et voluntati.

> (The Reason does not keep the sound of this voice to itself, but joyfully communicates it to the Will.[14])

In chapter xi St. Bernard had already elaborated this idea of the reason as the source of consolation and instruction to the erring will:

> Haec igitur et his similia intus suggerit ratio voluntati, eo copiosius quo perfectius illustratione spiritus edocetur. Felix sane, cujus voluntas sic cesserit et aquieverit consilio rationis.

> (These, and others like them, are the ideas which Reason suggests to the Will, the more abundantly the more perfectly she is in-

[13] *P.L.*, 182, 848C.
[14] Ibid., loc. cit.

structed by the light of the Spirit. Undoubtedly he is happy in whom the Will has submitted and agreed to the counsel of the Reason.[15])

The Dreamer in *Pearl* suffers through a will which does not listen to the voice of Reason: at its first mention the sweet sound is hardly attended to (17–22). The conflict is explicitly described later in the proem:

> A deuely dele in my hert denned,
> Þaʒ resoun sette myseluen saʒt.
> I playned my perle þat þer watʒ spenned
> With fyrce skylleʒ þat faste faʒt;
> Þaʒ kynde of Kryst me comfort kenned,
> My wreched wylle in wo ay wraʒte.   (51–6)

Lastly, the scent of the spices brings the sleep which makes the consoling revelation possible:

> Suche odour to my herneʒ schot;
> I slode vpon a slepyng-slaʒte
> On þat precios perle wythouten spot.   (58–60)

To find Reason as the opponent of Will is not surprising—this pair were responsible for many medieval debates. The second source of comfort, 'kynde of Kryst', is not quite so obvious. The phrase has usually been interpreted as 'the nature of Christ', but this seems unduly vague. I would translate 'Nature, through Christ', and this, I believe fits in with the poet's thought in the poem as a whole. As we shall see, the poet clearly regards the natural cycle of growth, leading to decay and renewal as an important aspect of God's laws for the world. In the same way the death of a human being leads to renewal, both bodily and spiritual. This, of course, although it takes place through the natural cycle of which death is a part, cannot be achieved by nature alone, since man does not, in fact, spring up again like the grass. It is only through the redemption that renewal is brought about for mankind. Hence the phrase 'kynde of Kryst' anticipates an important part of the poet's argument, as I hope to show in the chapters which follow.

15 *P.L.*, 182, 846A–B.

3

The doctrinal meaning of the consolation provided by Reason to the Will is not difficult to grasp, but as part of the description of the garden, the voices which bring comfort or revelation need explanation. The basis is to be found in the text of the Bible. In Genesis, Adam and Eve 'heard the voice of the Lord God', in Eden, while the Song of Songs contains much dialogue. Origen, for example, comments at length on 2. 14:

> My dove in the clefts of the rock, in the hollow places of the wall, shew me thy face. Let thy voice sound in my ears: for thy voice is sweet and thy face comely.

In this, and the preceding verse, he says, God calls the soul from the winter which we must take as 'the time when she is still tossed with the waves of her passions'. The voice of the soul itself, for which verse 14 asks, 'is sweet when it expounds the faith and the doctrines of the truth, when it unfolds God's dealings and his judgements'.[16] St. Bernard may have had such a passage in mind when he wrote in the *de Conversione* of the voice which Reason hears in the garden, and of the wisdom which Reason passes on to the Will, in his view the source of the winter of the unsubdued passions.

Now, the voice of God in Eden after the Fall, brought condemnation to Adam and Eve and recognition of their loss, and in gardens where this voice is heard, the emphasis is on the ominous gathering of shadows, on a wind which from a refreshing breeze has become stormy, cold, and blighting, and on a corresponding turbulence of the emotional atmosphere. The threatening, cloudy sky probably owes much to God's speeches to Moses out of storm and cloud (e.g. at Exod. 19, 16 ff.). The rushing wind owes something to the wind of Pentecost, and to fit the new ominousness of the scene, the refreshing cool of the evening changes to wintry cold.

---

[16] *Commentary on the Song of Songs*, III (IV), 15 (*P.G.*, 13, 188 f.; translation by R. P. Lawson, *Origen, the Song of Songs, Commentary and Homilies*, Ancient Christian Writers, XXVI (London, 1957), pp. 246 ff.

The Garden of Loss

This garden, like the Paradise of Delights, of which it is only another aspect, was also a much used *topos*. Though it is built up on the basis of the description of Eden after the apple has been eaten, it also owes something to the separation of the Bride and Bridegroom in the Song of Songs. The theme was developed in terms of winter, which brings the flowers of the garden to an end, by St. Gregory of Nyssa:

> Man's nature in the beginning flourished while it was in Paradise, growing fat and thriving on the water of the fountain there; and he flourished so long as he had the blossom of immortality and not the leaves. But when the winter of disobedience came and withered its roots, the blossom was shaken off and fell to the ground. Man was thus stripped of his immortality; the grass of virtue was dried up; the love of God was chilled by repeated sin; and the passions were stirred up into a great swell by stormy winds, causing many souls to be shipwrecked.[17]

St. Gregory the Great also writes of the stormy winds which carry off the leaves in a passage in the *Moralia in Job*:

> Quid est enim homo, nisi folium, qui vidilicet in paradiso ab arbore cecidit? Quid est nisi folium qui tentationis vento rapitur, et desideriorum flatibus levatur?

> (What is man who fell in Paradise from the tree but a leaf? What but a leaf, seized by the wind of temptation and blown by the winds of desire?[18])

Man's loss of immortality and subjection to death is thus bound up with the description of the garden of Eden. This association of ideas provides the frame for a poem in the *de Die Judicii*:

> Inter florigeras fecundi caespitis herbas
> flamine ventorum resonantibus undique ramis
> arboris umbriferae moestus sub tegmine solus
> dum sedi, subito planctu turbatus amaro,
> carmina prae tristi cecini haec lugubria mente,
> utpote commemorans scelerum commissa meorum
> et maculas vitae mortisque inamabile tempus
> iudiciique diem horrendo examine magnum.

[17] Musurillo, *From Glory to Glory*, p. 188 (Greek text in *P.G.*, 44, 869).   [18] xiii, 25 (*P.L.*, 75, 980).

Proem

(While I sat amidst the flowery grasses of the fertile turf with the
blast of the winds everywhere in echoing branches, under the
cover of the shady tree, alone and dejected, I was thrown into
confusion by a sudden bitter complaint. In the sadness of my
mood I sang these wretched verses, as remembering the offences
of my sins, the stains of my life and the hateful time of death, in
terrifying contemplation of the great Day of Judgement.[19])

This poem was attributed to Bede, which may have helped
to give it currency, especially in England. Whether or not the
poet of *Pearl* knew it, his opening garden is heavy with the same
emotions. He himself makes no mention of the trees which are
such an essential part of this garden, since it was 'amidst the
trees of paradise' that 'Adam and his wife hid themselves from
the face of the Lord God', but his illustrator is careful to shade
the sleeping figure of the Dreamer with a good selection of
them.[20]

There is much evidence that this shadowy garden, the Eden
of just fallen man, was associated with a voice bringing comfort
or revelation: God's voice, after all, was heard in it; and it
instituted the historical process of man's recovery. St. Augustine
had commented on the relevant passage in Genesis in *De Genesi
contra Manichaeos*.[21] This voice is also important to the commentator who, perhaps, gives best the troubled atmosphere of
the garden after the Fall. This is the anonymous author of
Quaestiones super Genesim:

> Quid est quod ad auram post meridiem, nisi quod lux ferventior
> veritatis abscesserat, et peccatricem animam culpae suae frigora
> constringebant. Ad auram namque post meridiem, primus homo
> post culpam absconsus, invenitur: quia enim meridianum
> calorem charitatis perdiderat, jam sub peccati umbra, quasi sub
> frigore aurae torpebat: sicut de eodem peccanti homine scriptum
> est: quia secutus est umbram. Charitatis enim calorem perdi-

[19] H. Löhe, *Be Domes Daege*, Bonner Beiträge, 22 (1907), pp. 7–8.
For an excellent discussion of the poem and its symbolism, see B. F.
Huppé, *Doctrine and Poetry* (New York, 1959), pp. 81 ff.

[20] This illustration is reproduced as the frontispiece in Gordon's
Pearl.

[21] *P.L.*, 34, 208 f.

derat, et verum solem homo deseruit, et sub umbra se interni
frigoris abscondit.

(What is the meaning of the breeze of evening except that the
more fervent light of truth has left, and the coldness of its
guilt grips the sinful soul? For in the evening breeze, the first
man after his sin is found hidden; because he has lost the midday
heat of charity, now he lies stupefied in the shadows of sin as in
the cold of the breeze, just as it is written concerning the same
sinning man, *Because he has followed the shadow*. He has lost the
heat of charity and has abandoned the sun and hidden himself
within the shadows of his inner cold.[23])

Even in this garden the voice of God is heard and brings hope of
mercy. The words 'Adam, where art thou', are to be understood as a call to repentance.[23]

A final example of a garden of this kind comes from the work
of an English poet. Lydgate, in 'An Holy Meditation' uses the
motif to introduce the words that his soul, standing for reason,
addresses to 'sensuality', the 'fleshly lust', or 'will', which makes
it impossible for him to solve his problem. The garden, in fact,
is the setting for meditation on a problem which has caused a
mental conflict:

> With greuous study annoyed was myn hert,
> Oute of þe which ne wist I howe tastert,
> But to þe grenes fast I can me hye,
> Wening þer to fynde remedye,
> But al for nought certain it wolde not be;
> For whane I hade sette me vnder a tree,
> What for þe floures and þe herbes greene,
> And noyse of briddes singing ay bytweene
> In hir wyse me thought crafftely,
> Þat suche a mirthe neuer noon herde I.
> Hir song made so myn herte for to accende
> Þat vnto studye holly I gan attende;
> And studying enforced I my thought
> To spirituel thing, and to noon oþer nought:

[22] *P.L.*, 93, 268C. Doubtfully ascribed to Bede. See Huppé,
Doctrine and Poetry, p. 82.

[23] *Quaest. super Gen.* (*P.L.*, 93, 280–81). Cf. Huppé, op. cit. p. 97,
n. 41.

But flesshly lust crepte in myn hert anoon
So slelely, þat neghe past was and goon
Al my spirituel affeccion,
Til oure lord god for my correcion
Of his gret might putte þane into my mynde
Repreving my flesshe in þis kynde,
My soule, I seye, spake þus my flesshe vn-to,
If yee wol here, þus he sayde, loo,—[24]

Lydgate's technique is, as often, uncertain, but there is no doubt that he is using an appropriate *topos* in an appropriate way to introduce a moral poem. He is not mechanically borrowing from the machinery of the poetry of courtly love, and a contemporary reader would have had no more difficulty than the readers of the *Roman de la Rose* in distinguishing the moral garden from the garden of the Love Visions. As Genius puts it:

Car, qui dou bel jardin carré,
Clos au petit guichet barré,
Ou cil amanz vit la querole
Ou Deduiz o ses genz querole,
A ce beau parc que je devise,
Tant par est beaus a grant devise,
Faire voudrait comparaison,
Il ferait trop grant mespreison
S'il ne la fait tel ou semblable
Come il ferait de veir a fable.

(For if anyone would compare the pretty, square garden, shut in by the little wicket gate, where the lover saw the carol danced by Mirth and his following, to the beautiful park which I have described, he would be greatly mistaken, if he failed to make it clear that he is comparing true with false.   (20279–88))

4

Most writers who use the *topos* of the garden, whether in association with love or morality, also use the *topos* of the seasons of the year. As a rule the garden is set in spring—this is

[24] *Minor Poems*, I, pp. 43 ff. ll. 25–46.

the case in the *de Die Judicii* and Lydgate's 'An Holy Meditation', as well as in the *Roman de la Rose*. Spring is, of course, naturally associated with the pleasures of a garden as well as with the pleasures of love, but the idea that its appearance as the setting for devotional works implies borrowing from the tradition of courtly writing will not hold. In an essay on the Middle English Lyric, E. K. Chambers wrote of the spring setting in vernacular religious lyric: 'For these poets the old setting of the *renouveau* has found a new meaning';[25] but, though it would be unwise to maintain that the two traditions never cross-fertilized each other, we must recognize that the association of Spring, and other seasons of the year, with moral and devotional themes was a very ancient one. R. T. Davies, in the introduction to his anthology of Middle English Lyrics, points out the traditional linking of Spring to the annunciation.[26] It was also associated both with the Nativity and the Crucifixion,[27] and was often described with all the elaboration and joyousness which we associate with the later lyrics. A single example, taken from St. Gregory of Nyssa, will show the kind of treatment which such descriptions could be given:

How lovely is the Creator's description of the springtime which He has made! To Him David says: The summer and the spring were formed by thee (Ps. 73, 17). He dissolves winter's oppressiveness, and tells us that the sadness of the season has passed, and with it the unpleasant rains. He shows us the meadows filled and blossoming with flowers. The flowers, He tells us, are in full bloom and ready for plucking; and so now the flower pickers can gather them either for making garlands or preparing perfume. Sounds of speech make the season joyful, the song of birds echoes in the glens, and the sweet voice of the dove resounds in our ears.[28]

[25] *Early English Lyrics*, E. K. Chambers and F. Sidgwick (London, 1937), p. 287.
[26] R. T. Davies, *Medieval English Lyrics* (London, 1963), p. 18.
[27] See Rahner, *Greek Myths and Christian Mystery*, chapter IV, where a wealth of examples are given.
[28] Translated by Musurillo, *From Glory to Glory*, p. 183–4 (*P.G.*, 44, 865A f.).

Here, as in many passages of this kind, more than one season is mentioned—the cycle as a whole, in fact, is at the back of the writer's mind. In later secular poetry the purpose of seasonal description is temporal only—although congruity of time and action is usually observed. In devotional writing the *topos* always has the function of developing the thought, and, since it is the cycle of the year as a whole which was most significant in argument, it is usually present, either explicitly or by implication in such passages.[29]

The *Pearl*-poet, as we have said, does not enter his garden in Spring, but he is at pains to give it a seasonal setting. He chooses the harvest month of August, a time of year which had very definite associations for him, as his other poems show. The idea is first introduced in stanza three in the sentence which enlarges on the biblical grain which dies to live by adding the idea of the loaded harvest wains. It is then directly stated in stanza four:

> To þat spot þat I in speche expoun
> I entred in þat erber grene,
> In Auguste in a hyȝ seysoun,
> Quen corne is coruen wyth crokeȝ kene. (37–40)

It has been suggested that the 'high season' in August refers to a feast of the Church, either the Assumption or Lammas,[30] and either would be appropriate in the context. Elsewhere, however, the poet shows the importance he attaches to the seasons as a part of the imagery, and, indeed, of the machinery of his poetry. In *Sir Gawain and the Green Knight* he has a long and important link passage in which he describes the four seasons of the year.[31] In *Purity* he takes full advantage of the conclusion of the story of the Flood, with its promise to mankind, in one of the finest passages in this rather uneven poem:

[29] For a fuller discussion of the significance of the topos for the *Pearl*-poet, see below, pp. 59 ff.

[30] See Gordon, *Pearl*, p. 47, note on line 39.

[31] Lines 500–33. See J. A. Burrow, *A Reading of* Sir Gawain and the Green Knight, pp. 33–6.

Sesounez schal yow never sese of sede ne of hervest,
Ne hete, ne no harde forst, umbre ne droȝþe,
Ne þe swetnesse of somer, ne þe sadde wynter,
Ne þe nyȝt, ne þe day, ne þe newe ȝerez,
Bot ever renne restlez—rengnez ȝe þerinne!   (523-7)

He is likely to have believed, with the author of the *Cursor Mundi*, that the earth knew no changing seasons before the Flood——

    . . . bituix Adam and noe
    Þe time was euer ilik grene,
    Þat nankin rainbow was sene,
    And þof na rain on erth fell
    Plente on erth moght man tell—   (1988-92)

a tradition which Jean de Meun blends with the perpetual happy Spring of the Golden Age which was brought to an end by Jupiter's division of the year into four (*Roman de la Rose*, 20190-5).

It is likely, therefore, that the chief importance of the harvest season in *Pearl* lay in its position in the cycle of the year. Just as the poet gives an original turn to the motif of the garden, when he makes its centre-piece not the fountain of life, nor the Tree, but the grave, so, instead of Spring he chooses the less obvious autumnal setting. Certainly the season in which 'al rypeȝ and roteȝ þat ros vpon fyrst' (*GGK*, 528), and which, while it was part of a change which brought an end to the Golden Age of perpetual Spring, yet bore witness to the power and providence of God, suits his theme of mortality and regeneration. But there were, I think, other overtones. If we, once more, turn to the writings of St. Bernard, we shall find that the cycle of the year comes to stand as a symbol of regeneration, and that it is closely linked to the moral garden. I have already cited the garden of the *de Conversione* with its 'scent of the field in full harvest.' Another extended treatment of the garden comes at the beginning of chapter III of the *de Diligendo Deo*. St. Bernard's theme is the Crucifixion, and he turns almost at once to the imagery of the Song of Songs. He writes of the Fruit of the Cross:

Haec sunt quippe mala punica, quae in hortum introducta dilecti sponsa carpit ex ligno vitae.

(These are pomegranates, which, brought into the Garden of the Beloved, the Bride plucks from the Tree of Life.)

He goes on:

Monumenta siquidem Passionis, fructus agnosce quasi anni praeteriti, omnium utique retro temporum sub peccati mortisque imperio decursorum, tandem in plenitudine temporis, apparentes. Porro autem Resurrectionis insignia, novos adverte flores sequentis temporis, in novam sub gratia revirescentis aestatem, quorum fructum generalis futura resurrectio infine parturiet sine fine mansurum. Jam, inquit, hiems transiit, imber abiit et recessit, flores apparuerunt in terra nostra: aestivum tempus advenisse cum illo significans, qui de mortis gelu in vernalem quamdam novae vitae temperiem resolutus, Ecce, ait, nova facio omnia: cujus caro seminata est in morte, refloruit in resurrectione; ad cujus mox odorem in campo convallis nostrae revirescunt arida, recalescunt frigida, mortua reviviscunt.

(We must understand the teaching of the Passion as the fruits of the last harvest: that is to say of all the times which have passed under the dominion of sin and death, and which have now ripened in the plenitude of time (Gal. 4, 4). And compare the trophies of the resurrection to the fresh flowers of the new age which is brought into flower by grace in a second summer. These flowers will yield, to the future general resurrection, fruits which will never fade. 'Already,' says the bride, 'winter is passed, the rain is over and gone, the flowers appear on the earth' (Cant. 2, 11–12). She wishes to say that summer has come with Him who has melted the ice of death to bring back the spring warmth of a new life, saying 'Behold, I make all things new' (Apoc. 21, 5). His flesh, sown in death, has flowered in the resurrection (I Cor. 15, 42); and the scent which flows through our whole valley renews what was withered, warms what was cold, revives what was dead.[32])

In this passage Winter is described and Spring; Summer and the harvest season are blended together—the cycle of the seasons has become fully significant of the spiritual and bodily regenera-

[32] *De Diligendo Deo*, III; *P.L.*, 182, 978C–979B.

tion which is the promise of the Christian faith. The time of the unfading fruits of the last harvest—which is also the time of the fresh flowers of the new age—is no bad one in which to enter into the garden of the grave. The imagery which St. Bernard uses in this passage is remarkably close to the third stanza of *Pearl*—a point to which we must return.

The actual description of the season in which corn is reaped with sharp sickles is reminiscent of the calendar illustrations in which the corn harvest is shown, usually for July or August. The foreground is always filled by the figures of the reapers, whose sickles make a sharp accent against the background of the uncut corn.[33] There may also be a suggestion of the final harvest in this detail. The same inconography was, in fact, used both for the calendar pictures and for the illustration of the symbolical corn and grape-harvest of the Apocalypse, where there is the same pictorial emphasis on the sickles:

> Mitte falcem tuam et mete, quia venit hora ut metatur, quoniam aruit messis terrae. Et misit qui sedebat super nubem falcem suam in terram, et demessa est terra . . .
>
> Mitte falcem tuam acutam et vindemia botros vineae terrae, quoniam maturae sunt uvae eius. Et misit angelus falcem suam acutam in terram et vindemiavit vineam terrae, et misit in lacum irae Dei magnum.

> 'Thrust in thy sickle and reap, because the hour is come to reap; for the harvest of the world is ripe.'
>
> And he that sat on the cloud thrust his sickle into the earth, and the earth was reaped . . .
>
> 'Thrust in thy sharp sickle and gather the clusters of the vineyard of the earth, because the grapes thereof are ripe.'
>
> And the angel thrust in his sharp sickle into the earth and gathered the vineyard of the earth, and cast it into the great press of the wrath of God (14, 15–16, 18–19).

In the Calendars the two harvests, of course, belong to different months, but in some illustrations of the Apocalypse they are

[33] The *Très Riches Heures du Duc de Berry* provides a good example, in the July miniature. The same scene, for the same month, also appears in the Grimani Breviary.

brought together as two panels within one frame, or as a composite picture, to illustrate chapter 14, 15–20.[34]

Gardens which derive from Genesis and from the Song of Songs are, thus, as common as their counterparts in the Love Visions, and were developed as a literary *topos* a good deal earlier. They all, whether they are wholly or partly allegorical, have in common a concern with man's original loss, which brought death into the world, and with the possibility of his recovery and regeneration. It is for this reason that the moral garden is linked to the *topos* of the Seasons of the Year—an important link in the argument which proves that God's Providence works for good in the natural world. For this reason, too, many writers expand the scriptural references to the voices in the gardens into an important feature, which brings hope and revelation. In the same way the sleep of the Song of Songs, traditionally associated with revelation, comes into prominence.

The *erber* of *Pearl* is not an entirely internalised moral garden, nor is it, like St. Bernard's in the *de Conversione*, a clearly defined allegory. But it is, through its associations with innumerable other gardens of the kind, a fit setting for a stormy mental conflict and for the beginning of hope. The central feature of the *erber* is not the *lignum vitæ* or *fons signatus*: it is, in striking contrast, the actual grave, introduced, as we have seen, in terms which allow no doubt of its literal and grievous significance. The grave in a garden of delights is no obvious *et in Arcadia ego*: it is the central motif around which the twin themes of the earthly and heavenly treasure, and of mortality and regeneration are organized. It is, therefore, to the imagery which centres on the grave which we must now turn if we are to understand just how the poet utilizes the garden-*topos*.

[34] Examples from a window at Vincennes and from a book-illustration are given by É. Mâle, *L'Art Religieux de la Fin du Moyen Âge*, p. 454 and p. 456. The grape-harvest is usually the September scene in the Calendars, and sickles, of course, do not feature in it. For the *Pearl* poet, it should be noted, the work of the Vineyard was that appropriate to an earlier month—'Keruen and caggen and man hit clos.' These activities are shown in March in the *Très Riches Heures*.

III

IMAGES OF
TRANSFORMATION

THE CENTRAL STANZAS of the proem (2 and 3) are the foci round
which the imagery of the proem itself, and of the poem as a
whole, is organized. Stanza 2, with its broken rhythms and in-
coherence of thought and feeling, establishes the reality of the
grave. Stanza 3 contains a clearly stated series of images which
relate to the theme of regeneration, both separately and as a
linked sequence.

In this stanza, as we have seen, the method is not that of
descriptio but of the statement of a proposition and of deduction
from it—in fact, of argument; and we are reminded that in the
Middle Ages imagery always relates to persuasion, and the support of argument, not to the creation of mood or atmosphere.
Stanza 3 brings together into one closely woven whole the
images of treasure, of spices, of flowers opening to the sun, of
unfading blossom and fruit, of grass grown from the dead seed,
and of harvested wheat:

> Þat spot of spyseȝ mot nedeȝ sprede,
> Þer such rycheȝ to rot is runne;
> Blomeȝ blayke and blwe and rede
> Þer schyneȝ ful schyr agayn þe sunne.
> Flor and fryte may not be fede
> Þer hit doun drof in moldeȝ dunne;
> For vch gresse mot grow of grayneȝ dede;
> No whete were elleȝ to woneȝ wonne.
> Of goud vche goude is ay bygonne;
> So semly a sede moȝt fayly not,
> Þat spryngande spyceȝ vp ne sponne
> Of þat precios perle wythouten spotte.

The separate images all possess a richness of association which has accumulated through a long tradition of use in Christian writing; but, more than this, the nexus as a whole also has the weight of tradition behind it.[1]

Since the logic by which such image-clusters arose is not now obvious, we must try to explore the links between the images, as well as their individual meaning.

2

GARDENS AND TREASURE

The poet is writing of a garden in the proem, and the images of plants and growth fit naturally into this frame. The link between the garden, and its plants and flowers, and treasure is not obvious to us, but it is not hard to show that it too would have been a natural association for the poet. Once more, the basis is to be found in the Bible. In Gen. 2, 10–12 the rivers of Eden are connected with treasure:

> Et fluvius egrediebatur de loco voluptatis ad irrigandum paradisum, qui inde dividitur in quattuor capita. Nomen uni Phison: ipse est qui circuit omnem terram Hevilath, ubi nascitur aurum; et aurum terrae illius optimum est: ibi invenitur bdellium et lapis onychus

> (And a river went out of the place of pleasure to water paradise, which from thence is divided into four heads. The name of the one is Phison: that is it which compasseth all the land of Hevilath, where gold groweth. And the gold of that land is very good: there is found bdellium, and onyx stone.)

In Revelations the passage which takes up the theme of the four streams and the Tree of Life in the description of the Heavenly Jerusalem is also closely connected with treasure, since, immediately after the description of the city in terms of jewels and gold, comes the description in terms of the water and the tree of Eden:

[1] Most of the passages quoted in the last chapter illustrate this aspect of the imagery. The citation from the *de Diligendo Deo* (p. 50) is especially important.

Et ostendit mihi fluvium aquae vitae splendidum tanquam crystallum, procedentem de sede Dei et Agni. In medio plateae eius et ex utraque parte fluminis lignum vitae adferens fructus duodecim, per menses singulos reddens fructum suum, et folia ligni ad sanitatem gentium.

(And he shewed me a river of water of life, clear as crystal, proceeding from the throne of God and of the Lamb. In the midst of the street thereof, and on both sides of the river, was the tree of life, bearing twelve fruits, yielding its fruits every month; and the leaves of the tree were for the healing of the nations (22, 1–2).)

The Song of Songs, too, mingles the imagery of treasure with that of the garden in the description of the Bridegroom and the Bride; for example:

Genae illius sicut areolae aromatum consitae a pigmentariis. Labia eius lilia distillantia myrrham primam. Manus illius tornatiles, aureae, plenae hyacinthis. Venter eius eburneus, distinctus sapphiris.

(His cheeks are as beds of aromatical spices set by the perfumers. His lips are as lilies dropping choice myrrh. His hands are turned and as of gold, full of hyacinths. His belly as of ivory, set with sapphires (5, 13–14).)

Ezechiel has a particularly striking reworking of the material of Genesis to produce a Paradise of Jewels which, besides affecting the development of the kind of imagery we are considering, influenced descriptions of Eden as the Earthly Paradise:[2]

In deliciis paradisi Dei fuisti, omnis lapis pretiosus operimentum tuum, sardius, topazius et iaspis, chrysolithus et onyx et beryllus, sapphirus et carbunculus et smaragdius; aurum opus decoris tui et foramina tua in die, qua conditus es, praeparata sunt.

(Thou wast in the pleasures of the paradise of God: every precious stone was thy covering: the sardius, the topaz and the jasper, the chrysolite and the onyx and the beryl, the sapphire and the carbuncle and the emerald: gold the work of thy beauty:

---

[2] Eccles. 2, 5–8, also associates a pleasure garden with treasure. For the Earthly Paradise and its surroundings, see below, pp. 89 ff.

and thy pipes were prepared in the day thou wast created (28, 13).)

It is not, indeed, surprising to find that the imagery of treasure and of the garden is linked by many other writers besides the *Pearl*-poet. An early instance of the association comes from St. Ephraem the Syrian, the poet in whose work so much of the imagery which we find to be typical of later writers has already crystallized:

> . . . Thy Paradise also, O Lord, looketh for the pure . . . In a spicy root the Son of David was brought to us, and from a dry ground flowed unto us the Fountain of mercies. How shall we reject that Fountain, which mercies have poured forth in dry lands? The key manifesteth itself unto him that seeketh it. Thy treasure rejoiceth in the thief that taketh it by violence, because Thou didst rejoice in that woman who from the hem of Thy garment took and stole a medicine for her plague . . . Thy silver, O Lord, sheweth mercy unto the empty, that he may be enriched thereby.[3]

In his *Rhythms on the Pearl*, St. Ephraem also links the jewel to the images of the tree and its leaf, to spice, to the root and stock, and, often, to the fountain.[4]

St. Bernard, as we have seen, associates both the treasure of Wisdom and pearls (with reference to the parable of the Pearl of Great Price), with the delights of the garden.

---

[3] From the translation of J. B. Morris, *Select Works of S. Ephrem the Syrian* (Oxford, 1847), pp. 152–3. St. Ephraem's works were influential in the Eastern Church, but it is unlikely that they were known to Western Medieval writers. Nevertheless his poems often illustrate traditions and usages which do reappear in the West. His long and very beautiful poem on the Pearl is particularly interesting. It shows a blend of biblical with Eastern imagery which can still be traced in many later works, Latin and vernacular (see below, pp. 141 ff.) On St. Ephraem's works see *Dictionnaire Théologique*, col. 188–93; *Dictionnaire Biblique*, col. 1889–91; Rubens Duval, *La Littérature Suriaque* (Paris, 1899), pp. 331–8; C. Ferry, *S. Ephrem Poète* (Paris, 1877); E. Emereau, *S. Ephrem le syrien, son œuvre littéraire grecque* (Paris, 1918).

[4] Ibid. The tree and leaf, p. 94; spice, p. 97; the fountain, pp. 97, 100, etc.; the root, stock, p. 100; medicine of life, p. 97.

Images of Transformation

Sapientia est, cujus pretium nescit homo . . . Sanctum est, margaritae sunt, nec faciet ipse quod prohibet.

(Wisdom is a treasure whose value no man can reckon (Wisdom 7, 14) . . . It is a holy thing: these things are pearls, nor will He do what He Himself forbade (i.e. allow them to be cast away. Matt. 7, 6; Luke 10, 21).[5])

With this spiritual treasure, still within the context of his long exposition of the garden, he contrasts earthly gold: 'The hearts of men are not better satisfied by gold than their bellies would be by gold.'[6]

The very popular and influential *Stimulus Amoris*, attributed to St. Bonaventura, also links the image of the garden to treasure: I quote from Hilton's version:

Lo now the gate of paradise is opened and through virtue of his blood is put away the burning pliant sword. Lo Jesu, that is the tree of life, is set in midst of paradise, thirled throughout in stock and in branches. If thou wilt have part of this fruit, lay thy foot of love in holes of this tree. Lo! how the treasure of wisdom and of endless charity is opened. Go by the breaches of that wound and thou shalt find delices of wisdom and of love.[7]

This, as well as the treasure of Wisdom 7, 14, is the treasure in the Casket—here used of the Incarnation. It is used of the Virgin birth in *Purity*, together with the image of the rose sprung from the Root of Jesse:

For loke fro fyrst þat he lyʒt wythinne þe lel Mayden,
By how comly a kest he watz clos þere, . . .
And þer watz rose reflayr where rote hatz ben ever,   (1069–70, 1079)

The same association is to be found in a carol by Audelay:

Angelis ther cam out of here toure
To loke apon this freschele floure,
Houe fayre he was in his coloure,

[5] *de Conversione ad Clericos*, xiii (*P.L.*, 182, 848B).
[6] Ibid., xiv (*P.L.*, 182, 849A).
[7] *The Goad of Love*, ed. C. Kirchberger (London, 1952), p. 52. The same passage also has the imagery of spices as medicine and food. See below, p. 75 ff.

57

And hou sote in his sauour,
    And to behold
How soche a flour myght sprynge in golde.[8]

The reference here to the flower growing in gold is so brief that
we might miss its force if we did not know of the habitual
blending of the imagery of flowers and treasure and remember
with Herbert that:

> Thou hast but two rare cabinets full of treasure,
>   The *Trinitie* and *Incarnation*.[9]

Dunbar uses the same cluster of images of the Virgin, and
includes those of the spice and the wheat, to which we must
presently return:

> Spyce, flour delice of paradys,
>   That baire the gloryus grayne.
> Imperiall wall, place palestrall,
>   Of peirles pulcritud;
> Tryumphale hall, hie trone regall
>   Of Godis celsitud;
> Hospitall riall, the lord of all
>   Thy closet did include;
> Bricht ball cristall, ros virginall,
>   Fulfillit of angell fude.[10]

[8] Greene, *The Early English Carols*, 172, st. 5, p. 130.

[9] 'Ungratefulness', *The Works of George Herbert*, ed. F. E. Hutchinson (Oxford, 1959), p. 82. See R. Tuve, *A Reading of George Herbert*, p. 141, and cf. 'To all Angels and Saints', *Works*, pp. 77–8, where the same images are used, including the mixed one 'a flower of his rich crown' (ll. 21–2). Herbert uses the 'crown imperiall' to bring together, through a pun, treasure and flowers in 'Peace'. The crown, of course, also bears the sense of the reward of the just, and symbolizes perfection. See below, pp. 165–8.

[10] *The Poems of William Dunbar*, ed. W. Mackay Mackenzie (Edinburgh, 1932), p. 162. Some words are ambiguous. *Spyce* could, as often, mean 'species', though this would require an unusual absolute use. *Grayne* could mean 'branch', as the editor suggests, but this does not fit the 'angell fude' so well as 'grain (of wheat)'. *Angell fude* is manna, and manna is normally equated with the bread of the sacrament, the body of Christ. (For a discussion of this equation, with illustrations, see R. Tuve, op. cit. pp. 161 f.) *Peirles*, too, could mean 'peerless' or 'of pearls'. As *margarita* is commonly used of the Blessed

Flower and jewel thus become interchangeable images, in poems addressed to the Virgin or to Christ. They could also stand interchangeably for the virtues, either in general, or for one selected according to the writers needs. Thomas de Hales blends plant and jewel imagery in his *Love Ron*, where the virtue which the maiden has to guard is 'tresur' and 'ymston':

> Mayde, al so ich þe tolde,
>   þe ymston of þi bur
> He is betere an hundred folde
>   Þanne alle þeos in heore culur;
> He is i-don in heouene golde
>   and is ful of fyn amur.
> Alle þat myhte hine wite scholde,
>   he schyneþ so bryht in heouene bur.[11]

While she preserves this treasure she is 'sweeter than any flower' (151), 'sweeter than any spice' (168).

Flower and jewel could stand, too, for the blessed soul in heaven, as well as for the virtues by which heaven was gained. The *Pearl*-poet uses the rose as well as the pearl for his beatified maiden, and Dante uses much jewel-imagery, including that of the pearl, in his descriptions of the souls of the blessed in the *Paradiso*.[12]

3

GROWTH AND DECAY AND THE UNFADING FLOWERS

In *Pearl* the imagery of plants and the cycle of growth and decay is linked to the theme of mortality and regeneration. This cycle of natural growth can be thought of in different ways. It

---

[11] Carleton Brown, *English Lyrics of the Thirteenth Century*, no. 22, ll. 177–84, p. 73.

[12] For a fuller discussion, see the chapter on the Symbolism of the Pearl and Rose, below, pp. 169–72.

Virgin in Latin hymns the latter is not in any way improbable. For another instance of linked flower and jewel imagery used of the Virgin, see *Medieval English Lyrics*, ed. R. T. Davies, p. 199. For instances in Latin hymns, see, e.g., Mone, *Hymni Latini Medii Aevi* (Freiburg, 1853–5) II, nos. 338, 341, 350.

can, for example, be related to the whole order of nature, as governed by the wider cycle of the seasons, which in turn take their place in the universal order. Day and night, the movement of the stars, the seasons, the growth and decay of plants are thus linked to form a *topos* in the strict sense of the term: they help to elaborate an argument which relates mortality to immortality.[13] Tertullian, for example, used the sequence in support of the resurrection of the body: the physical world, he says:

> ... signatum et ipsum humanae resurrectionis exemplum in testimonium vobis. Lux cottidie interfecta resplendet et tenebrae pari vice decedendo succedunt, sidera defuncta vivescunt, tempora ubi finiuntur, incipiunt; fructus consummantur et redeunt, certe semina non nisi corrupta et dissoluta fecundius surgunt; omnia pereundo servantur, omnia de interitu reformantur.

> (... is itself a signed portrait of the resurrection of mankind for a testimony to you. Daily the light is slain, and shines anew: darkness by the same sequence departs and returns: constellations which have died come to life again: seasons end and begin: fruits ripen and return: certainly grain rises in greater fertility only after it has decayed away and dispersed: all things are preserved by being destroyed, all are brought into shape again out of perdition.[14])

[13] This is, in fact, the Stoic argument to prove the order and divinity of the universe. The most important source for Christian writers was probably Cicero, *de Natura Deorum*, II. See E. Zeller, *Stoics Epicureans and Sceptics* (London, 1880), chapter vii, and E. V. Arnold, *Roman Stoicism* (Cambridge, 1911), §248, pp. 225–6.

[14] *Apologeticum*, 48, 7–8 (*Corpus Scriptorum Ecclesiasticorum Latinorum*, lxix, pp. 114–15. Translated by Evans, *de Resurrectione Carnis*, p. xiii.). The whole pattern seems to have been commonly taken over by Christian writers. Evans, p. 226, cites a passage from Minucius Felix (*Octavius*, 34), which, by adding the flowers and leafy trees is even closer to the sequence of *Pearl*. 'Vide adeo quam in solacium nostri resurrectionem futuram omnis natura meditetur: sol demergit et nascitur, astra labuntur et redeunt, flores recidunt et revivescunt post senium arbusta frondescunt, semina nonnisi corrupta revirescunt: ita corpus in saeculo ut arbores in hiberno: occultant virorem ariditate mentita.' Other early Christian examples are Clement of Rome, *Epist.* I, 24; Theophilus, *ad Autolycum*, I, 13.

The emphasis, in such passages, is always on the complete cycle, thought of as a whole. The succession from spring, through the harvest season, to winter, means life as well as death —not in the modern sense of a triumph of the life-force over its opposite, but because the process as a whole is designed to bring about renewal through mortality. The growth of dead seed and quiescent root can, therefore, figure forth man's hopes of immortality. Thus St. Bernard, in a passage on the four seasons, hymns winter as significant of spiritual regeneration:

O vernalis temperies, o aestiva venustas, o autumnalis ubertas: et, ne quid videar praeteriisse, o quies et feriatio hiemalis! Aut certe, si hoc magis probas, sola tunc hiems abiit et recessit.

(O mildness of Spring, O beauty of Summer, O fruitfulness of Autumn, and, lest I should seem to pass it over, O rest and leisure of Winter—or rather, if you will, there is only Winter, which comes and goes.[15])

Very closely connected with this idea, and indeed merging with it, is the idea of the cycle of growth as a direct expression of God's providence. Gavin Douglas uses this *topos* in its most usual form in the prologue to the tenth book of his *Eneados*, ll. 6–15:

Quhou mervallus beyn divisions of thi gracis,
Distribut so to ilk thing in all placis!
The son to schyne our all, and schaw his lyght,
The day to laubour, for rest thou ordanyt nycht;
For diuers causys schupe seir sessionis and spacis.

Fresche veir to burgioun herbis and sweit flouris;
The hait symmyr to nurys corn all houris,
And breid all kynd of fowlis, fysch, and beste;
Hervyst to rendir hus frutis maiste and leste:
Wyntyr to snyb the erth wyth frosty schouris.

The argument usually starts with a mention of the cosmos as a whole, and continues with the division of day and night, followed by the seasons. The pattern was established early—the ultimate source is the Book of Wisdom, 7, 17–21; it was used by

[15] *In Cant.* xxxiii, 6 (*P.L.*, 183, 954B). Cf. Vaughan 'The Seed Growing Secretly', *Works*, p. 510 f., especially ll. 25 ff.

such an influential writer as St. Augustine,[16] and a passage in Boethius follows the same plan.[17] In such treatments of the *topos* the seasons inevitably play an important part. In *Pearl*, the natural cycle is hinted at in the Dreamer's hope that the flowers and fruit which grow from the grave will not decay— that is that the natural order will be suspended. Emphasis also falls on Autumn, the harvest season, both as the season in which he enters the garden, and as part of the imagery of stanza 3. But the Dreamer has to learn that it is precisely through the cycle which brings decay that the flowers and fruit attain an immortality beyond change. His imagery is well chosen to express this paradox, since it is essentially ambivalent. Mortal flowers *must* fade in order to qualify for immortality. The flower is thus a symbol, from one point of view, of transience, and even of what is most worthless on earth.[18] From another point of view it becomes a symbol of immortality, and of the highest spiritual reward.

The fading flower and fruit have a biblical origin. Many poets borrowed their imagery from Isaiah 28, 4:

> Et erit flos decidens gloriae exsultationis eius, qui est super verticem vallis pinguium, quasi temporaneum ante maturitatem autumni, quod, cum adspexerit videns, statim, ut manu tenuerit, devorabit illud.

> (And the fading flower, the glory of his joy, who is on the head of the fat valley, shall be as a hasty fruit before the ripeness of

---

[16] *de Vera Religione*, I, xxix, 52 (*P.L.*, 34, 145). Cf. Origen, *On the Song of Songs*, III (*P.G.*, 13, 174).

[17] *de Consolatione Philosophiae*, I, m. 2 (cf. IV, pr. 6).

[18] Jung notes the ambiguity of the rose symbol in connection with alchemy. See *Mysterium Conjunctionis* (*The Collected Works*, vol. 14, translated by R. F. C. Hull, London, 1963), §421, p. 306. It can stand not only for transitory beauty but even for 'the lust of the world (*voluptas mundi*)'. The rose was used in this sense by Aelfric in his *Homily on the Assumption of St John*. The apostle, who stands above all for purity, exhorts his erring disciples not to prefer flourishing briefly like the rose to eternal bliss: 'Bicgað eow paellene cyrtlas, þaet ge to lytelre hwile scinon swa swa rose, þaet ge hraedlice forweornian. Beoð blow-ende and welige hwilwendlice, þaet ge ecelice waedlion.' On other aspects of the symbolism of the rose, see below, pp. 169–72.

autumn: which when he that seeth it shall behold, as soon as he taketh it in his hand, he will eat it up.[19])

A familiar example from the 14th century is the lyric 'An Autumn Song':

> Nou skr(y)nketh rose & lylie flour
> þat whilen ber þat suete sauour
> in somer þat suete tyde;
> ne is no quene so stark ne stour,
> ne no leuedy so bryht in bour
> Þat ded ne shal by-glyde.[20]

Flowers can thus be a symbol of mortality. Gregory the Great writes in the *Moralia in Job*:

Mundus tot floribus brevi siccandis repletur, quot hominibus.— Quasi flos etinim egreditur, quia nitet in carne; sed conteritur, quia redigitur in putredinem. Quid enim sunt nati homines in mundo, nisi quidem flores in campo? Tendamus oculos cordis in hanc latitudinem mundi praesentis, et ecce quasi tot floribus quot hominibus plenus est. Vita itaque in carne, flos in feno est.

(The world, just as it is, is filled briefly with withering flowers, so with men. For, just as the flower, man comes forth that he may shine in the flesh; but he wastes away that he may be returned as putrefaction. For what are men born on earth unless flowers in a field? Bend the eyes of our heart over the extent of this present world, and lo! it is full of flowers as of men. Life therefore in the flesh is flower in its withering.[21])

The flowers perish, but this is not the whole story. 'Nothing perishes except with a view to salvation',[22] man is returned as putrefaction in order, as St. Gregory goes on to say, to suffer re-creation:

quia ad illam speciem redit ad quam percipiendam creatus fuerat si in paradiso positus peccare noluisset.

[19] Cf. Isaiah 40, 6–8, and Job, 14, 2.
[20] Carleton Brown, *Religious Lyrics of the Fourteenth Century*, no. 10, ll. 1–6, p. 11.
[21] *In Job* XI, l. 67 (*P. L.*, 75, 983–4). Quoted and translated by B. F. Huppé, *Doctrine and Poetry*, p. 85.
[22] Nihil deperit nisi in salutem. Tertullian, *de Resurr. Carnis*, Evans, p. 34.

(For all things return to that beauty for which they were destined at our creation, had we not sinned in Paradise.[23])

The mortal flowers, as Spenser puts it, 'Doe worke their owne perfection' through change,[24] and find an immortal counterpart:

> These are thy wonders, Lord of love,
> To make us see we are but flowers that glide:
> Which when we once can finde and prove,
> Thou hast a garden for us, where to bide.[25]

It is, indeed, characteristic of imagery of this kind, that the very object which stands for mutability should come to stand for its opposite, immutably fixed in heaven as the symbol of immortality.

For the *Pearl*-poet the flowers which grow from the grave 'schyneȝ ful schyr agayn þe sunne'. In his literal description of the returning Spring in *Sir Gawain and the Green Knight* he had used the same motif. There the earthly flowers 'bide a blysful blusch of þe bryȝt sunne', which, in the drought of Autumn, is destined to wither them. In *Pearl* the unfading flowers open to the Sun of Righteousness, and are a symbol of eternal life gained through the grave. Similarly, in Vaughan's 'Regeneration' the garden contains:

> . . . a banke of flowers, where I descried
> (Though 'twas mid-day,)
> Some fast asleepe, others broad-eyed
> And taking in the Ray.[26]

[23] *In Job* XII, v, 7 (*P.L.*, 75, 990 f.). Quoted and Translated by Rahner, *Greek Myths and Christian Mystery*, p. 248.

[24] *Faerie Queene*, VII, vii, 58. When Nature gives her verdict on the mutability debate she argues on the same lines as Tertullian and St. Gregory the Great.

[25] Herbert, 'The Flower', *Works*, p. 167.

[26] *Works*, p. 399. On the nature of this garden, see above, pp. 42 ff. The imagery of this poem is discussed at length by R. A. Durr, *On the Mystical Poetry of Henry Vaughan* (Cambridge, Mass., 1963), pp. 79 ff. He does not, however, relate the poem to Gen., chapters 2 and 3, and, although it is most valuable on many points, his explanation seems out of focus. The garden is one of loss and exile, as the concluding lines show: 'Lord, then said I, / On me one breath, And let me dye before my death!' To this Vaughan adds Cant. 5, 17, 'Arise, O North,

Dante, too, plays on the idea of the real sun as the source of
the vital heat on which all growth and fruition depend, and the
Heavenly Sun through which all goodness comes into being, in
his description of the work on earth of St. Benedict:

> Questi altri fuochi tutti contemplanti
>   uomini fuoro, accesi di quel caldo
>   che fa nascere i fiori e'frutti santi,

> (These others, all contemplatives at root,
> Were quickened by that warm enkindling fire
> Which giveth birth to holy flower and fruit.
> *Paradiso*, xxii, 46–8)

and the simile which follows points the parallel to the natural
sun:

> . . . L'affetto che dimostri
>   meco parlando, e la buona sembianza
>   ch' io veggio e noto in tutti li ardor vostri,
> Così m' ha dilatata mia fidanza,
>   come 'l sol fa la rosa, quando aperta
>   tanto divien quant' ell' he di possanza.

> (. . . The affection which thou hast displayed,
> Speaking with me and the benign intent
> Which by your glowing you have each conveyed
> Dilate me, and make me newly confident
> As when the sun the rose encourages
> To open to the utmost of its bent. *Paradiso*, xxii, 52–7)

With a slight shift in emphasis, Paradise itself becomes for Dante
a rose blooming under a Sun which creates an eternal Spring:

> Nel giallo della rosa sempiterna,
>   che si dilata ed ingrada e redole
>   odor di lode al sol che sempre verna,
> qual è colui che tace e dicer vole,
>   mi trasse Beatrice . . .

---

and come thou South-wind, and blow upon my garden, that the spices
thereof may flow out', showing that the rushing wind which brings
the voice of God is still associated with the spices. Cf. Richard of
St. Victor, *Explicatio in Cant. Cant.* xxxi, where the south wind is the
'Spiritus sui consolationem' (*P.L.*, 196, 494A).

Proem

(To the yellow of the Rose whose leaves dilate,
  Tier over tier, perfumed with praises quired
  To the Sun that doth eternal Spring create,
Me, like to one made mute, who yet desired
  To speak, Beatrice onward drew . . .[27] *Paradiso*, xxx, 124–8)

while the Blessed Virgin is a fair garden in heaven, flowering beneath Christ's rays:

> Perchè la faccia mia sì t' innamora,
>   che tu non ti rivolgi al bel giardino
>   che sotto i raggi di Cristo s' infiora?

> (Why does my face enamour so, that thou
>   On the fair garden hast no glance bestowed
>   Which flowers beneath Christ's rays?
>   *Paradiso*, xxiii, 70–2)

In *Pearl*, not only flowers but also fruits are unfading. St. Bernard used this motif in the passage already quoted from the *de Diligendo Deo*.[28] For Dante the Saints themselves fill Heaven with eternal fruit:

> . . . Ecco le schiere
>   del triunfo di Cristo e tutto il frutto
>   ricolto del girar di queste spere!

> ('Behold the assembled hosts,' Beatrice said,
>   Behold Christ triumphing, and all the fruit
>   These spheres have in their circling harvested.
>   *Paradiso*, xxiii, 19–21)

In England the *Myroure of Oure Ladye*, the fifteenth-century commentary on the services of Sion Monastery, has the following passage in explanation of a verse and response in the Monday Service at Matins:

Responce. *Benedicta.* Blessed be the erthe whose flowres. fade not. whose fruyte ys lyfe. of all that lyue. geuyng noryshynge to all mankynde. Verse. *Vere*, For southe thys erthe ys the vyrgyn mother. the floures are her workes. her sonne ys the fruyte.[29]

---

[27] Cf. St. Bernard, on the mid-day Sun of Heaven: 'O eternal solstice, where the day never passes, O mid-day Sun, O softness of eternal Spring' (*In Cant.* xxxiii, 6 (*P.L.*, 183, 954B)).

[28] Above, p. 50.

[29] Ed. J. H. Blunt, *E.E.T.S.*, xix (London, 1873), p. 181.

Images of Transformation

The *Pearl*-poet brings the imagery of the flowers and growing plants into close relation to the grave. That this was a well-established variant of the *topos* is suggested by the reappearance of very similar associations in the work of two seventeenth-century poets. In 'The Seed growing Secretly' Vaughan writes first of

> thy humble grave
> Set with green herbs, glad hopes and brave;

and continues:

> O calm and sacred bed where lies
> In deaths dark mysteries
> A beauty far more bright
> Than the noons cloudless light
> For whose dry dust green branches bud
> And robes are bleach'd in the *Lambs* blood.[30]

Herrick's 'Dirge of Jephthah's Daughter' is particularly interesting as testimony to the persistence of the whole nexus of imagery. He even apostrophizes the maiden as 'Pearle of praise' and goes on, after the real, fading flowers have been laid on her grave—

> The Daffadill,
> And other flowers . . .
> The Primrose, and the Violet—

to play with the idea of the 'seed of life': all other pleasures, like buried seed, are laid in the grave, one alone, the pleasure of mourning for her, is left outside it. The grave itself is described in terms of a Paradise of sweets, spice, and perpetual spring:

> Sleep in thy peace, thy bed of Spice;
> And make this place all Paradise:
> May Sweets grow here! & smoke from hence,
> Fat Frankincense:
> Let Balme, and Cassia send their scent
> From out thy Maiden-Monument.

[30] *Works*, p. 512, ll. 22–36.

Proem

May no Wolfe howle, or Screech-Owle stir
A wing about thy Sepulcher!
No boysterous winds, or stormes, come hither,
To starve, or wither
Thy soft sweet Earth! but (like a spring)
Love keep it ever flourishing.[31]

Herrick would have had no difficulty in appreciating the development of the imagery in the proem of *Pearl*, nor would he have doubted that it turned on 'the harmlesse and unhaunted ground' where innocence was buried.

The flowers which grow from the Pearl's grave are given colours, and these are named in a line which moves slowly and with weight:

Blomeȝ blayke and blwe and rede
Þer schyneȝ ful schyr agayn þe sunne.

This insistence on detail in a part of the poem where, as we have seen, such detail is very sparingly used, is obviously important.[32] It would be likely to set the mind of a contemporary reader working in the direction of the flowers of the virtues.

The blossoms of immortality, in fact, very easily shift their emphasis a little, and become the very virtues by which man regains his place in the Garden of God. St. Gregory of Nyssa passes straight on from his account of the winter of disobedience which put an end to the flowers of Paradise, to speak of the flowers of the virtues, which grow in the Spring of the Redemption:

For the flowers of life are the virtues, which blossom now, and bring forth their *fruit in season* . . . Do you see, He says, the meadow blossoming with flowers? Do you see chastity shining

[31] L. C. Martin, *The Poetical Works of Robert Herrick* (Oxford, 1956), pp. 359 ff.

[32] The Chaucerian translation of the *Roman de la Rose* mentions 'floures yelowe, white, and rede' (1433), and blue is added in the *Parlement of Foules* 1. 186. But these colour lists, like the other details in the description, merely add to the brilliance of the scene, and are introduced without special emphasis in passages which, unlike the stanza we are considering, depend for their whole effect on the amassing of visual detail.

like a fragrant lily? Do you see the rose of modesty, and the
violet, the *good odour of Christ*? Why not make a garland of
these?[33]

In the *Vitis Mystica* of St. Bonaventura the imagery of the
flowers is elaborated:

> Propterea *exinanavit semetipsum* Filius Dei, *formam servi acci-
> piens*, et plantatus est in terra nostra et corporis nostri deformi-
> tatem accepit et fronduit, floruit, fructus plurimos attulit, ut per
> hoc, quod nostrae humanitati unitus fuit, Deitati suae nos
> uniret. Sed quia sine flore non pervenitur ad fructum, floruit
> benignissimus Dominus meus Iesus. Qui sunt eius flores nisi
> virtutes? Floruit autem admirabiliter et valde singulariter et
> excellenter vitis haec inclyta, non uno florum genere, sicut aliae
> vites et arbores, sed omnium in se florum speciem continebat:
> violam scilicet humilitatis, lilium castitatis, rosam patientiae et
> caritatis, et crocum abstinentiae.

> (Therefore the Son of God emptied Himself, taking the nature
> of a slave, and was planted in our earth, and accepted the de-
> formity of our body, and put forth leaves, flowers, and, above all,
> fruit, so that, as He was united to our humanity, He might unite
> us to his Godhead. But, because there can be no fruit without
> flowers, my most gracious Lord Jesus brought forth flowers.
> What are His flowers but the virtues? So this glorious vine
> flowered in a wonderful, and indeed in a unique and excellent
> way, not with flowers of a single kind, like other vines and trees,
> but having in itself the beauty of all kinds of flowers: the violet
> of humility, the lily of chastity, the rose of patience and love, and
> the crocus of abstinence.[34])

The flowers of the virtues, *par excellence*, are thus violet, lily,
and rose,[35] flowers of the three colours blue, white, and red,

[33] *Commentary on the Song of Songs (P.G.*, 44, 872B). Translation
by Musurillo, *From Glory to Glory*, p. 189. Cf. the comment on the
lilly of the valley (*P.G.*, 44, 840C), Musurillo, p. 173.

[34] *Vitis Mystica*, xiv (*Decem Opuscula*, ad Claras Aquas, 1926), p.
448.

[35] The fourth, the crocus, is more unusual. Rose, lily and violet are
commonly used in connection with Christ, and also His Mother. This
is especially common in the Latin Hymns (for one combining all three
flowers, addressed to the Virgin, see Mone, *Hymni Latini*, II, p. 184).
The flowers are also commonly used of Saints, particularly of those

specified in *Pearl*. There is, I think, no doubt that the *Pearl*-poet's flowers which, by springing from mortality indicate immortality, also, like those of St. Gregory, suggest the virtues growing in the soil of human life and surviving the grave; but this is an idea which, for a good reason, the poet has left in the background and we shall do his poem no service by putting it into the foreground. If he had wished to ultilize more than a suggestion of the symbolism of the flower colours he would no doubt have done so. It was not a subject on which a medieval poet was likely to be gravelled for lack of matter. The expanded *Vitis Mystica* devotes numerous chapters to its exposition.[36] Nor would it have been very appropriate to his poem. Death took his Pearl before there was time to cultivate the flowers of the virtues:

> Þou lyfed not two ȝer in oure þede;
> Þou cowþeȝ neuer God nauþer plese ne pray.   (483–4)

Nevertheless, the point of the poet's unusual treatment of the parable of the Vineyard[37] is that, through baptism, the child did in fact enter the vineyard, and laboured there for a short space in the sense that she committed no deadly sin for 'þe innocent is ay saf by ryȝt' (684).

[36] *P.L.*, 184, 635 ff.

[37] Cf. Gordon, p. xxvi. D. W. Robertson (*M.L.N.*, lxv, p. 152), cites a parallel from Bruno Astensis (twelfth century).

---

who, like the Pearl-Maiden were part of the Virgin host of the Lamb. Sigebert of Gembloux (*c*. 1030–1112) described the 'virginalis sancta frequentia' in such terms:

> Hi pervagantes prata recentia
> pro velle querunt serta decentia,
>   rosas legentes passionis
>   lilia vel violas amoris.

(ed. Dümmler, *Passio Sanctae Luciae*, st. 19, *Abhandl. d. Kgl. Akad.* Berlin, 1893.) Reprinted and translated by Helen Waddell, *Medieval Latin Lyrics* (London, 1938), p. 158–9.

4
TREASURE AND MORTALITY

If gardens and the plants which grow in them are linked to mortality, so, in its turn, is the imagery of treasure, which, we have already seen linked to the garden.

In *Pearl*, as elsewhere, flower and jewel are interchangeable images, and they are used in close association with the theme of death. In the Maiden's speech in ll. 257 ff. the images of the jewel in the casket and the flower in the garden are intertwined:

> Sir, ȝe haf your tale mysetente,
> To say your perle is al awaye,
> Þat is in cofer so comly clente
> As in þis gardyn gracios gaye,
> Hereinne to lenge for euer and play.   (257–61)

and in the next stanza the 'gemme þat þe watȝ lef' (266) becomes the mortal rose, which, in its immortal transformation becomes a jewel again:

> Bot, jueler gente, if þou schal lose
> Þy ioy for a gemme þat þe watȝ lef,
> Me þynk þe put in a mad porpose,
> And busyeȝ þe aboute a raysoun bref;
> For þat þou lesteȝ watȝ bot a rose
> Þat flowred and fayled as kynde hyt gef.
> Now þurȝ kynde of þe kyste þat hyt con close
> To a perle of prys hit is put in pref.   (265–72)

The image of the rose is picked up later in the sense of the unfading flower in Heaven, and proves the Dreamer's acceptance of the Maiden's teaching:

> And þou so ryche a reken rose,
> And bydeȝ here by þys blysful bonc
> Þer lyueȝ lyste may neuer lose.   (906–8)

The images of flower and jewel are a gentle way of presenting the facts of mortality. The Maiden, however, does not neglect to drive the lesson home by returning to the theme of the grave in its worst aspect. At l. 320 she uses the image of the clinging clay which had already been used in the proem:

> Er moste þou ceuer to oþer counsayle:
> Þy corse in clot mot calder keue.
> For hit watȝ forgarte at Paradys greue;
> Oure ȝorefader hit con mysseȝeme.
> Þurȝ drwry deth boȝ vch man dreue.
> Er ouer þys dam hym Dryȝtyn deme.   (319–24)

She returns to the idea later, at the climax of her description of the heavenly Pearl as the Bride of the Lamb:

> Lasse of blysse may non vus bryng
> Þat beren þys perle vpon oure bereste,
> For þay of mote couþe neuer mynge
> Of spotleȝ perleȝ þat beren þe creste.
> Alþaȝ oure corses in clotteȝ clynge,
> And ȝe remen for rauþe wythouten reste,
> We þurȝoutly hauen cnawyng;
> Of on dethe ful oure hope is drest.   (853–60)

The linked imagery of treasure and flowers in relation to the grave is in fact woven through the poem.

St. Erkenwald—and it is a good reason for ascribing it to the *Pearl*-poet[38]—also links treasure in general and pearls in particular to the grave. The theme of this poem is God's mercy to the good pagan. The scene is set in London in the time of Bishop Erkenwald, where work is in progress on the 'principal temple' of the town, which was to be rededicated after its earlier heathen use. The workmen uncover a tomb in which is found a body, richly clothed and undecayed. The handling of the story is interesting. The theme is a common hagiographical one; but, through the poet's treatment and the imagery he uses, it becomes not merely an account of a particular miracle but of a manifestation of God's grace operating with, not against, the

---

[38] On the authorship of St. Erkenwald, see Savage, *St. Erkenwald* pp. xlviii ff.; Fr. Storman has kindly pointed out to me that the same unusual interpretation of psalm 23 (Vulgate) as referring to two distinct categories of the saved occurs in *Pearl*, stanza 57, and *St. Erkenwald*, ll. 277–9, which seems to point strongly to common authorship.

natural cycle. Great stress is laid not only on the absence of decay in the body and clothes of the good pagan judge but also on the riches and beauty—among which gold and pearls are singled out—which have been miraculously preserved. They are described in detail:

> Araide on a riche wise, in rialle wedes:
> Al with glisnande golde his gowne wos hemmyd,
> With mony a precious perle picchit þeron,
> And a gurdille of golde bigripide his mydelle;
> A meche mantel on lofte with menyver furrit,
> Þe clothe of camelyn ful clene, with cumly bordures;
> And on his coyfe wos kest a coron ful riche,
> And a semely septure sett in his honde.
>
> Als wemles were his wedes, with-outen any tecche,
> Oþer of moulynge, oþer of motes, oþir moght-freten,
> And als bryȝt of hor blee, in blysnande hewes,
> As þai hade ȝepely in þat ȝorde bene ȝisturday shapen. (77–88)

The bishop expresses his wonder at the preservation of the clothing: the body might have been embalmed, but he knows of no means of saving cloth from natural decay:

> Þi body may be enbawmyd, hit bashis me noght
> Þat hit þar ryve ne rote, ne no ronke wormes;
> Bot þi coloure ne þi clothe, I know in no wise
> How hit myȝt lye by monnes lore and last so longe. (261–4)

The body replies that these earthly riches have been preserved by 'þe riche Kynge of reson' (267). The bishop considers that if such a reward has been granted the body, the soul must also have 'of his grace summe brawnche' and, again picking up the word 'rich', which is woven through the passage, asks to be told:

> ... of þi soule, in sele quere ho wonnes,
> And of þe riche restorment þat raȝt hyr oure Lorde! (279–80)

This brings the poem to its point: the suspension of the natural order of decay for the body has not brought any benefit to the soul which 'sittes ... Dwynande in þe derke dethe, þat dyȝt us oure fader' (293–4). Once the bishop has baptized the

73

body, and the soul has been received in heaven, the poem reaches its conclusion in the full restoration of the natural order:

> Wyt this cessyd his sowne, sayd he no more;
> Bot sodenly his swete chere swyndid and faylide,
> And alle the blee of his body wos blakke as þe moldes,
> As roten as a rottok þat rises in powdere.
> For as sone as þe soule was sesyd in blisse,
> Corrupt was þat oþer crafte þat covert þe bones;
> For þe ay-lastande life, þat lethe shalle never,
> Devoydes uche a vayneglorie, þat vayles so litelle.   (341–8)

The theme of earthly and heavenly treasure is, in fact, worked out in *St. Erkenwald* in close association with the theme of mortality and regeneration; and, in the most literal sense, the discussion takes place over an open grave.

There are some signs, though it is a less common usage, that the pearl itself was immediately linked to mortality, as a symbol of the defeat of the ravages of the grave. I have already quoted Bacon on the tradition that the pearl's lustre could survive burial in a literal sense.[39] Tertullian compares the body to pearls, in an argument concerned with resurrection which has also been quoted.[40] Donne, who may have this passage in mind, has the same image:

> In the generall resurrection upon naturall death, God shall work upon this dispersion of our scattered dust, as in the first fall, which is the Divorce, by way of Re-union, and in the second, which is Putrifaction, by way of Re-efformation; so in this third, which is Dispersion, by way of Re-collection; where mans buried flesh hath brought forth grasse, and that grasse fed beasts, and those beasts fed men, and those men fed other men, God that knowes in which Boxe of his Cabinet all this seed Pearle lies, in what corner of the world every atome, every graine of every mans dust sleeps, shall recollect that dust, and then recompact that body, and then reinanimate that man, and that is the accomplishment of all.[41]

[39] See above, p. 24.
[40] See above, p. 9.
[41] *The Sermons of John Donne*, ed. E. M. Simpson and G. R. Potter, VII (Berkeley and Los Angeles, 1954), p. 115.

In a context like this the treasure comes to stand for an immortality gained through mortality and so comes to share the ambivalence of the flower image, signifying what is gained as well as what is lost, and standing for eternal value as well as earthly dross. If such a tradition was known to the *Pearl*-poet and his readers it would certainly have enriched his poem, but we cannot, of course, be sure that it was familiar in fourteenth-century England.

5

THE SPICES

The spices in the proem of *Pearl* serve a double purpose. They are, as we have seen, an important feature of the moral garden which is derived from the combination of Genesis and the Song of Songs, and, in the fourth stanza, they are part of the literal description of such a place. In the third stanza, however, they are part of the imagery which the poet assembles round the idea of death and loss.

As images spices have two main and interlocking associations. They are linked to the ideas of medicine and of unction.[42] Both associations come together in the Gospels in the precious ointment of Luke 7, 37–50 (Matt. 26, 6–13), with which the woman who had been a sinner anoints Jesus, and in the spices bought later by the women 'that coming they might anoint Jesus' (Mark 16, 1). Spices thus become part of the imagery of incarnation and redemption. They are used of Christ, and, as we have already seen, of the Blessed Virgin.[43] They are, of course, also associated with the regeneration of the soul, since, as unction and medicine, they stand for Christ's healing and priestly power; and with mortality, since they are particularly associated with His death and burial. It is not, therefore, surprising to find spices as part of the imagery centring on the

[42] 'Spices are a species of medicament.' Origen, *On the Song of Songs* I, 3 (*P.G.*, 13, 90). In Exodus 30, 22–5, Moses was commanded to make the unction with spices. Medicinal ointment and unction are linked in Origen's commentary on the *Song of Songs* (e.g. loc. cit.).

[43] See my article 'Langland on the Incarnation', *R.E.S.*, N.S., xvi (1965), pp. 349 ff., and above, p. 58.

75

grave. Whether, like flower and jewel, they can also stand for the beatified soul is not easy to say. The Dreamer addresses the maiden as '*specyal spice*' (938), but the word is ambiguous; it could mean merely 'kind' (of thing), a variation of the common use of 'þing' to mean 'maiden'.[44]

Spices can certainly stand for the virtues through which the soul earns its reward, and by which its healing manifests itself. Hilton's *Goad of Love* provides a good example, in which spice is also thought of as medicine and food:

> Lo the spicer's shop is opened to the full of all sweet spicery, full of medicinable ointments, Gracia dei and salve is there enough. Go into it and get thee medicine for to heal thee, and restore thee and keep thee in holiness. What spicery that thee liketh and what lectuarie thou covetest, there take it, meekness and mildness, patience and soberness, chastity and cleanness, charity and softness and such other delicate confections, if thou love them there mayst thou have them.[45]

The spices thus take their place in this series of images of regeneration, and are of the same kind, with the same general significance, as the flower and the treasure.

6

SEED AND ROOT

When he uses the imagery of the seed and, by implication, of the root, the *Pearl*-poet is invoking one of the richest complexes of associations available to the medieval poet; but these associations are not always what the modern reader would expect. As Hugo Rahner warns us 'the Fathers of the church . . . when they spoke of roots and flowers, could imply things to which our ears are no longer attuned.'[46]

---

[44] See *O.E.D.*, Thing, sb. 10. The same difficulty arises over the use of *species* ('spice' or 'species') in Latin hymns. The *Love Ron*, however, has an unambiguous phrase: 'swetture þan eny spis' (l. 168). *Pearl*, l. 235, *special spece*, suggests 'species'. Both phrases may have been current.

[45] *The Goad of Love*, ed. C. Kirchberger, p. 52.

[46] *Greek Myths and Christian Mystery*, p. 180–1.

In the case of the seed, the most important source for the Christian Middle Ages is undoubtedly St. Paul's elaboration—already metaphorical—of John 12, 24–5 in 1 Cor. 15. He has, besides the idea of dying to live, the 'bare grain'—the seed which is insignificant in comparison with the plant—and the idea that every seed reproduces its own kind:

> Insipiens, tu quod seminas non vivificatur, nisi prius moriatur; et quod seminas, non corpus quod futurum est seminas, sed nudum granum, ut puta, tritici aut alicuius ceterorum; Deus autem dat illi corpus sicut vult et unicuique seminum proprium corpus. . . . Sic et resurrectio mortuorum. Seminatur in corruptione, surget in incorruptione.

> (Senseless man, that which thou sowest is not quickened, except it die first. And that which thou sowest, thou sowest not the body that shall be; but bare grain, as of wheat, or of some of the rest. But God giveth it a body as he will; and to every seed its proper body . . . So also is the resurrection of the dead. It is sown in corruption; it shall rise in incorruption (1 Cor. 15, 36–8, 42).)

St. Augustine, too, is an important source: he writes both of the power of the seed, so disproportionate to its size, and of its determining nature in *On Christian Doctrine*, 1, 33, 37, and mentions 'the force of minute seeds generating species and numbers, and everything in its kind preserving its proper mode'. The reference to number shows that he is thinking not only of the seed of plants, though the reference to the 'force of minute seeds' shows that this idea is present, but of the philosophical concept of seed as a creative principle.[47]

From the idea of the seed as determining the form of the plant, comes the Christian metaphor of the seed as the divinely implanted likeness in man, the image of God, obscured by the fall, which can be restored through grace. The seed, in this sense, is

[47] Cf., e.g., Plutarch, *Moralia*, 'There are, in fact, some who state that fire is the first principle of the universe and, like a seed, creates everything out of itself and receives all things into itself when the conflagration occurs' (Loeb edn, with translation by H. Cherniss and W. C. Helmbold, vol. xii, 1957, p. 291 f.).

like the withered flowers renewed in a new spring, or the green shoots which branch again in regeneration.[48]

The *Pearl*-poet transforms his Pearl, lost in the ground, to a seed in the earth, and the image is entirely appropriate to his theme. Whether or not, like Donne, he intends also to glance at a pun on 'seed-pearl' is uncertain.[49] From this seed grow plants and flowers, which have their roots below, in the grave.

The root is not quite so fundamental as the seed as originator of the plant, but it contains the vital substance which gives form and being to leaves and flowers. When Lydgate wrote of the plant in winter:

> In Rootys restith / the vertu vegetatyff
>
> > (*Secrees*, 1446)

or Chaucer, in the Prologue to the *Canterbury Tales*, of the regenerative action of Spring showers, which

> The droghte of March hath perced to the roote,
> And bathed every veyne in swich licour
> Of which vertu engendred is the flour,   (2–4)

they are both in strict accord with Cicero:

> in arborum autem et earum rerum quae gignuntur e terra radicibus inesse principatus putatur.
>
> (With trees and plants the ruling principle is believed to be located in the roots.[50])

The terms in which he defines 'the ruling principle' throw a good deal of light on the root-image, which, like the seed, means far more than a mere cause of origin, a stage of development left behind and superseded by what grows from it:

> Principatum autem id dico quod Graeci ἡγεμονικόν vocant, quo nihil in quoque genere nec potest nec debet esse praestantius;

[48] Cf. Durr, *On the Mystical Poetry of Henry Vaughan*, pp. 125 ff., where a number of references are collected.

[49] The compound is not recorded before the sixteenth century in English, and seems to have been first used of ornamentation on cloth. See *O.E.D.*, seed-pearl.

[50] *De Natura Deorum*, II, 11 (edited with a translation by H. Rackham, Loeb Classical Library, Cambridge, Mass., 1951, pp. 150–1).

ita necesse est illud etiam in quo sit totius naturae principatus esse omnium optimum omniumque rerum potestate domina-tuque dignissimum.

(I use the term 'ruling principle' as the equivalent of the Greek *hēgemonikon*, meaning that part of anything which must and ought to have supremacy in a thing of that sort. Thus it follows that the element which contains the ruling principle of the whole of nature must also be the most excellent of all things and the most deserving of authority and sovereignty over all things.[51])

In this sense the root, though it is buried in the earth and must, to fulfil its destiny, give rise to the flowers which reach up to heaven, is the basis and condition of man's salvation. It has the power to survive 'winter', the cutting back of the shoots through sin—St. Gregory of Nyssa's 'winter of disobedience'.

St. Gregory the Great develops the idea in a way which brings root and seed close together:

Potest etiam radix justi ipsa natura humanitatis intellegi, ex qua subsistit. Quae videlicet radix senescit in terra cum natura carnis deficit in pulverem redacta. Cujus in pulvere truncus emoritur, quia exstinctum corpus a sua specie dissipatur. Sed ad odorem aquae germinat, quia per adventum sancti Spiritus resurgit: *Et faciet comam quasi cum primum plantatum est*, quia ad illam speciem redit ad quam percipiendam creatus fuerat si in paradiso positus peccare noluisset.

(By this root we may understand the nature of man, that nature that is the essential part of him. Even as a root ages in the ground and gradually begins to die, so it is with man, who, according to the nature of his flesh, resolves himself at the last into ashes. The root becomes dust, and the beauty of man's body suffers corruption. But the fragrance of the living water causes the root to revive, and similarly, the human body is recreated when the Holy Ghost descends. For all things return to that beauty for which they were destined at our creation, had we not sinned in Paradise.[52])

[51] Ibid., loc. cit.

[52] *In Job*, XII, v, 7 (*P.L.*, 75, 989 f.). See Rahner, op. cit. p. 248. Cf. St. Augustine, *Enarrat. in Psalmos*, 51, 12 (*P.L.*, 36, 607C), and St. Gregory the Great, *Registri Epistolarum*, ix, cviii (*P.L.*, 77, 1035). Quisquis in ejus radices (caritatis) se inserit, nec a viriditate deficit, nec a

Proem

In the Middle English Lyric a very similar train of thought is often found, as a rule linked to the Root of Jesse, a natural association of ideas. A carol of the fifteenth century, for example, plays on the idea of the root of the healing plant from which all good things grow:

> O of Jesse thow holy rote,
> That to thi pepill arte syker merke,
> We calle to the; be thow oure bote,
> In the that we gronde all owre werke.
>
> Thy laude ys exalted by lordes and kynges;
> No man to prayse the may suffice;
> Off the spryngith vertu and all gode thynges;
> Come and delyuere vs fro owre malice.
>
> Off the may no malice growe,
> That thou thyselue arte pure godenesse;
> In the be rotedde what we showe,
> And graunte ows blisse after owre decesse.[53]

The idea of root or seed reproducing its proper kind is present here, as it is in *Pearl*: 'Of goud vche goude is ay bygonne.'

Another lyric on the Root of Jesse plays, much as the *Pearl*-poet does, on the idea of seed, root and healing flower:

> There is a floure sprung of a tre,
> The rote therof is callid Jesse;
> A floure of pryce;
> There is non seche in paradise!

God himself sows the seed in Bethlehem, where the angel finds Mary '[In] medis here herbere', and from it springs a flower 'yet bers the prys / As most of hele / To slake oure sorous eueredele'.[54]

A carol of the Eucharist uses the images of flower and spice

[53] Greene, *The Early English Carols*, no. 1, p. 1.
[54] Ibid., no. 172a, p. 129.

---

fructibus inanescit, quia humorem fecunditatis opus efficax non amittit. (Whosoever grafts himself into its roots (Charity's) neither falls away from greenness nor becomes empty of fruits, because effective work loses not the moisture of fecundity.) See also Rahner, op. cit. pp. 259 ff., for this development in relation to the mandrake root.

in connection with the root in a way which is hardly intelligible
unless we remember how they have been linked elsewhere:

> Of alle the spyces that I knowe,
> Blyssid be the qwete flour.

> Qwete is bothe semely and sote;
> Of alle spyces that is bote;
> The vertu spryngit out of the rote,
> So blyssid be the qwete flour.[55]

Both *spyce* and *flour*, it is true, are ambiguous here. *Spyce* could
mean 'kind', 'species', rather than 'spice', and *flour* could mean
'flour' for making bread, perhaps in its original sense 'fine
flour', i.e. the 'flower, best part, of the wheat'. It is very possible
that there is deliberate word-play in this carol. *Bote*, 'remedy',
however, is unambiguous, and fits in with 'spice' as medicine.
The fact that wheat is not a spice, and does not, in the normally
accepted sense, bear a flower, would not disturb the poet who is
concerned with associations of ideas not with visual images.

7

WHEAT

The final image in the cluster is that of the wheat, which, in
accordance with John 12, 24–5 and 1 Cor. 15, grows from the dead
seed. We have, in fact, already encountered it in the illustration
from Dunbar and in the Eucharist carols just quoted.

In relation to the seed, in fact, the wheat is part of a whole
complex of plant imagery. It has, however, more specialized
associations. It is harvested: and, further, it is made into bread.

As bread it stands, obviously, for the body of Christ. Dunbar,
writing of the incarnation uses it in this way and links it to spice
and flower:

> Spyce, flour delice of paradys,
> That baire the gloryus grayne . . .
> . . . ros virginall,
> Fulfillit of angell fude.[56]

[55] Ibid., no. 320, p. 220.
[56] *Poems*, p. 162, ll. 71–2, 79–80. This poem is built up of reminis-
cences of Latin hymns to the Virgin. In these the linking of the bread

In *Pearl*, however, this aspect of the wheat, as providing life-giving bread, is not specifically mentioned. The poet speaks rather of harvest, as the result of sowing:

> No whete were elleȝ to woneȝ wonne.

In the Harvest we have an image very like those based on flower and fruit: it stands, on the one hand, for mortality and, on the other, for the final gathering of God's own harvest into blessedness.

The ambivalence of the image is well brought out by Langland's use of it. In Passus vi of *Piers Plowman* (B), to work with Piers at ploughing and sowing stands for right participation in this mortal life. But the good workers in these earthly fields are promised a share in a harvest which the very rise of the verse shows to be more than this world's:

> Ac who so helpeth me to erie or sowen here ar I wende,
> Shal haue leue, bi owre lorde, to lese here in heruest,
> And make hem mery there-mydde . . .   (vi, 67–9)

and,

> At heighe pryme Peres lete the plowe stonde,
> To ouersen hem hym-self, and who-so best wrouȝte,
> He shulde be huyred ther-after, whan heruest-tyme come.
> (vi, 114–16)

The Eucharist carols illustrate well the blending of the imagery of wheat, harvested as bread, with flower, and root. Exactly the same complex reappears in the seventeenth century in Herbert's 'Peace':

> Then went I to a garden, and did spy
>   A gallant flower,
> The Crown Imperiall: Sure, said I,
>   Peace at the root must dwell.
> But when I digg'd, I saw a worm devoure
>   What show'd so well.

---

and manna (angel's food) is common. See, e.g., Mone, *Hymni Latini*, II, nos. 504, ll. 305–8; 507, ll. 161–2; 555, ll. 48–57. See also Greene, *Carols*, p. 219, no. 318, sts. 3–4; p. 221, no. 321, sts. 1–2. Cf. Gregory the Great, *Epist.* xxviii, 'Because a grain of wheat, falling into the earth has died, that it might not reign in heaven alone.'

Images of Transformation

At length I met a rev'rend good old man,
Whom when for Peace
I did demand, he thus began:
There was a Prince of old
At Salem dwelt, who liv'd with good increase
Of flock and fold.

He sweetly liv'd; yet sweetnesse did not save
His life from foes.
But after death out of his grave
There sprang twelve stalks of wheat:
Which many wondring at, got some of those
To plant and set.

It prosper'd strangely, and did soon disperse
Through all the earth:
For they that taste it do rehearse,
That vertue lies therein,
A secret vertue bringing peace and mirth
By flight of sinne.

Take of this grain, which in my garden grows,
And grows for you;
Make bread of it: and that repose
And peace, which ev'ry where
With so much earnestnesse you do pursue,
Is onely there.[57]

It is, once again, clear that a linked sequence of images owes its existence and long-continued vitality not to its ornamental value, or to any incidental beauty, but to the fact that it expresses a train of thought.

8

Our examination of the imagery of the proem has been lengthy and has taken some devious routes, but it has, I believe, shown that the images are all closely linked to each other and to the theme of mortality and regeneration and that, therefore, the subject of the poem is the death of a person and not loss in any other form. Further, it is clear that the imagery of

[57] *Works*, p. 125, ll. 13–42. See 'Langland on the Incarnation', pp. 355 f.

treasure, of the garden, of the plant in all its parts and aspects, of spices, wheat, and harvest, forms an inextricably linked whole; not brought together by the poet but joined by long traditional use. It is not, therefore, possible to interpret the poem as developing its themes through the juxtaposition of contrasted groups of images; for example, by opposing the artificiality and non-organic quality of treasure and jewels to the natural imagery of the plant.[58] The imagery is complex and is capable of conveying subtle variations of thought, but it is cut out of whole cloth.

Another conclusion which cannot be avoided is that the way in which the images of the poem are introduced supports the development of its triple form. What is pure imagery, even simile, in the proem becomes, as we shall see, a part of the literal description of the Earthly Paradise in the next section, to undergo a further transformation in the final section when the Earthly Paradise is replaced by a vision of Heaven itself and the New Jerusalem, which, if it can be thought of as existing in naturalistic terms at all, is separated by sphere upon sphere from an Earthly Paradise situated at the highest point of the actual earth.

The poet, in fact, uses his imagery structurally, and in this he is, of course, in sharp contrast to some of the sources we have quoted: by the lesser devotional prose-writers, by many composers of hymns, by a poet like Dunbar in the 'Ballat of Our Lady' such imagery is often used in a cumulative way. It is, indeed, more homogeneous than the modern reader might think at first glance, but, nevertheless, it serves to amass impressive detail, and to create an effect of heaped riches. The poet of *Pearl*, like Dante, and like Langland at his best, uses the image-clusters thematically, in a way which, because it is typical of certain of the poets of the seventeenth century is often called metaphysical.[59] It is certainly an imagery intended to develop

[58] See W. S. Johnson, 'The Imagery and Diction of the *Pearl*', *E.L.H.*, xx (1953), pp. 161 ff.

[59] See L. L. Martz, *The Poetry of Meditation*, pp. 91 ff., for an interesting and cautious discussion of the relation of medieval and seventeenth-century technique.

the thought and argument of the poem not to create mood—the main function of imagery for poets since the romantic revival. For this reason it is impossible to grasp the form and purpose of the work unless we approach the foundation which the poet lays in the proem in accordance with his intentions.

Part Two

THE DREAM

I

THE EARTHLY PARADISE

I

THE DREAMER, who had fallen asleep in a garden, finds himself, in the next section of the poem, in a very different setting. He is still in a *locus amœnus*, but, instead of the garden behind the wall or the park with its palisade, he is now in an open landscape with rocks, trees, and a river as its salient features. Curiously enough, it is in this landscape that critics have seen the closest resemblance to the Garden of Love of the *Roman de la Rose*. Osgood, for example, is emphatic on the subject:

> In *The Pearl* appears also the setting familiar to any reader of the *Roman de la Rose* or its descendants . . . In the principal scene of the poem are the familiar trees, birds, flowers, fruits, meadow and river, and precious stones; but towering cliffs of crystal are superadded, and all is much more spacious, resplendent, and sublime than in the poet's predecessors and contemporaries.[1]

Gordon is even more definite:

> The framework of the poem as a whole—a vision seen in a dream —is the form popularized by the *Roman de la Rose*. And the influence of that poem, or the school of poetry derived from it, is clear in the general conception of the heavenly region in which the dreamer finds himself, the flowery garden, bright, clear, and serene.[2]

Dorothy Everett has more to say of the differences:

> . . . throughout the opening descriptions there are reminiscences, verbal and otherwise, of the Garden of Love in the *Roman de*

[1] *Pearl*, p. xv.
[2] *Pearl*, p. xxxii.

la Rose . . . the trees, the birds, the river of the country of the poet's vision could not fail to remind his readers of that beautiful garden. Yet the details—the 'flaumbande hweȝ' of the birds, the tree-trunks 'blwe as ble of ynde,' the emeralds, sapphires and other gems that lie at the bottom of the stream—are peculiar to this description and less realistic than those in the *Roman*; for this land is more remote from normal experience than the Garden of Love, and surpasses it in beauty.[3]

Here the emphasis falls on points which we must in a moment take up. A hint of dissension, of a radical kind, comes from D. W. Robertson:

> Much of the detail in *Pearl* or *Piers Plowman* involves symbolic or scriptural materials combined to form pictures of things which cannot be seen in the terms used to describe them, like the colorful forest along the river in *Pearl* or the Castle of Caro in *Piers Plowman*.[4]

As was the case with the garden of the opening, it is obviously important to decide whether the poet has drawn his material from the bright world of the *Roman de la Rose* or from a non-visual symbolism based on the Bible—or whether, perhaps, he has done neither, but has utilized a convention of a different type, which would have been equally ready to his hand. Since understanding of the poem depends on appreciation of the convention in which the poet writes, the problem is a vital one. The solution, clearly, must come from within the poem itself, and this provides two lines of attack: first, the Dreamer's own statement about the place in which he finds himself; secondly its features and the technique of the description.

In stanza 12 the Dreamer sums up his impressions:

> Forþy I poȝt þat Paradyse
> Watȝ þer o[u]er gayn þo bonkeȝ brade.
> I hoped þe water were a deuyse
> Bytwene myrþeȝ by mereȝ made;
> Byȝonde þe broke, by slente oþer slade,
> I hoped þat mote merked wore.
> Bot þe water watȝ depe, I dorst not wade,
> And euer me longed ay more and more.   (137–44)

[3] *Essays on Middle English Literature*, pp. 90–1.
[4] *A Preface to Chaucer*, p. 280.

The Earthly Paradise

Apart from l. 140, which is textually obscure, this is a clear statement. He is of the opinion that beyond the water must lie the walled city (*mote*) of Paradise.[5] But the water forms an impassable barrier—it is too deep for wading.

It is clear, I think, that this is not merely a comparison with Paradise designed to heighten the effect.[6] The poet makes a careful and accurate statement: from his observation of the country he is in his Dreamer concludes that Paradise, which he thinks of as a walled city, must be found beyond the water. It cannot be seen at present; doubtless a 'slope or vally' conceals it. This careful attention to topography is in strong contrast to the casually hyperbolical comparisons of the Love Visions and romances.

It is not likely that, at this stage, the Dreamer expects to see Heaven itself, the actual New Jerusalem, the abode of the Lamb, on the other side of the water: by the walled city of Paradise he means rather the Earthly Paradise (later, he calls it 'Paradys *erde*', 248), the resting-place of Enoch and Elias; a place from which Heaven is not far off, and a natural and proper meeting-place for the blessed spirits of the dead and the living. In the *Divina Commedia* it is in the Earthly Paradise, on the Summit of the Mount of Purgatory, that Dante first encounters Beatrice, and the nearness of such places to Heaven is often stressed. In

[5] On the difficulties of l. 140, see Gordon, *Pearl*, p. 52, note to ll. 139–40. I take *deuyse* to mean 'division', 'dividing line', and *mereȝ* as a synonym of 'water(s)', as its use in l. 1166 suggests. It is possible, however, that it implies water laid out in ornamental pools—a familiar feature in paradisial surroundings. Cf. Isaiah 41, 18, 'aperiam in supinis collibus flumina et in medio camporum fontes, ponam desertum in stagna aquarum et terram inviam in rivos aquarum'; the next verse contains the tree-list already remarked on (above p. 36). In l. 138 the manuscript reads *oper*—'Paradise was there, or facing those broad banks.' *Ouer*, giving the phrase *ouer gayn*, 'over against', gives better sense, and I have adopted it.

[6] For the use of this device in Love Visions and romances, see the references collected by Osgood, *Pearl*, p. 61, note to l. 137. The indications are, in such cases, that it is the Earthly Paradise which is meant, not Heaven. Thus, Machaut, in the 'Dit dut Vergier', 13, expressly names the *paradis terrestre*.

the Old English version of Lactantius' *Phoenix* for example, the Happy Land is a place

> Þǽr bið oft open, ēadgum tōgēanes,
> onhliden hlēoþra wyn, heofonrīces duru.[7]

It is in keeping with the theme of 'ay more and more' that when the Dreamer does, in fact, see a *'mote'*, a walled city, he is vouchsafed a vision of Heaven itself, not of the terrestrial, though unapproachable city of Paradise.

The Earthly Paradise was, in fact, a real place, located on earth, and, theoretically at least, within the reach of a traveller.[8] Its protecting wall (whether of fire, natural mountain or rock, or in the form of a rampart)[9] is insisted on by all writers, and it is often thought of as a castle or city: so much the poet could have gathered from Mandeville and from the Alexander romances. It is situated at the earth's highest point—and for that reason it was untouched by Noah's flood. Moreover, 'it is so high that it toucheth nere to the cyrcle of the Mone'.[10] Dante uses all this when he places Purgatory on the lower slopes of the mountain which culminates in the Earthly Paradise, and it is from here that the journey through the heavenly spheres begins with the circle of the moon.

The Dreamer of *Pearl*, therefore, considers that he is somewhere on earth—'I ne wyste in þis worlde quere þat hit wace', and he is gradually convinced that he has reached that inacces-

[7] N. F. Blake (ed.) (Manchester, 1964), ll. 11–12: 'There the door of heaven is often opened to the blessed; joyful melody is revealed.' The Old English poet expands his Latin original here.

[8] Cf. H. R. Patch, *The Other World According to Descriptions in Medieval Literature* (Cambridge, Mass., 1950), p. 134: 'The Garden of Eden was universally believed to exist, and, although cut off from ordinary approach, was supposed still to be waiting for the saints before their ascent to Heaven.' Medieval maps often showed its location. Traditionally, it had been moved by God, after the departure of Adam and Eve, and placed beyond an impassable barrier.

[9] Ample illustration of each kind of barrier will be found in Patch's book, *passim*.

[10] *The Voiage and Travayle of Syr John Maundeville Knight*, ed. John Ashton (London, 1887), p. 211. This idea had patristic authority. See Patch, op. cit., pp. 142 ff.

sible place where a river guards the walled castle of the terrestrial paradise. He has reached this place 'in Godeʒ grace', and he may be remembering Mandeville's comment and apology for his own failure: 'no man may passe there but through speciall grace of God'.[11]

2

The Earthly Paradise, like every other place fit for human habitation in the medieval world, was enclosed. Whether it is thought of primarily as a garden or as a castle—it is often both—a wall of some sort defends it from all casual approach. But outside the wall of Paradise lies open country, and it is through this country that the four-fold river of Eden flows. The Garden of Love, of course, has a somewhat similar approach. There is, however, a difference. The Garden of Love, as far as the *Roman de la Rose* is concerned, is approached through a pleasant, but ordinary, countryside. It is springtime: flowers and birdsong help to make the landscape agreeable and the water is clear and adds to the beauty of the scene. But the wonders all lie within the Garden. The Earthly Paradise, however, extends its influence over the surrounding countryside. The rivers which flow out of it wash down jewels, or fruit, or leaves with marvellous properties, and the natural features—cliffs, rocks, the river itself, are not of a kind ordinarily encountered.[12]

[11] *The Voiage and Travayle of Syr John Maundeville Knight*, p. 212.

[12] Many sources were available for the detailed description of the Earthly Paradise and its surroundings. For a poet of the late fourteenth century the Alexander Romances, especially the *Iter ad Paradisum* and its derivatives would probably be the most important. (See G. Cary, *The Medieval Alexander* (Cambridge, 1956), pp. 19–21, and M. M. Lascelles, 'Alexander and the Earthly Paradise in Medieval English Writings', *M. Aev.*, V. 31, 79, 173 ff.) *Mandeville's Travels* also describe the Earthly Paradise at length. They were immensely popular in England in the fourteenth and fifteenth centuries, and by 1400 would have been available in French, Latin, or English (see J. E. Wells, *A Manual of the Writings in Middle English*, pp. 433 ff.). Apart from these, innumerable works contain references to the tradition (see Patch, op. cit., *passim*). Arabic eschatological writings, too, shared many of the features of the Earthly Paradise descriptions. One work at least belonging to this tradition, the *Liber Scalae*,

When, therefore, the Dreamer finds himself journeying through a land of marvels he is following in a familiar track; but not one which is likely to lead to any imitation of the Garden of Love, or which owes its characteristics to that tradition.

There is, too, another consideration which is of importance here: medieval art, visual and literary, distinguished sharply between open landscape and enclosed scene. What was appropriate to the one was by no means appropriate to the other.

A garden, with its enclosing wall or hedge, is always a place in which something happens, something is found or done. Landscape, on the contrary, however beautiful in itself, was something through which one passed on the way to action or discovery—and it is landscape, open country with natural features, which the *Pearl*-poet describes. The distinction can be seen in even the most abstract treatment of the two topics. For the devotional writers the garden or other enclosure represents a state which may or may not contain in itself the seeds of change. Landscape, open country, is a figure for something to be passed through in order to reach one's objective. Thus, for St. Bernard, and others, the garden represents the Church, in which man finds rest and regeneration. For William of St. Thierry open country is the *regio dissimilitudinis*, a country which the soul must leave far behind as it travels towards perfection.[13]

---

[13] See especially the *Expositio altera super Cant. Cant.*, *P.L.*, 180, 494B, where the *regio dissimilitudinis* is the pasture of the goats, the land of exile of Cain, and is contrasted with the Soul's lodging with God—'ibi cubabo tecum'. A similar scheme is found in the Middle English lyric, 'In a valey of þis restles mind'. Valley, mountain, meadow, and hill represent the country of the search. The quest is ended when: 'My loue is in hir chaumbir: holde ʒoure pees; / Make

---

was available in Latin and French in the fourteenth century, and one of its MSS seems to have been written in England (see M. Manzalaoui, 'English Analogues to the *Liber Scalae*,' *M. Aev.*, XXXIV (1965), pp. 21 ff.). The Moslem Paradise described was the permanent abode of the blessed, but it seems likely that, since it by no means agrees with the Christian concept of Heaven, a fourteenth-century reader would equate it rather with the tradition of the Earthly Paradise, or the Islands of the Blessed.

The Earthly Paradise

Medieval painting followed the same convention, as is well known. In fourteenth- and even fifteenth-century work only journeys, hunts, or battles are seen against a landscape setting;[14] other events are enclosed in gardens, buildings, even architectural frames which seem irrelevant to the theme, like those which often surround the Infant Christ in the crib. Even when landscapes, in later painting, do lie beyond a garden wall, or are seen through a window, their function is to help to lead all the lines of the painting inwards to the central, enclosed scene.

The Calendar scenes, it is true, often show a springtime walk though open country: but even here the castle is usually close at hand.[15] When the characters of the *Decameron* varied the day's entertainment by taking a little exercise they did not stray far from their castle walls.[16]

[14] On the contrast of the enclosed garden and the world beyond in medieval art, see K. Clark, *Landscape into Art* (London, 1949), pp. 9 ff. There are, however, exceptions. Suso, as often, takes an independent line: 'Many men nowadays go to look over the hedge of thorns, and walk beside the moat the long day through, without daring to risk the thorny barrier with resolute and free will, in order to break through into a land fair, vast, and full of the flowers of spiritual beauty' (*Grosses Briefbuch*, VIII, ed. K. Bihlmeyer, *Heinrich Seuse, Deutsche Schriften* (Stuttgart, 1907), pp. 431–2).

[15] Clarke, op. cit., p. 12, emphasizes the importance of the calendar scenes for the development of profane art in the fifteenth century. For their importance as possible models for descriptions in poetry, see Rosemond Tuve, *Seasons and Months, Studies in a Tradition of Middle English Poetry* (Paris, 1933), pp. 143 ff. The walk into the country is charmingly illustrated by the April and May miniatures in the *Très Riches Heures du Duc de Berry*. April shows a betrothal scene, and the participants have not strayed far from the walled garden shown on the right. May has a garlanded cavalcade of knights and ladies, accompanied by musicians. The castle is seen to be close at hand, beyond a belt of trees. The Grimani Breviary has a country walk for April, with a jester to entertain the company, but, with the castle still in sight, two of the ladies have already seated themselves to play with a lapdog.

[16] When a journey of two miles was undertaken on foot it required considerable preparation and organization (*Decameron*, Third Day, Prologue).

3e no noise, but lete hir slepe' (F. J. Furnivall, *Political, Religious, and Love Poems, E.E.T.S.*, 15 (1866), pp. 180 ff., ll. 105–6).

The Dream

Vision literature, on the whole, also favours the enclosure. Dante, in the *Inferno*, is soon within the walls of Hell: Chaucer spends little time in the desert in the *House of Fame*. In *Pearl* the Dreamer expresses the preference of his age when he voices his dissatisfaction with a life in the open with the question:

> Haf ȝe no woneȝ in castel-walle,
> Ne maner þer ȝe may mete and won? (917–18)

The landscape in which the Dreamer finds himself is thus a setting which would inevitably produce certain associations and expectations in the reader. It may be the scene of an encounter, but sooner or later it will lead the traveller to the enclosure which signifies permanence to the medieval mind, and is the right place for definitive events or decisions, as distinct from transitional states or discussions.

It is clear by now that this landscape has little to do with the walled garden of the *Roman*, but there is still the question, raised by Robertson, of whether it is a symbolical or allegorical scene, not intended to be 'visualized'. The average reader's first impressions are likely to be in immediate revolt against this view. Sharpness of detail, the richness of what seems a studied appeal to the senses, a vivid clarity in the development of the description, all seem to point one way. A closer examination of the technique of the poem seems to me to show that these pointers are not to be ignored and that the reader's spontaneous impression is the right one.

In the proem the poet tended to use *descriptio* for a purpose commonly recommended by the rhetoricians[17] of influencing the reader's view of the object or person described. In this section he is using it for the other great purpose for which it was an inevitable tool—the development of narrative. In fact, as Faral notes, description, especially of scenes, is always very close to narration.[18]

The main organizing factor of the *descriptio* in the second section of *Pearl* is the movement of the Dreamer's figure: in l. 67, 'I bere þe face . . .'; in l. 101, 'I welke ay forth . . .'; in

---

[17] See above, p. 11.
[18] *Les Arts Poétiques*, p. 82.

l. 107, 'I wan to a water . . .'. The movement of the solitary figure is only lightly indicated, but it is enough to allow the landscape to be viewed from different directions and distances. The other organizing factor, a usual one in medieval description, is the natural passage of the eye from mass to detail: from cliffs and forests to rocks and trees, and to details of the trees; from a distant view of the river and its banks to a close-up. The fact that this description, unlike the description of the proem, is organized in this essentially visual way is in itself enough to disprove the assertion that the poet is making 'pictures of things which cannot be seen in the terms used to describe them'.[19]

3

The Dreamer, in fact, makes the traditional *iter ad Paradisum*, although, through God's grace, he makes it without the traditional difficulties, and it is only with the final stages, where the river is the only barrier left, that the poet is concerned.

The scene, as a whole, is enclosed by cliffs:

> I knew me keste þer klyfeȝ cleuen,   (66)

and these are emphasized by the repetition of ll. 73–4, where the cliffs are part of 'þo downeȝ sydeȝ'—that is of hills. In fact, this is high country and, if we think of the poet as on lower ground, looking towards the forest which clothes the lower

[19] Robertson, *A Preface to Chaucer*, p. 280. The rhetoricians do not give rules for the construction of descriptive passages, but their examples are logically planned. For instance, Matthieu de Vendôme describes a garden in the order flowers—trees—the birds in the trees, so that the eye travels up from the ground (Faral, op. cit., p. 81). The poets usually surpass the theorists. One of the best organized of medieval descriptions is that of the Green Knight's castle in *Sir Gawain and the Green Knight*, where the eye first takes in the whole mass, then travels from the lowest point, where the wall plunges into the moat, upwards to the ramparts, and then inwards to the various buildings within the wall. The passage ends with a summing up in which the first confused glimpse 'As hit shemered and schon þurȝ þe schyre okeȝ', resolves itself into a sharply etched design, which stands out against the sky as if 'pared out of papure' (*Sir Gawain*, 764–802). See also below, III, ii, pp. 214 ff.

slopes, then making his way towards the flatter ground of *fryth*, *playn*, and *reuerez* (water-meadows), he would seem to have provided a good solution to the problem of a Paradise which is situated at the highest point of the world but is approached by a river. He has, in fact, placed it in a mountain valley, overhung by sheer cliffs, and surrounded by forests which still contain outcrops of rock.

A desire to rationalize and a knowledge of the probabilities of mountain scenery might have produced this description: but it seems more likely that the poet relied on *auctoritas* than on observation: in this case the Alexander romances, with or without suggestions from Mandeville, would have done most of the work for him.

The *Iter ad Paradisum* has the journey through rocky country beside a river which deafens with its noise and is too swift for navigation. Paradise, when it is reached, is not to be penetrated by the living, but is guarded by a wall. From its inhabitants comes the gift of the 'Wonderstone' to Alexander. This outweighs all the matter in the world until it is covered with a little dust, when it weighs nothing at all. It is a parable of Alexander's pride, which will be destroyed by death. Alexander's revelation thus has much in common with that of the Dreamer in *Pearl*. Both concern the relation of the treasure of earth and the pride of life to mortality, and in each case the journey results in self-knowledge.

The *Wars of Alexander* (*de Preliis*) has the story of Alexander's journey to the land of the Sun. To reach this he passes through a dark valley, and comes to a high land, surrounded by diamond cliffs, and full of marvels:

> And þus þai dryfe furth þe driȝt of daies foure score,
> Till at þai come till a cliffe, as þe clause tellis,
> Ane egge þat was all ouire of Adamand stanes,
> With, hingand in þe rughe roches, rede gold cheynes.
> Þan was þare graythed of degreces for gomes vp to wynde,
> Twa thousand be tale & fyue trew hundrethe.[20]

[20] *The Wars of Alexander*, ed. W. W. Skeat, *E.E.T.S.*, E.S., XLVII, 4874–9. I quote from the English version, since it is possible that it was known to the poet of *Pearl*. Even if it was not, it shows a reworking

The Earthly Paradise

At the top, 'þat touched to þe cloudes', is a palace, a temple and a garden—the realm of the Sun:

> It was so precious a place, and proudly a-tired
> Þare was na place it a pere, bot paradyse selfe. (4904-5)

Alexander and his men have already (4787 ff.) climbed a huge mountain at the top of which they find marvellous and dangerous beasts. This forms the barrier to the dark valley, into which they descend (4803 ff.). In spite of the darkness, which was so thick

> Þat þai miȝt fele it with þaire fiste, as flabband webbis, (4807)

this valley has some of the features of the surroundings of Paradise. There are streams, bright as silver, and fruit 'brethand as mirre'. When they climb out of it they come to a plain, which, again, has paradisial features: it has 'Revers . . . ricchest of þe werd' (4822), and fruit-bearing trees, while the ground is red. Then comes the diamond cliff, the final barrier before the paradisial land of the Sun, where revelation comes from the trees which prophesy.

Mandeville's account of the Earthly Paradise reproduces much of the material of the Alexander romances. He places the trees of the Sun and Moon 'that spake to Kyng Alexander', in a wilderness of wild beasts in the land of Prester John. His Earthly Paradise is approached through another wilderness of hills and rocks, which is dark by day and night. It is guarded by a wall, and from it run the four rivers, the first of which is Phison—'in that river are many precious stones and much *Lignum Aloes* & gravel of golde'. It stands at the highest point of the world 'nere to the cyrcle of the Mone', and it cannot be approached by any man 'for by land he may not go for wylde beastes which are in the wyldernesse, and for hylls and rocks where no man may passe. Nor by those ryvers may no man

---

of the material within a similar stylistic convention. For discussion of the interrelationship of the poems in this group, see I. Gollancz and M. Day, *Sir Gawain and the Green Knight* (*E.E.T.S.*, 210, 1940), pp. xiii ff.; H. L. Savage, *St. Erkenwald*, pp. xlviii ff.; Menner, *Purity*, pp. xix ff.; Marie Borroff, *Sir Gawain*, pp. 52 ff. The question is by no means settled.

passe, for they come with so great course and so great waves that no ship may saile against them.'²¹

Some of this material is repeated in Mandeville's description of the Vale Perilous, which is also full of jewels and precious stones, in association with the river Phison, but which is also full of devils, and contains the entry to Hell.²² The strongest associations of the material are, in fact, with death: writers pass easily from brilliant jewels to darkness and to the after-life.

Alexander's two journeys have been compared to the journey of Gilgamesh through the dark mountain to the Garden of the Sun, which flourished beside the Waters of Death. This Garden has jewelled trees, with fruit of carnelian and leaves of lapis lazuli, and 'for thorns and thistles there were haematite and rare stones, agate, and pearls from out of the sea'. It is approached through a great mountain guarded by scorpions, and through twelve leagues of impenetrable darkness. Normally the way and the Garden are inaccessible to men 'no mortal man has gone into the mountain . . . no mortal man has gone this way before, nor will, as long as the winds drive over the sea'.²³ Gilgamesh finds a maiden there, Siduri, the wine-maker. She corresponds to the female guide of many later journeys to paradisial lands.²⁴ Whether the adventures of Gilgamesh were in fact later transferred to Alexander, or whether the similarities result from the use of a common tradition, the fact remains that in both cases the significance of the story is of submission to the law of death. Alexander learns through the Wonderstone. Gilgamesh loses the flower of eternal youth, and learns the truth that for mankind 'there is no permanence'.

The *Morte Arthure* seems to draw, though perfunctorily, on much the same tradition in the Dream of Fortune (3227 ff.). Like Alexander, the king first encounters a wilderness of 'wykkyde bestez', and then, after going on through the forest

²¹ *The Voiage and Travayle*, ed. Ashton, pp. 207 f., 210 ff.
²² *Ibid.*, 196 ff.
²³ *The Epic of Gilgamesh*, English Version by N. K. Sandars, Penguin Books (London, 1960), pp. 96 ff.
²⁴ Ibid., p. 104. On the Maiden as the inhabitant and guide in the Earthly Paradise, see below, pp. 114 ff.

comes to 'a medowe, with montayngnes enclosyde' (3238) where silver vines bearing golden grapes are to be found. Here there is no climbing, and the relation of the forest to the mountain barrier is not very clear. The subject of the revelation is, once more, the inevitability of death and the transitoriness of power and glory.

Huon of Burdeux, Lord Berners's translation of the French prose Romance made in about 1525,[25] is a late version of a journey through landscape of this type, but in some ways it has the closest resemblance to *Pearl*.

This romance may, as its editor suggested,[26] be independently based on Eastern tales, but it seems clear that, in the main, it is a reworking of Alexander's marvellous journeys.[27] Huon reaches the top of the cliff by air, in the claws of a gryphon, so that the description of the surrounding landscape is given as he leaves the garden of the fountain and apple tree of youth. As in *Pearl*, a river and rocks are important features.

The revelation, which concerns Huon's future, comes from an angel, who appears in a blaze of light:

> sodaynely there aperyd to hym a lyght shynynge, that he thought he was rauysshed in the heuen amonge the aungellys/ therwith he harde a voyse angelicall. (p. 435)

The angel instructs him to pick the apples of youth, and Huon is more fortunate than Gilgamesh, in that he does not actually lose the apples, but they are finally all given away, the third 'which I kepte for my selfe' (p. 567), to the Emperor, as a ransom for Huon's imprisoned wife.

There is, thus, a strong tendency for journeys to paradisial lands to lead to knowledge concerning mortality and the limitations of humanity in the face of death. This concept seems to have been stamped on the material from its earliest develop-

[25] *Duke Huon of Burdeux*, ed. S. L. Lee, *E.E.T.S.*, XLI–XLIII (1882–7).

[26] Ibid., I, p. xxvii.

[27] Huon and Alexander both travel along a river, and through a region of darkness. Huon's rock is, too, suggestively named 'the rocke of Alexander'.

ments in Eastern legend and mythology. The *Pearl*-poet, in
fact, is not giving a grim twist to the happy country of romance
and Love Vision, but is writing of a land in which men are
traditionally brought face to face with the reality of their nature,
from which they return, if not disappointed, at least sadder, as
well as wiser.

4

The *iter ad Paradisum* is thus a journey through well-established
surroundings, which leads to a well-established type of result.
The details used in the description of these surroundings in
Pearl, far from being a mere piling up of 'commonplaces in
contemporary poetry',[28] all fit into an accepted picture of the
terrestrial paradise and its approaches.

The first details which catch the Dreamer's eye are the cliffs
and 'rych rokkeȝ', which we have already discussed. Next the
poet turns to the woods and the details of the trees: these are
very unlike either the 'homly' or the more exotic trees which are
listed in the *Roman*. The trees of the *Roman* are for use and
pleasure. They provide wholesome fruit, or they are praised, in
the Chaucerian version, since, 'for to seen it was solas' (1378);
and their names recall the traditional tree-lists which are an
inseparable part of the description of the pleasure ground.[29] The
trees in *Pearl* have nothing in common with this tradition.
They are not named—indeed, they belong to no familiar species:
their trunks are brilliant blue, and their leaves are silver. These
shimmer and reflect the light in a way which is described with
loving precision:

[28] Osgood, *Pearl*, p. xiv.
[29] On the tree-lists and their sources, see J. A. W. Bennett, *The
Parlement of Foules*, pp. 70–3; see also above, I, ii, n. 6. The distinction
between the trees for use and for pleasure in a paradisial garden had
been made by Philo, commenting on Gen. 2, 8 ff. This is another
indication of the very complex ancestry of this material. (See Philo,
On the Account of the World's Creation Given by Moses, liv., *Philo with
an English Translation*, by F. H. Colson and G. H. Whitaker, I, p. 120,
The Loeb Classical Library, 1962.)

The Earthly Paradise

As bornyst syluer þe lef on slydeȝ,
Þat þike con trylle on vch a tynde.
Quen glem of glodeȝ agaynȝ hem glydeȝ,
Wyth schymeryng schene ful schrylle þay
                    schynde. (77–80)

This undoubtedly is, as Gordon suggests, an example of the
working of the poet's visual imagination, but it is also very like
the description of the Trees of the Sun and Moon in the
Alexander story. The Tree of the Sun in the *Wars of Alexander*,
shakes its golden leaves before it utters a prophecy:

Þan schogs hire þe son-tree & schoke hire schire leues,
And with a sweȝand swoȝe þis sware scho him ȝeldis. (5018–19)

Something like this may have suggested the far more effective
interplay of light and sound on metallic leaves in *Pearl*.

Trees with silver and gold leaves and jewelled fruit are found
in texts which have little to do with the Earthly Paradise and,
conversely, descriptions of the Earthly Paradise and its surroundings are sometimes more commonplace. In the *Purgatorio* the Earthly Paradise is made marvellous by the strange
procession which moves through the wood, not by the strangeness of the trees themselves.[30] Nevertheless, both the Alexander
romances and Mandeville associate a land of marvellous trees
with the approach to Paradise, and there seems little doubt that
the poet of *Pearl* does so too.

The description of the silver leaves, with its insistence on
shimmering light and movement has, however, been compared
to Dante's description of the forest which borders the Earthly
Paradise in the *Purgatorio*. He writes, it is true, of 'le fronde,
tremolando' (xxviii, 10), but the effect is one of movement and
sound, not light:

                ma con piena letizia l 'ore prime,
                    cantando, ricevìenco intra le foglie,
                    che tenevan bordone alle sue rime.

---

[30] *Purgatorio* xxix. The 'alberi d'oro' (43), are in fact the candle-
sticks of the vision, and not part of the wood, which shelters them with
'verdi rami' (35).

> (And from a full throat singing loud and gay
> Welcomed the first thrills in the leaves, that bore
> A burden to the descant of their lay.   xxviii, 16–8)

It is possible that Dante is here using the motif of the singing trees, which is sometimes associated with the Earthly Paradise.[31] The words which the *Pearl*-poet uses—*trylle* and *schrylle*—could be used of sound, but there seems little doubt that he intends to give an effect of light, and, although it is still possible that *trylle* was suggested by Dante's *tremolando*, neither Dante nor any other known source can parallel the peculiarly vivid effect of the combined impressions of sight, touch, and sound as the silver leaves slide over one another and create a shimmering alternation of light.

The blue tree-trunks seem to be unique to the poet of *Pearl* although the trunks of trees are often mentioned as 'bright' or 'of gold' in contrast to leaves and fruit.[32] Here again, it is possible that we have a verbal reminiscence of Dante in an earlier description in the *Purgatorio* vii, 64 ff., which also uses the material of the Earthly Paradise. Here Dante has a string of similes to describe the brilliance of the colours of the flowers, among them:

> Oro e argento fine, cocco e biacca,
> indaco, legno lucido, sereno.

> (Gold and fine silver, crimson, pearly white,
> Indigo, smooth wood lustrous in the grain.   vii, 73–4)

It is possible that either the poet misunderstood the Italian or that his memory brought back to his mind the unusual colour word, indigo, and fused it with the polished wood which immediately followed it in the *Purgatorio*. The shining metallic tree-trunks of the typical description of this kind would then become 'as blwe as ble of Ynde'.

After the description of the leaves on the trees, the Dreamer's eye travels down again to the ground, where

[31] Patch, op. cit. Index, under Trees.
[32] E.g. *Destruction of Troy*, 4960, 'the bole was of bright gold'; cf. *Wars of Alexander*, 5002 ff.

> Þe grauayl þat on grounde con grynde
> Wern precious perleȝ of oryente:
> Þe sunnebemeȝ bot blo and blynde
> In respecte of þat adubbement. (81–4)

This motif is repeated and elaborated in stanza 9, in the description of the river which forms the climax of this passage. Its banks are first described 'as fyldor fyn'; then, as the Dreamer comes nearer, the thin thread of gold resolves itself into 'bonkeȝ bene of beryl bryȝt'. The sound of the water—as we have seen, a feature of the *Iter ad Paradisum*—is emphasized:

> Swangeande swete þe water con swepe,
> Wyth a rownande rourde raykande aryȝt. (111–12)

But like all the details which are reminiscent of the wild and difficult country of the *Iter* and the other Alexander romances, this becomes a source of added pleasure.

In ll. 114–20, comes a brilliant set-piece of *descriptio* of the jewels in the water:

> As glente þurȝ glas þat glowed and glyȝt,
> As stremande sterneȝ, quen stroþe-men slepe,
> Staren in welkyn in wynter nyȝt;
> For vche a pobbel in pole þer pyȝt
> Watȝ emerad, saffer, oþer gemme gente,
> Þat alle þe loȝe lemed of lyȝt,
> So dere watȝ hit adubbement.

Since it is stated in Genesis itself that the river Phison is associated with gold and jewels, it is not surprising that, as we have already seen, they are commonly found in rivers which flow from Paradise. Patch has collected innumerable examples. The passage from the beginning of the *Roman de la Rose* has, however, been closely linked to these lines in *Pearl*, and Gollancz[33] even saw a development from the French:

> Si vi tot covert e pavé
> Le fonz de l'eve de gravele (120–1)

to the English translation:

> Tho saugh I well
> The botme paved everydell
> With gravel, ful of stones shene, (125–7)

[33] *Pearl*, p. 123, note to l. 113.

and thence, with further heightening, to *Pearl*. But in fact, this part of the *Roman* does not use the tradition of the paradisial river of jewels at all. This comes later in the fountain in the Garden of Love with its twin crystals, and in the fountain in the Shepherd's Garden at the end.

The opening of the *Roman*, in fact, draws on another tradition, one which is typical of classical pastoral description and which can be traced from Theocritus through the late Latin lyric.[34] In this the shining pebbles and the clear water are a part of the natural beauty and pleasure of the place and nothing more, and if jewels and crystal or precious metal are mentioned, it is as comparison only.

Fountains and streams with jewels in them are not, of course, unknown in Love Vision and romance (the fountains inside the two gardens of the *Roman* are cases in point). But it is the descriptions which are most closely associated with the Earthly Paradise which are nearest to *Pearl*. Mandeville several times introduces the gravel of gold or precious stones. There is the river in which are many precious stones and 'gravel of golde',[35] there is the 'great floud that cometh from Paradise and it is full of precious stones, and no drop of water, and it runneth with great waves into the gravely sea'.[36] There is also the lake in Ceylon which is full of jewels and from which a river runs to the sea.[37] In the *Journal of Friar Odoricus* there is also a shore where at low tide pearls, rubies, diamonds, and many other jewels can be picked up.[38]

[34] See Curtius, *European Literature and the Latin Middle Ages*, p. 185 ff. In the *Purgatorio*, Dante has a Theocritan stream, in keeping with the naturalistic trees. He saves the river of jewels for the *Paradiso*. Bernardus Silvestris also places a stream of this kind in Eden in *De Mundi Uuiversitate*, I, iii, 330 ff., ed. Barach and Wrobel, *Bibliotheca Philosophorum Mediae Aetatis*, I (Innsbruck, 1876).

[35] *The Voiage and Travayle*, ed. Ashton, p. 211. This is the river Phison, which flows from Paradise.

[36] Ibid., p. 190, also of a river which flows out of Paradise.

[37] *Mandeville's Travels*, Cotton Titus C., XV, p. 131. The pearls in this lake were tears shed by Adam and Eve as they left Paradise.

[38] English version, ed. Ashton in *The Voiage and Travayle*, p. 237. The original was one of Mandeville's most important sources. The river, or shore, with a gravel of jewels or gold, is thus one of the most

Huon of Burdeux has the same motif when Huon emerges from the underground river, and his ship is grounded in shallow water:

> then he sawe before hym all the grauell in the water were medelyd with presyous stones / when Huon sawe that / he toke a scope and cast into the shyppe so moche of those presyous stonys that it gaue as great a light as thoughe · x · torchys hade bene brynnynge. (p. 442)

Here the precious stones give out light, as do those in the river in *Pearl*. Their radiance is even more striking in another description in *Huon of Burdeux*, although it misses the effect of flashing, moving light which is common to Dante and the *Pearl*-poet:

> the whyche streme ran and fell into the great ryuer where as the shyppe laye; and when he was enteryd into this streme he sawe ye goodlyest presyous stonys that euer he sawe, they were so fayre and so rych that the value coude not be estemyd, the grauell of the streme that issuyd out of the fountayne were all precyous stonys, and they cast such lyght that al the mountayne and rocke dyd shyne therof, wherof Huon had great maruayle. (p. 439)

Dante, as we have said, used a river of the Theocritan kind to border his Earthly Paradise in the *Purgatorio*. He saves the river of jewels for a later passage, in the *Paradiso*, where it undergoes a brilliant transformation and acquires a symbolical sense not dreamed of by the writers on the Earthly Paradise. There is a general similarity in the two passages, in the treatment of the jewels as turning the water to fire, although the description in *Pearl* is literal, while Dante's is symbolical. If they are read side

---

widespread motifs. It is found in Arabic sources (see Manzalaoui, 'English Analogues to the *Liber Scalae*', *M. Aev.*, XXXIV, p. 28), but it is unlikely that, as Manzalaoui suggests, such works were particularly influential in spreading it. Most examples could be accounted for by Mandeville alone. Cf. e.g. Spenser, *Faerie Queene*, III, iv, 18 ff.; Milton, *Paradise Lost*, iv, 237 ff. Even in Finland a paradisial island of maidens is magically endowed with a gravel of pearls and jewels (*Kalevala*, Runo, xxix; see the translation of W. F. Kirby, *Everyman's Library*, 260 (London, 1962, p. 44)).

by side both the differences and the similarities will be clear. The *Pearl*-poet's version has already been quoted. Dante's runs:

> E vidi lume in forma di rivera
> fluvido di fulgore, intra due rive
> dipinte di mirabil primavera.
> Di tal fiumana uscìan faville vive,
> e d' ogni parte si mettìen ne' fiori,
> quasi rubin che oro circunscrive.
> Poi, come inebriate dalli odori,
> riprofondavan sè nel miro gurge;
> e s' una intrava, un' altra n' uscìa fori.
>
> (And I beheld, shaped like a river, light
> Streaming a splendour between banks whereon
> The miracle of spring was pictured bright.
> Out of this river living sparkles thrown
> Shot everywhere a fire amid the bloom
> And there like rubies gold-encrusted shone;
> Then as if dizzy with the spiced perfume
> They plunged into the enchanted eddy again:
> As one sank, rose another fiery plume.
>
> *Paradiso*, xxx, 61–9)

No description of a river of jewels in the literature of the earthly Paradise, as far as I know, comes as close to the *Pearl*-poet's as this. Nevertheless, Dante is following a different tradition, one in which Heaven itself is described, on the basis of Ps. 35, 10, 'For thee is the fountain of life, and in Thy light we shall see light.'

Alain de Lille, in his *Anticlaudianus* has an elaborate description of a fountain and river of light of this type, which is three-fold, since it symbolizes the Trinity:

> Hic videt irrigui fontis radiare nitorem,
> Qui praedives aquis reliquo conspectior amne,
> Sidera luce domat, praecellit mella sapore;
> Cujus deliciis cedit Paradisus, odore
> Balsama vincuntur, nardus submittitur illi.
>
> (Here she saw splendour flowing out from a moistening fountain, which, far more beautiful than any other stream, richer in

its water by far, tames the stars with its light, surpasses honey with its savour; to these delights Paradise yields the prize, they conquer balsam with their scent, nard makes submission to them.)

The streams are ablaze with a light not unlike fire:

> Qui mulcens urit, urendo mulcet, et ardens
> Mitigat, incendens demulcet, temperat urens.

(Which soothes as it burns, in burning soothes, and burning also alleviates; blazing, caresses; burning, assuages.[39])

This passage may well have given some hints to the poet who could cut through its amazing verbiage. The three main elements in Dante's description, the blazing fire, the scent, and the flowers, are all present in the *Anticlaudianus*, while the jewels might be inferred from the references to the richness of the stream.

There is, however, another handling of the theme of the heavenly Fountain, which is even more striking and which, although the details are different, is nearer in total effect to Dante's heavenly river. This is the chapter on 'Jesus the Fount of Light' in St. Bonaventura's *Arbor Vitae*. This chapter is built round a number of biblical texts, culminating in the quotation of Ps. 35, 10:

Ad hunc fontem vitae et luminis curre cum desiderio vivo, quaecumque es, anima Deo devota, et cordis intima vi ad eum exclama; 'O inaccessibilis decor Dei excelsi et purissima claritas lucis aeternae, vita omnem vitam vivificans, lux omne lumen illuminans et conservans in splendore perpetuo mille millena lumina fulgurantia ante thronum Divinitatis tuae a primaevo diluculo! O aeternum et inaccessibile, clarum et dulce pro-fluvium fontis absconditi ab oculis omnium mortalium, cuius profundum sine fundo, cuius altum sine termino, cuius ampli-tudo incircumscriptibilis, cuius puritas imperturbabilis'; ex quo fluvius procedit *olei laetitiae; qui laetificat civitatem Dei*, et torrens ignei vigoris, *torrens*, inquam, *voluptatis divinae*, quo laetabunda ebrietate potati, caelestes illi convivae hymno incessabili iubilant.

[39] J. Wright (ed.), *Satirical poets of the Twelfth Century* (Rolls Series), II, p. 373.

Hoc nos oleo sacro perunge huiusque torrentis desiderabilibus guttis sitibundas refocilla fauces arentium cordium, ut *in voce exsultationis et confessionis* decantemus tibi cantica laudis, experientia teste probantes, quoniam apud te est fons vitae, et in lumine tuo videbimus lumen.

(To this fountain of life and light run, O souls devoted to God, with intense desire, and with all the power of your inmost hearts cry out to Him: 'O inaccessible beauty of God on high, and purest clarity of eternal light; Life, giving life to all that lives, light, giving light to every light, and preserving in eternal radiance a thousand times a thousand lamps shining before the throne of your divinity from the primeval dawn. O eternal and inaccessible, clear and sweet stream issuing from the fountain hidden from all mortal eyes, whose depths has no bottom, whose scope no limit, whose extent cannot be circumscribed, whose purity cannot be troubled'. From this stream comes the oil of gladness which gladdens the city of God, and the rushing, fiery torrent, the torrent, truly, of the divine delight, which fills with joyful inebriation the guests at the heavenly feast, who sing an unending hymn of praise.

Let us anoint ourselves with this sacred oil; revive the dry throat of our parched hearts with the longed-for drops of this torrent, so that amid loud cries of joy and thanksgiving, we may sing a song of praise to You and learn by experience that with You is the fountain of life and in Your light we see light.[40])

The lesser lights and the thousand times a thousand lamps correspond in meaning to Dante's sparks. For the jewels we have to turn back a few pages, where Christ the Radiant Spouse, the Lamb of the heavenly marriage, is described clad in a long tunic 'in which He shall shine as if covered with all manner of precious stones'.[41] It would not be hard for a poet's imagination to conflate the two passages.

Dante's treatment of the material is, of course, unique. The description is, for one thing, part of a great development on the theme of light in canto xxx. For another, while it is presented as what Dante actually saw, and has all the urgency and immediacy of direct reporting, it is also only a foreshadowing of ultimate

[40] *Decem Opuscula*, pp. 203–4.
[41] *Decem Opuscula*, p. 201.

reality. Beatrice comments, 'Il fiume e il topazii / ch'entrano ed escono e 'l rider dell' erbe / son di lor vero umbriferi prefazii.' ('The river and the topazes / That enter and issue, and the smiling flowers, / Are of their truth foreshadowing prefaces (xxx, 76–78).) This treatment results in a heightening of the material which could hardly be surpassed. If, as seems likely, the same material is used by Jean de Meun in the *Roman de la Rose* (20, 279 ff.) we can see its adaptation in the opposite direction: everything is flattened rather than heightened, in a way which is in keeping with the more discursive style of Genius's sermon. The fountain itself, apart from its triple form, is naturalistically described. The light which does not burn or dazzle is derived from the carbuncle, not the stream, and it is from the jewel, too, that the scent comes. The *Pearl* seems to represent a middle position between the two. The direct experience is there, and the urgency of the Dreamer's emotional involvement in what he sees. But the stream remains earthly, albeit placed at a most significant point of earth. It foreshadows, and in a sense merges with, the river which flows from the throne of God, but without losing its own earthly nature.

In the next stanza of *Pearl* comes the detail of the scent of the fruit, 'As fode it can me fayre refete'. Scent which feeds, whether of fruit, flowers, or spices, is often referred to in descriptions of the Earthly Paradise, or of lands associated with it. It is to be found, for example, in the 'Vision of St. Salvius', in the *Historia Francorum*, of Gregory of Tours, and in the *Account of Elysaeus*.[42] In the Alexander romances the inhabitants of the country near Paradise live on balm gathered from the trees. The motif could be transferred to the context of divine imagery, and in a Latin hymn the Blessed Virgin is called the rose without thorns which produces the flower with a life-giving scent.[43]

---

[42] See Patch, op. cit., pp. 97 and 149. In the *Epistola ad Aristotelem* the people of the land live on the balm from the trees (balm is, of course, always associated with scent.) In the *Iter* spice is pressed from the leaves which float down the river from Paradise. (See M. M. Lascelles, *M. Aev.*, V, 185.) Vincent of Beauvais linked the spices to the prolongation of life which resulted from drinking the water—a common motif: Mandeville himself, as well as Huon of Burdeux, drank the water of youth.   [43] Mone, *Hymni Latini*, II, p. 9.

Mandeville provides an interesting example of the way in which the topography of the Earthly Paradise overlaps with that of other inaccessible regions. 'There is,' he says, 'another yle that men call Pitan, men of this lande till no lande, for they eate nought and they are smal, but not so smal as Pigmes. These men liue with smell of wild aples.'[44] His ultimate source is Pliny (book vii, 2) and, although the whole of this section of his work is dominated by the nearness of Paradise, he presents his near-pigmies quite prosaically as an interesting piece of ancient geographical lore.

For his birds, with their flaming hues and beating wings, it is certain that the *Pearl*-poet drew on Mandeville, though probably at one remove. If, as seems likely he wrote *Pearl* after he wrote *Purity*, he is here copying and adapting his own translation of Mandeville in that work:

Þe coperounes of þe c[ov]acles þat on þe cuppe reres
Wer fetysely formed out in fyloles longe,
Pinacles pyȝt þer apert þat profert bitwene,
And al bolled abof wyth braunches and leves,
Pyes and papejayes purtrayed withinne,
As þay prudly hade piked of pomgarnades;
For alle þe blomes of þe boȝes wer blyknande perles,
And alle þe fruyt in þo formes of flaumbeande gemmes . . .

Upon hit basez of brasse þat ber up þer werkes,
Þe boȝes bryȝt þer abof, brayden of golde,
Braunches bredande þeron, and bryddes þer seten
Of mony [curious] kyndes, of fele-kyn hues,
As þay wyth wynge upon wynde hade waged her fyþeres.
Inmong ȝe leves of þe [launces] lampes wer grayþed,
And oþer louflych lyȝt þat lemed ful fayre.   (1461–8, 1480–6)

This rather overloaded description of the cups is greatly compressed in *Pearl*. In fact, the poet takes from it only details. He transfers the striking and beautiful epithet 'flaumbeande' from the jewels to the birds (he did not find it in the French Mandeville). He takes over the beating of the birds' wings,

[44] Ashton, *The Voiage and Travayle*, p. 193.

which is a mechanical device in *Purity*, to become the accompaniment to the song of living birds in *Pearl*.[45]

When the poet gave the birds in *Pearl* the flaming hues of the jewels in *Purity*, he may also have had another context at the back of his mind. In the *Wars of Alexander*, when Alexander is on his way to the Trees of the Sun and Moon, just before he comes to the dark valley, he goes through a miraculous forest where:

> ʒit bred þar briddis in þa braunches at
> blith was & tame,
> And if a man had þaim hent or with his hand touchid,
> Þan floʒe þar flawmes out of fire before & be-hind. (4782–4)

This seems to be a curious combination of the legend of the Phoenix with the flaming barrier which guards the Earthly Paradise.

All the details which go to make up the description of the blissful country in *Pearl* are, thus, associated with descriptions of the surroundings of the Earthly Paradise, rather than with the Garden of Love. Moreover, this part of the earth emerges as something which is, again and again, described not only for its own sake—though it is one of the wonders of the world—but because it is a point at which earth touches the boundaries of heaven, and this life the life hereafter. We have seen that in early epic the hero is sent to this land to learn the lesson of his humanity, and to gain a treasure which can never be put to use in the world. Even in the latest versions, the twin themes of self-knowledge and mortality are still firmly linked to accounts of the Earthly Paradise. The Garden of Love, although it may be an offshoot of the same tradition, could never serve a purpose like that of the *Pearl*-poet, but the journey to the Earthly Paradise is, by long use, perfectly adapted to his needs.

[45] Menner, *Purity*, pp. 109–10, notes to these lines, compares the phrasing of the French Mandeville, and considers that the poet had direct recourse to this text. The comparison of birdsong to musical instruments is, of course a commonplace. For a discussion of this motif, and the possible influence of Mandeville on Spenser, see J. A. W. Bennett, *The Parlement of Foules*, p. 116.

II

ENCOUNTER

I

THE WHOLE ACTION OF *Pearl* involves only two persons: the Dreamer and the Maiden. The vision of the New Jerusalem does, it is true, introduce the figure of the Lamb, and describes the Heavenly Host of which the Maiden is one, but there are only two speaking parts in the poem, and only these two are presented fully, in the round. Just as it was essential to decide what kind of a garden we were dealing with in the proem so, obviously, it is of the first importance to determine to what kind these figures belong—whether they are realistically[1] presented as what we should call 'characters' in the narrative, whether they are personifications which play a part in a clear-cut allegorical scheme, or whether they are used to help to elaborate a more complex symbolism.

It will be best to take the figure of the Maiden first, since the Dreamer is mainly presented through his relationship to her. She first appears at a point when the landscape description of section iii, with its refrain of 'more and more' and its accumulation of comparatives within the stanzas has built up to a climax at which:

> More meruayle con my dom adaunt:
> I seȝ byȝonde þat myry mere
> A crystal clyffe ful relusaunt;
> Mony ryal ray con fro hit rere.
> At þe fote þerof þer sete a faunt,
> A mayden of menske, ful debonere;
> Blysnande whyt watȝ hyr bleaunt.

---

[1] By the terms 'realistic', 'real', 'realism', I mean only to indicate direct presentation, as against allegorical.

Encounter

I knew hyr wel, I hade sen hyr ere.
As glysnande golde þat man con schere,
So schon þat schene an-vnder shore.
On lenghe I loked to hyr þere;
Þe lenger, I knew hyr more and more. (157–68)

This crowned and shining figure recalls the guides of many other visions. She is like 'a crouned quene, most of honoure',[2] or like the shining angelic guide of *Huon of Burdeux*. She has something in common with the impressive figures of Boethius's Lady Philosophy, Alain de Lille's Dame Nature, or Langland's Holy Church.[3] Like their's, her garments and equipment are in part symbolical. She wears white for purity, and she has on her breast the pearl of great price. Like Lady Philosophy her nature is apparent from her countenance. Boethius saw 'a womman of ful greet reverence by semblaunt, hir eien brennynge and cleer-seynge over the comune myghte of men'.[4] The Pearl-Maiden has 'Her semblaunt sade for doc oþer erle' (211). 'Sad' here, does not, of course, mean 'sorrowful', in the modern sense, but it does not mean merely 'grave' either: it is, rather, 'steadfast'; 'beyond the changes of earthly emotion'.[5]

But, although there are resemblances between the way in which the Pearl-Maiden is described and the way in which a Lady Philosophy or a Dame Nature is presented, there are also differences—and these are of such a kind as to suggest that she is not, as they are, a straightforward allegorical figure, the personification of an idea. Such personifications are, necessarily, described in a comparatively simple way—to elaborate their appearance beyond a certain point would be to obscure the ideas they stand for. Moreover, the allegory is often developed by

[2] Carleton Brown, *Religious Lyrics of the Fourteenth Century*, no. 132, p. 234.
[3] Peter Dronke's statement that 'The principal inspiration for the "reproachful beloved"' (he includes the Pearl-Maiden in this category), 'in medieval European literature is clearly Boethius's *Philosophia*' seems, however, a dangerous oversimplification (*Medieval Latin and the Rise of European Love-Lyric*, I (Oxford, 1965), p. 91, n. 1).
[4] Chaucer's translation, ed. Robinson, *The Works of Geoffrey Chaucer*, p. 321 (I, pr. i, 4–7).
[5] See C. S. Lewis, *Studies in Words* (Cambridge, 1961), pp. 79 ff.

details introduced as a part of their personal description which could not form part of a realistically conceived picture. Philosophy, for example, is said to have a robe which depicts (according to the commentator Chaucer read) the active and contemplative life, with ladders between 'by which degrees men myghten clymben fro the nethereste lettre to the uppereste' (I, pr. i, 27–36). Alain de Lille's nature has a robe on which all the birds and beasts have their being. But, although the colours are symbolical, and the pearl at her breast has a figurative meaning, the appearance of the Pearl-Maiden is described with a richness of detail which is like the entirely realistic description of *Sir Gawain and the Green Knight*. Lines like these describe an object beautiful in itself—they do not develop an allegorical sense:

> A pyȝt coroune ȝet wer þat gyrle,
> Of mariorys and non oþer ston,
> Hiȝe pynakled of cler quyt perle,
> Wyth flurted flowreȝ perfet vpon.
> To hed hade ho non oþer werle;
> Her here leke, al hyr vmbegon,
> Her semblaunt sade for doc oþer erle,
> Her ble more blaȝt þen whalleȝ bon.
> As schorne golde schyr her fax þenne schon,
> On schyldereȝ þat leghe vnlapped lyȝte.
> Her depe colour ȝet wonted non
> Of precios perle in porfyl pyȝte.[6]   (205–16)

---

[6] Compare also the description of 'hir beau biys' (197 ff.) with its details concerning borders and 'lappeȝ', with that of Gawain's 'vrysoun' (ll. 608 ff.), 'Enbrawden and bounden wyth the best gemmeȝ / On brode sylkyn borde, and bryddeȝ on semeȝ.' In both descriptions, no doubt, the colours, jewels, and devices are appropriate to the characters and add something to our knowledge of them, but the details are presented as what an onlooker would have actually seen. A similar technique is used by Langland for the description of Lady Meed; but, although she is certainly an allegorical figure, she is not used in the same way as the simpler personifications in *Piers Plowman*—she acts out a complex part for which the development of something near what we should call 'character' is necessary. She may, too, have been intended to remind the reader of a real woman. (On Langland's technique in the presentation of Lady Meed, see 'Lady Meed and the Art of

There is significance, too, in the way in which the Dreamer's recognition of the figure which confronts him is worked out. Recognition is usually important in visions which use a guide of this kind. But it is usually a delayed recognition. This is because the purpose of the vision is to recall a Dreamer, who has gone astray, to his former good purpose (represented by the figure which appears to him) and some space is needed to make the situation clear. Boethius's recognition of Lady Philosophy is thus delayed until she has driven off the poetical muses who have been misleading him, and until she has made a good many speeches. Langland's Dreamer, similarly, is slow enough in his recognition of Holy Church to allow time for the important speeches in which she explains herself. In Pearl, however, the recognition is quite differently managed; it is the Dreamer who defines what he sees, and who calls the maiden's attention to himself, and the whole experience is presented in terms of his emotional reaction to the encounter. Recognition, in fact, comes to him at the first possible moment. His exclamation, 'I knew hyr wel, I hade sen hyr ere—' comes after only two lines of description and he returns her greeting by naming her himself, and defining her importance to him:

> 'O perle,' quod I, 'in perleȝ pyȝt,
> Art þou my perle þat I haf playned,
> Regretted by myn one on nyȝte?' (241–3)

Recognition of a personification is normally followed by a request for the exposition of the ideas for which she stands. In fact, it is to recall these ideas to mind that the vision is devised, and the intention is to rescue the Dreamer from just such a state of regret as line. 243 describes. In Pearl, however, instead of this state being due to neglect of the principles for which the personification stands and to the cultivation of their opposites (this was the case with Boethius, with Dante, with Langland's Dreamer) it is the separation itself, seen as an event in the real world, which is blamed as the source of sorrow:

Piers Plowman', by A. G. Mitchell, *The Third Chambers Memorial Lecture*, University College, London, 1956.) On the colour-symbolism of *Pearl* and *Gawain*, see below, p. 162.

'What wyrde hatȝ hyder my iuel vayned,
And don me in þys del and gret daunger?
Fro we in twynne wern towen and twayned,
I haf ben a joyleȝ juelere.' (249–52)

Just as separation itself is the cause of sorrow, so reunion alone, in the paradisial setting in which the Pearl has been found, would, or so the Dreamer thinks, be a sufficient cure:

'Now haf I fonde hyt, I schal ma feste,
And wony wyth hyt in schyr wod-schaweȝ.' (283–4)

This is in striking contrast to Boethius's question as to why, for what purpose, he is visited by Philosophy, or Dante's prayer to Virgil for practical help in getting past the beasts, or Langland's Dreamer's urgent request to Lady Holy Church for guidance as to how his soul may be saved. It is true that, whether he will or not, the Dreamer of *Pearl* is to learn from the Maiden, but her appearance to him is not handled primarily from this point of view.

The immediate recognition, the emotional reaction, the reference back to an event, not an idea, all point away from personification and towards realism. In fact, particularly when we compare it with other appearances and other recognitions in vision literature, the scene is only fully intelligible if we understand it in terms of what we should call 'real' characters. This impression is borne out by the combination of tenderness and awe with which the Dreamer regards the Maiden—even at the crowning moment of the vision when he sees her in bliss among the following of the Lamb he calls her 'my lyttel quene'—and by the references, which are scattered through the poem, to her existence before she was lost.

She is referred to in terms of family relationship:

Ho watȝ me nerre þen aunte or nece. (233)

There are references to her age, made in terms of human life on earth:

'Þow wost wel when þy perle con schede
I watȝ ful ȝong and tender of age.' (411–12)

and:

> 'Þou lyfed not two ȝer in oure þede;
> Þou cowþeȝ neuer God nauþer plese ne pray,
> Ne neuer nawþer Pater ne Crede.' (483-5)

These lines are most easily and naturally interpreted to refer to a human being; it is only with the greatest difficulty
and ingenuity that they can be made to fit a personification.[7]

If the Maiden represents a 'real' person, now translated to a
state of blessedness, so must the Dreamer; and the insistence on
her infancy, on the relationship, and on his possessive love for
her, all suggest that he stands for a father who mourns the
death of a daughter. This is borne out by the choice of the pearl
itself as the main symbol—one of its traditional associations is
with littleness[8]—and, in the discussion of salvation, by the
insistence on the texts which relate to little children. If we
accept all this, the situation which gives rise to the poem is,
perhaps, enough in itself to account for the way in which the
main figures are treated and for their divergence from the usual
types to be found in vision literature. Nevertheless, the poet did
chose to cast the work within this convention, and it seems,
therefore, worth asking whether he drew on literary precedent
as well as on his own experience in his presentation of Dreamer
and Maiden. It is, I think, likely that he did, since, even if we
are convinced that the characters are presented as fundamentally
'real', the poem as a whole is by no means fully realistic. The
Maiden is the centre of a cluster of symbols which are as important to our understanding of her as her relationship to the
Dreamer; and, as we shall see, the Dreamer himself cannot be
understood to correspond to the personality of the poet but is,
at most, only an abstraction from it, presented in a way which

---

[7] See especially Sister Mary Madaleva, *Pearl: a Study in Spiritual
Dryness* (New York, 1925), the most consistent attempt to interpret
the *Pearl* as pure allegory. Most critics who thought of the *Pearl*
as primarily an allegorical poem explained such passages as this by
postulating an 'elegaic element'. See, for example, J. B. Fletcher, 'The
Allegory of the *Pearl*', *J.E.G.Ph.* xx (1921), pp. 1 ff.

[8] See below, pp. 155-7.

does, at times, make us see him as something not unlike a personification.[9]

As far as the Maiden is concerned it seems to me that the poet could have found in the *Divina Commedia* a precedent for the treatment of figures as part allegorical, part humanly individual, which, while they merge easily into a symbolical way of writing, can be approached with human feelings of tenderness and affection as well as with awe. More than this, if we examine the way in which the figures of Dreamer and Maiden and their conversation are developed in *Pearl* and compare it with passages in the *Purgatorio* and *Paradiso* which place Dante in a similar situation, we shall find numerous similarities of detail and plan.

2

Among the guides of the *Divina Commedia* two maidens are more fully drawn than the rest. Of these, Beatrice is a figure further removed from life and more closely associated with symbolism.[10] Matilda, on the other hand, though she, too, is an allegorical figure, is treated with a combination of gravity and tenderness which comes very near to the method used in the description of his maiden guide by the *Pearl*-poet.[11] We are, I think, reminded of Matilda through the total impression the Pearl-Maiden makes on us, but of Beatrice by the pattern of events in which she plays her part, and by the details of what she says.

[9] See Gordon, *Pearl*, pp. xiv ff., for a good discussion of the problems raised by the 'fictitious I' in the poem, and, further, below, pp. 134–6.

[10] What Dante really meant by the figure of Beatrice, is a matter which must, of course, be left to specialists on the subject. I have tried here merely to point out what would have seemed obvious to an English reader of the fourteenth century, who could hardly miss the allegorical element, since it would be a familiar device, and one that he would expect to find in the treatment of serious subjects, and who, as a poet, would be particularly interested in the technical mastery of the Italian poet.

[11] I am indebted to unpublished notes made by Dorothy Everett in my comparison of Matilda and the Pearl-Maiden. She is not, of course, to be held responsible for my conclusions.

Encounter

Matilda, like the Pearl, is first seen on the farther bank of a stream which borders the Earthly Paradise:

> e là m' apparve, sì com' elli appare
> subitamente cosa che disvia
> per maraviglia tutto altro pensare,
> una donna soletta che si già
> cantando e scegliendo fior da fiore
> ond' era pinta tutta la sua via.

> (And then appeared (as in a sudden light
> Something appears which from astonishment
> Puts suddenly all other thoughts to flight)
> A lady who all alone and singing went,
> And as she sang plucked flowers that numberless
> All round about her path their colours blent.
> (*Purgatorio*, xxviii, 37–42))

The paradisial flowers have, of course, been described earlier in *Pearl*.

In both poems the maiden is given the same blend of natural, characteristic behaviour and the stylisation which her status as something more than human demands. Matilda is thus described:

> Come si volge con le piante strette
> a terra ed intra sè donna che balli,
> e piede innanzi piede a pena mette,
> volsesi in su i vermigli ed in su i gialli
> fioretti verso me non altrimenti
> che vergine che li occhi onesti avvalli.

> (Even as a lady turns round in the dance
> With feet close to each other and to the ground
> And hardly foot beyond foot doth advance,
> Toward me with maiden mien she turned her round
> Upon the floor of flowers yellow and red,
> Holding the while her modest eyes earth-bound.
> (*Purgatorio*, xxviii, 52–7))

The Pearl-Maiden, who can feel no grief, and who addresses her father out of the agelessness of eternity is presented with a similar emphasis on 'womanliness', and her response is similarly

expressed in terms of graceful movement, with which the movement of the verse keeps pace:

> Ho profered me speche, þat special spece,
> Enclynande lowe in wommon lore,
> Caʒte of her coroun of grete tresore
> And haylsed me wyth a lote lyʒte.   (235–8)

After her introductory speeches, Matilda, like the Pearl-Maiden,
leads her interlocutor along the stream, and through the leafy
wood and shows him a greater vision.[12]

There are, thus, a number of general similarities in presentation between the two maidens. When we come to compare the
Pearl-Maiden and Beatrice, the parallels become closer, and the
question of even verbal echoes arises.

The first encounter of Dante with Beatrice, like that of the
Dreamer with the Pearl, is described at length; and there are
similarities both in details and in the general treatment of the
two episodes. Some may be coincidental, arising from the basic
likeness of the subject-matter, but they seem so numerous that
it is hard to dismiss them all as chance resemblances.

Both maidens appear in a blaze of light, Beatrice 'clothed in
the colour of a living flame' (*Purgatorio*, xxx, 33), the Pearl-
Maiden in a shining glory of white and gold. This, it is true, is a
common feature of Vision literature, but one detail in the
description of the *Pearl* seems to point to a knowledge of the
Divina Commedia. In an earlier passage of the *Purgatorio* (vii,
75), and one from which the *Pearl*-poet seems likely to have
derived his indigo tree-trunks,[13] comes the striking comparison
of the fresh green of the grass to the brilliance of a newly split
emerald. The idea of the heightened brightness of the sliced
surface of something in itself bright, seems to be behind the
unusual phrase of *Pearl*, also cast in the form of a simile, 'as
glysnande golde þat man con schere' (165)—'gold sliced
through'.

Dante at once reflects on the length of time that has passed
since he saw Beatrice:

[12] See further below, pp. 208 ff.
[13] See above, p. 104.

Encounter

> E lo spirito mio, che già cotanto
> tempo era stato che alla sua presenza. . . .

The Dreamer, too, recognizes the Pearl as someone he had
formerly seen and known:

> I knew hyr wel, I hade sen hyr ere . . .
> On lenghe I loked to hyr þere;
> Þe lenger, I knew hyr more and more.
> $(164 \ldots 167–8)$

The result in both cases is a spirit overcome and abashed:

> E lo spirito mio, che già cotanto
> tempo era stato che alla sua presenza
> non era di stupor, tremando, affranto . . .

> (My spirit that a time too long to name
> Had passed, since, at her presence coming nigh,
> A trembling thing and broken it became,
> *(Purgatorio, xxx, 34–6))*

> Bot baysment gef myn hert a brunt.
> I seʒ hyr in so strange a place,
> Such a burre myʒt make myn herte blunt. (174–6)

The Dreamer receives a blow to the heart: Dante is struck and
pierced through by 'l'alta vertù' which emanates from Beatrice,

> Tosto che nella vista mi percosse
> l'alta vertù che già m' avea trafitto
> prima ch' io fuor di puerizia fosse.

> (When smote my sight the high virtue that, ere
> The years of boyhood were behind me laid,
> Already had pierced me through, as with a spear,
> *(Purgatorio, xxx, 40–2))*

When she addresses him she unveils herself so that he can see
her face:

> vidi la donna che pria m' apparìo
> velata sotto l' angelica festa,
> drizzar li occhi ver me di qua dal rio.
> Tutto che 'l vel che le scendea di testa . . .

The Dream

(I found the gaze of her I had seen appear
  Erewhile, veiled, in the angelic festival,
  Toward me, this side the stream directed clear;
Howbeit the veil she had from her head let fall . . .
                 (*Purgatorio*, xxx, 64–7))

The Pearl raises her head and the Dreamer too is pierced:

> Þenne vereȝ ho vp her fayre frount,
> Hyr vysayge whyt as playn yuore:
> Þat stonge myn hert ful stray atount.   (177–9)

Dante, in dismay, turns to appeal for help to Virgil:

> volsimi alla sinistra col rispitto
>   col quale il fantolin corre alla mamma
>   quando ha paura o quando elli è afflitto
> per dicere a Virgilio: . . .

> (With such trust as a child that is afraid
>   Or hurt, runs to his mother with his pains,
>   I turned me to the left, to seek me aid
> And say to Virgil: . . . (*Purgatorio*, xxx, 43–6))

The Dreamer, who is alone, 'dorste not calle', but expresses at length his dread of what may happen:

> More þen me lyste my drede aros.
> I stod ful stylle and dorste not calle;
> Wyth yȝen open and mouth ful clos
> I stod as hende as hawk in halle.
> I hoped þat gostly watȝ þat porpose;
> I dred onende quat schulde byfalle,
> Lest ho me eschaped þat I þer chos,
> Er I at steuen hir moȝt stalle. (181–8)

Dante uses 'regalmente' of Beatrice at xxx, 70. In the longer passage of description which is devoted to the Pearl, mention is made of her 'araye ryalle':

> Þat gracios gay wythouten galle,
> So smoþe, so smal, so seme slyȝt,
> Ryseȝ vp in hir araye ryalle,
> A precios pyece in perleȝ pyȝt. (189–93)

Encounter

A comparison of Dante's description of his state of mind through the simile of the melting show and stanza 19 of *Pearl* suggests a more complicated relationship:

> Sì come neve tra le vive travi
>   per lo dosso d' Italia si congela,
>   soffiata e stretta dalli venti schiavi,
> poi, liquefatta, in sè stessa trapela,
>   pur che la terra che perde ombra spiri,
>   sì che par foco fonder la candela;
> così fui sanza lacrime e sospiri
>   anzi 'l cantar di quei che notan sempre
>   dietro alle note delli etterni giri; . . .
> lo gel che m' era intorno al cor ristretto,
>   spirito e acqua fessi, e con angoscia
>   della bocca e delli occhi uscì del petto.

> (As on the chine of Italy the snows
>   Lodged in the living rafters harden oft
>   To freezing, when the North-East on them blows,
> Then, inly melted, trickle from aloft,
>   If from the shadeless countries a breath stirs,
>   Like in the flame a candle melting soft,
> So was I, without sighs and without tears,
>   In presence of their singing who accord
>   Their notes to music of the eternal spheres . . .
> The ice that round my heart had hardened woke
>   Warm into breath and water, and from my breast
>   In anguish, through mouth and through eyes, outbroke.
>   (*Purgatorio*, xxx, 85–99))

In *Pearl* a similar state of mind is described in unusual terms:

> A manneȝ dom moȝt dryȝly demme,
> Er mynde moȝt malte in hit mesure.
> I hope no tong moȝt endure
> No sauerly saghe say of þat syȝt,
> So watȝ hit clene and cler and pure,
> Þat precios perle þer hit watȝ pyȝt. (223–38)

It seems to me possible that Dante's phrasing and thought may lie behind these lines and that *dryȝly demme* and *malte* should be taken in a more literal and concrete sense than is sometimes done—that is 'dammed up', 'brought to a full stop', corresponding to Dante's *congela*, and 'melted', 'let loose again', corresponding to *liquefatta*: 'a man's judgement would be struck into total immobility (like the frozen snow in the rafters) before his mind could melt into the full comprehension of it': i.e. be freed to flow round it, and so take its measure. The phrase *'malte in hit mesure'* is unusual and syntactically difficult however it is taken; the image would seem to be of water freed to flow round and over an object.

If the poet has, in fact, Dante's lines at the back of his mind, he would seem to have rejected the long simile in favour of a brief metaphor which hesitates between his favourite image of water (*demme*) and ice (*malte*). Although he makes frequent use of a string of short similes—also a favourite device of Dante's,[14] the *Pearl*-poet never adopted the long simile—and, indeed, in spite of the fact that it got off to a good start in Lagamon's *Brut*,[15] this type of simile was seldom, if ever, used by poets of the alliterative revival.

It is not surprising that each poet should speak of his period of longing for the lost one:

> Tant' eran li occhi miei fissi attenti
> a disbramarsi la decenne sete,
> che li altri sensi m' eran tutti spenti.

> (So fastened were mine eyes, and so intent
> The ten years' thirst of longing to abate,
> That the other senses were annulled and spent,
> (*Purgatorio*, xxxii, 1–3))

> 'O perle,' quod I, 'in perleȝ pyȝt,
> Art þou my perle þat I haf playned,
> Regretted by myn one on nyȝte?
> Much longeyng haf I for þe layned,
> Syþen into gresse þou me aglyȝte.' (241–5)

---

[14] As Osgood pointed out (*Pearl*, p. 57, note to l. 76), strings of short similies are characteristic of the *Pearl*-poet, who also uses them in *Purity* and *Patience*.

[15] See *Selections from Laȝamon's Brut*, ed. G. L. Brook, with a Preface by C. S. Lewis (Oxford, 1963), p. x.

But it is more surprising that the maidens' replies should
follow similar lines. Both accuse their interlocutors of error:

> Tuttavia, perchè mo vergogna porte
>   del tuo errore, e perchè altra volta,
>   udendo le serene, sie più forte,
> pon giù il seme del piangere ed ascolta:

> (Howbeit, that now the shame thou carry still
>   For thine error, and at the Siren's plea
>   Another time thou be of stronger will,
> Lay aside the seed of weeping; hark to me.
> <div align="right">(<i>Purgatorio</i>, xxxi, 43–6))</div>

> 'Sir, ȝe haf your tale mysetente,'   (257)

Both poets say that their heroes have concerned themselves
with valueless, transitory things:

> Piangendo dissi: 'Le presenti cose
>   col falso lor piacer volser miei passi,
>   tosto che 'l vostro viso si nascose.'

> (Weeping I said: 'Things of the passing day,
>   Soon as your face no longer on me shone,
>   With their false pleasure turned my steps away'.
> <div align="right">(<i>Purgatorio</i>, xxxi, 34–6))</div>

> 'Bot, jueler gente, if þou schal lose
>   Þy ioy for a gemme þat þe watȝ lef,
>   Me þynk þe put in a mad porpose,
>   And busyeȝ þe aboute a raysoun bref;
>   For þat þou lesteȝ watȝ bot a rose
>   Þat flowred and fayled as kynde hyt gef.   (265–70)

Both maidens cite their buried and dispersed bodies as proof of
what they say:

> 'sì udirai come in contraria parte
>   mover dovìeti mia carne sepolta.
> Mai non t' appresentò natura o arte
>   piacer, quanto le belle membra in ch' io
>   rinchiusa fui, e sono in terra sparte.'

> (Hear how my buried body should have spurred
> And on the opposite path have furthered thee.
> Nature or art never to thee assured
> Such pleasure as the fair limbs that did house
> My spirit, and now are scattered and interred.
>
> (*Purgatorio*, xxxi, 47–51))

> Now þurȝ kynde of þe kyste þat hyt con close
> To a perle of prys hit is put in pref.
> And þou hatȝ called þy wyrde a þef,
> Þat oȝt of noȝt hatȝ mad þe cler;
> Þou blameȝ þe bote of þy meschef,
> Þou art no kynde jueler.   (271–6)

In the *Paradiso* Beatrice reproves Dante for believing himself on earth:

> e cominciò: 'Tu stesso ti fai grosso
> col falso imaginar, sì che non vedi
> ciò che vedresti se l' avessi scosso.
> Tu non se' in terra, sì come tu credi;
> ma folgore, fuggendo il proprio sito,
> non corse come tu ch' ad esso riedi.'

> (And spoke: 'Thou makest thyself dense of wit
> With false fancy, so that thou dost not see
> What thou would'st see, wert thou but rid of it.
> Thou'rt not on earth, as thou supposest thee:
> But lightning from its own place rushing out
> Ne'er sped as thou, who to thy home dost flee.'
>
> (*Paradiso*, i, 88–93))

For a rather different reason, the Pearl-Maiden makes the same point. He had believed that she was on earth:

> Þre wordeȝ hatȝ þou spoken at ene:
> Vnavysed, for soþe, wern alle þre.
> Þou ne woste in worlde quat on dotȝ mene;
> Þy worde byfore þy wytte con fle
> Þou says þou traweȝ me in þis dene,
> Bycawse þou may wyth yȝen me se.   (291—6)

Both Dante and the Dreamer are said to be indulging in mad or frenzied behaviour:

Ond' ella, appresso d' un pio sospiro,
li occhi drizzò ver me con quel sembiante
che madre fa sovra figlio deliro,

(She, sighing in pity, gave me as she gazed
The look that by a mother is bestowed
Upon her child in its delirium crazed,
(Paradiso, i, 100–2))

'Me þynk þe put in a mad porpose, . . .
Wy borde ȝe men? So madde ȝe be! . . .'   (267, 290)

Lastly, what Dante is able to say in earnest:

. . . 'Madonna, sì devoto
com' esser posso più, ringrazio lui
lo qual dal mortal mondo m' ha remoto.'

('My Lady,' I answered, 'more devoutly none
Could thank Him, and I thank Him yet again,
Who hath removed me from yon mortal zone.'
(Paradiso, ii, 46–8))

is, in *Pearl* a part of the Dreamer's misunderstanding of his situation:

'Now haf I fonde hyt, I schal ma feste,
And wony wyth hyt in schyr wod-schaweȝ,
And loue my Lorde and al his laweȝ
Þat hatȝ me broȝt þys blys ner.'   (283–6)

As the Maiden points out, she is not, in fact, in the country in which he thinks she is.

Whether these similarities do in fact point to the *Pearl*-poet's knowledge and use of the *Divina Commedia* is not an easy question. It is not, I think, beyond the bounds of possibility that they arose because both poets were treating of similar material, and provided similar solutions to comparable technical problems. But even if this were so (and I am inclined to think that the balance of the evidence is in favour of a closer relationship), the important thing would still be that we do, towards the end of the fourteenth century, find an English poet who shows an ability to handle complex material and a technical mastery which can profitably be discussed in terms of a comparison with the great Italian poet. Chaucer apart, this is rare enough to call for remark.

Certainly, even if the *Pearl*-poet is allowed to owe a debt to Dante, it will still be his preservation of the decorum of his own poem that will strike us most forcibly. He never forgets, as Chaucer seems sometimes to do in the *House of Fame*, the smaller scale of his own poem, or, serious as he is, the different key in which it is planned. However we understand Beatrice, whether as an emanation of God or as a human beloved transfigured, one thing about her is clear. Through her intervention Dante is raised to a participation in the Divine Love and knowledge: he is a sharer in the final mystical vision. The Pearl-Maiden does not bring about this result, and the Dreamer's relationship to her is not of such a kind that she could do so.[16] The plan of the poem, and the peculiar structure of the final sections mean that the Dreamer is excluded from the vision of the Heavenly City.[17] He is not to cross the river, nor to be vouchsafed a vision of Heaven from within. There is no room for the philosophical and scientific discussion of the *Divina Commedia*, still less for the political prophecy which is such an important part of Dante's work. *Pearl* remains a more intimate, and a far simpler work and the balance through which the maiden's human characteristics never dislimn into either allegory or metaphysics is exquisitely preserved. Dante's in-

[16] Dronke's mention of her in the company of 'reproachful beloveds' which includes Beatrice, thus needs modification (*Medieval Latin and the Rise of European Love Lyric*, p. 91, note 1). Manzalaoui's suggestion that she is to be compared with the beloved maiden of Mohammedan eschatological tradition who welcomes the soul in paradise, and who is sometimes thought of as a guide and inspiration to the spirit while it is still on earth is, also, not entirely acceptable ('English Analogues to the *Liber Scalae*', *M. Aev.*, XXXIV (1965), pp. 21 ff.). The poet might, indeed, have taken some hints for the presentation of his maiden from the arabic derived *Liber Scalae*, which he could have read. But his Maiden is still of a different kind, since she represents the soul of a person who once lived, and with whom the Dreamer had the special relationship of father to child, not of lover to beloved.

[17] See further, below, pp. 121–2, 230 ff.

fluence, in fact, if it is present in *Pearl,* is pervasive, but never obtrusive, and never overloads the work with something which stands out as foreign to it.

The general similarity in the handling of the dialogue in the two poems is well summed up by Dorothy Everett:

> Small as the scale of *Pearl* is compared with Dante's poem, the method is essentially the same. In both, the process of enlightenment is presented by means of a dialogue between a mortal seeking it and a celestial being, once a loved mortal, who now possesses knowledge, by virtue of her position in heaven. In both, the poet has, as it were, split himself into two, so that he can present at once his ignorance and uncertainty and his knowledge and confidence; and since his serene confidence, and even his power to understand, was not achieved unaided, but was the result of divine revelation both direct and through the teaching of the Church, the person of the instructor is rightly represented as insusceptible of human emotion, remote and incomprehensible, while the person of the instructed remains human and prone to emotion, and for that reason able to arouse emotion. Though the dialogue form is often used in medieval literature to convey instruction, the similarity here is unusually close; and it is between something so fundamental to each poem that it affords far better grounds for thinking that the poet of *Pearl* knew the *Divina Commedia* than some of the lesser parallels that have been cited.[18]

Good as these grounds are, we could, I think go even farther, and see the influence of the *Divina Commedia* on much of the descriptive technique of *Pearl.* In fact, what Clemen said of Chaucer is equally applicable to the *Pearl*-poet:

> Surely Dante's influence must underlie this description at once so precise, so realistic and yet so truly a part of experience. What influenced Chaucer in the *Divine Comedy* was not the basic conception, the thoughts, the 'content'; it was Dante's method of presentation, the intensity, precision, and perception with which he reproduced sensuous detail, visual impressions of movement and light for the most part, but also of sounds. Chaucer must have been impressed at discovering a poet who

[18] *Essays on Middle English Literature,* p. 95.

131

portrayed marvels and visions as if they belonged to reality, yet expressed his own reactions so vividly that everything seemed to be happening at that very moment and to himself.[19]

3

In his presentation of the figure of the Maiden-guide, as we have said, the poet's own experience must be at least reflected. The final form, however, which this experience takes in the poem is likely to have been influenced by models which the art and thought of his day made available to him. Besides the *Divina Commedia*, there are other contexts, in which comparable figures appeared, which could have influenced his treatment of the Pearl-Maiden.

Feminine figures who are regarded with love as well as with awe by the man they guide to celestial heights take a number of different forms during the Middle Ages. These range from shadowy figures which belong to metaphysics rather than to poetry, to a human beloved who, in a moment of metaphorical hyperbole may take on some of their characteristics.[20] It does not seem to me that the Pearl-Maiden has any place in this company. There is another group, however, in which, I believe the poem itself justifies us in placing her. This takes in, as its upper limit the Blessed Virgin as Mediatrix, and includes the virgin Saints. The Maiden does, in fact, mediate between the Dreamer and God: she obtains special grace for him so that he is granted a vision of the Heavenly Jerusalem:

> 'Bot of þe Lombe I haue þe aquylde
> For a syʒt þerof þurʒ gret fauor.'   (967–8)

She also stands between him and God as the voice both of his own reason and of what is divinely reasonable—this is es-

---

[19] *Chaucer's Early Poetry*, pp. 90–1.

[20] Such figures, or ideas, e.g. 'Sapientia', 'Nous', even 'Anima-Mundi', are discussed at length by Dronke, *Medieval Latin and the Rise of European Love Lyric*, I, chapter ii, 'The Background of Ideas'. It may be felt that he underrates the part played by hyperbole and paradox in love-poetry. See also C. S. Lewis, *The Allegory of Love*, chapters i and ii.

pecially noticeable in her opening speeches, though it is also her rôle throughout the debate.

It is perhaps for this reason that the poet insists on her place among the holy Virgins, and that he treats her throughout the poem in terms that would be applicable to a Virgin Saint. As we shall see, the pearl itself is very commonly used as an image in hymns devoted to such saints, and is not restricted merely to St. Margaret.[21] But, more than this, as a queen of heaven, the maiden is in some sense compared to the Blessed Virgin herself —the poet is quick to modify the comparison. The Maiden's spontaneous hymn of praise sweeps away the Dreamer's doubts as to who is the supreme queen of heaven:

> 'Cortayse Quen,' þenne sayde þat gaye,
> Knelande to grounde, folde vp hyr face,
> 'Makeleȝ Moder and myryest May,
> Blessed bygynner of vch a grace!'   (433–6)

Further than this, I believe, the poet cannot go. Although he places the figure of his Maiden in a paradisial setting, and allows a wealth of imagery and symbolism to cluster round her, he never forgets, or lets his reader forget, that she does, in fact, represent a particular blessed soul, who had a separate and individual existence on earth. She brings comfort to the Dreamer principally for this reason—his first need is for reassurance as to the state of an individual after death. Certainly, the poet generalizes from her case, and uses it as an example of the way in which God's laws operate, and certainly she expounds these laws to him. But at no time in the poem does she bring about any mystical union in divine knowledge for the Dreamer. The end of the poem, indeed, is organized with the greatest care to prevent any such impression—and the coda expressly disclaims the intention.[22]

[21] See below, pp. 43, 166.
[22] See below, pp. 227 ff.

The Dream

4

We have already said a good deal about the figure of the
Dreamer—indeed, almost everything said about the Maiden
reflects on him. It only remains to see if there is anything of
special importance for the understanding of the poem about the
way in which the poet utilized what was an essential part of the
vision convention. Dreams and visions, it is evident, cannot take
place without dreamers or visionaries. In practice, however, it
became usual to treat figures which were originally no more than
a mere starting-point for what was to be revealed, as an integral
part of the whole.[23] This operated in two ways: first, if the
Dreamer was constantly present and involved in his dream, its
events tended to become more and more internal to his own
mind—so that at times the Dreamer-figure becomes something
like a personification in his own mental drama. Secondly such
figures gave an opportunity for the poet to speak now with an
assumed voice, as one of his own characters, now with his own,
as someone who interrupts and comments on his work. Since a
Dreamer of this kind can never have the same complete separation from the author-figure as a character less intimately bound
up in the narration, this can lead to very complex effects.

If we take the first case, where the Dreamer becomes a pro-
tagonist in his own inner drama, and thereby tends to lose some
of his identity, the most obvious example is the Dowel section
of *Piers Plowman*. Here the Dreamer, referred to as 'Will' (no
doubt because that was the poet's name)[24] becomes 'will', in
fact—that is acts out his part as that particular mental faculty,
split off from, and made to debate with, the other mental faculties and activities, which, united, make up his personality as a

[23] The Apocalypse provides a prototype for this kind of visionary;
Hermas, in the *Shepherd*, is treated in the same way. In these cases
the revelation is merely channelled through the Dreamer—the important
thing is for him to communicate it to the world at large, and he is not
shown as especially affected by it from point to point.

[24] On William Langland as the name of the poet of *Piers Plowman*,
see G. Kane, *Piers Plowman, The Evidence for Authorship* (London,
1965). A similar coincidence of name may lie behind *Pearl*: the
child's name may have been Margaret, or one of its forms.

whole. The result is a curious attenuation of all the figures—
Nevill Coghill calls them 'phantoms' and 'ghostly informants'[25]
—in which the Dreamer shares, though he is robust enough
elsewhere.

There are, I think, signs of the same tendency to flatten the
Dreamer into a personification in *Pearl*. We have seen that, in
the proem, his problem is described as that of will in conflict
with reason. In so far as the Maiden speaks with reason's voice,
the Dreamer necessarily tends to stand for his own will, the
faculty in need of correction. But I think that, for several
reasons, the narrowing down of the Dreamer figure into a single
aspect of himself which is so striking in the vision of Dowel, is
never allowed to go beyond a certain point in *Pearl*. One obvious
reason for this is the fact that the story is not developed in terms
of an allegorical action: the Maiden speaks with the voice of
reason not because she *is* reason but because, through a train of
events in the real world, she has come to occupy a position in
which there can be no mental conflict, and no opposition of
reason and will. She is shown as occupying this position in a real
sense, not through an action played out by personifications.

Another reason is the very delicate balance which is maintained throughout the poem between the Dreamer as father of
the child and the Dreamer as the awestruck contemplator of a
veray avysyoun. There are many points in the poem at which a
tone of voice or a turn of phrase reminds the reader of the basic
situation and—an important part of the plan, to which we must
return[26]—lowers the tension from the visionary sublime to
something more familiar. To give only two instances, there is the
appeal, with its rapid, almost tremulous rhythm, from reason to
sentiment of:

> 'And, quen we departed we wern at on;
> God forbede we be now wroþe,
> We meten so selden by stok oþer ston.' (378–80)

Words like this can only be addressed by one person to another
—they would make nonsense as between abstractions. Or there

[25] *The Vision of Piers Plowman*, translation by Henry W. Wells,
introduction by Nevill Coghill (London, 1935), p. xxi.
[26] See below, pp. 221 ff.

are the words of shocked reproof, with the familiar form of address 'damysel', and the staccato exclamations:

> 'Of countes, damysel, par ma fay,
> Wer fayr in heuen to halde asstate,
> Oþer elleȝ a lady of lasse aray;
> Bot a quene! Hit is to dere a date!'   (489–92)

Blunt, colloquial speech between abstractions is certainly not unknown in vision literature. We find it in *Piers Plowman*, for example, playing a signal part in the debate of the Daughters of God.[27] But it does, of necessity, make us regard the figures that use it in a special light. If the context of the poem proves that they are indeed personifications, then we at least know that they are personifications which play an unusual role, and call forth an unusual reaction. In *Pearl* such speeches are a part of our anchorage in the real world.

George Kane has shown with what subtlety Langland exploits the possibilities of differentiation between the *persona* of the Dreamer-poet and that of the author who speaks from an authoritative position, as it were from outside and above the poem.[28] The poet of *Pearl* is, I think, aware of this means of expression, but he makes sparing use of it. Considering the small scale of his work, indeed, it would hardly be possible for him to elaborate the device. He does, however, speak authoritatively, and with information which is not available to the Dreamer at this point, when, in the proem, he gives a diagnosis of his malady in terms which are of the utmost importance for the understanding of his plan:

> I playned my perle þat þer watȝ spenned
> Wyth fyrce skylleȝ þat faste faȝt;
> Þaȝ kynde of Kryst me comfort kenned,
> My wreched wylle in wo ay wraȝte.   (53–6)

[27] B-Text passus xviii. See Nevill Coghill, 'God's Wenches and the Light that Spoke' in *English and Medieval Studies Presented to J. R. R. Tolkien*, edited by Norman Davis and C. L. Wrenn (London, 1962), pp. 200 ff.

[28] Op. cit., chapter iv, 'Signatures', pp. 52 ff.

After this the Maiden's is the authoritative voice, until the very end, when her words of reproof are taken up and elaborated in lines which repudiate the Dreamer and his errors:

> Lorde, mad hit arn þat agayn þe stryuen,
> Oþer proferen þe oȝt agayn þy paye.
>
> To pay þe Prince oþer sete saȝte
> Hit is ful eþe to þe god Krystyin;
> For I haf founden hym, boþe day and naȝte,
> A God, a Lorde, a frende ful fyin.   (1199–204)

This is a final, weighty, summing up, which does not admit of any doubt or contradiction. It is certainly not the voice which, often hesitantly or with dubious logic, counters the Maiden's arguments in the debate section.

III

SYMBOLS OF PERFECTION

I

FROM THE *Divina Commedia* the poet of *Pearl* could have learnt how to present figures which, while they always remained human and individual, were yet, in an important sense, also the vehicles of symbolism. It is, indeed, hard to see where else he could have acquired this blend of the modes of realistic and symbolical writing.

Dante used the symbolism of numbers and of colours to help to convey this extra dimension of his characters.[1] For the Middle English poet the pearl itself is the main symbol. In the proem, as I have suggested, it was effective because it could stand for both earthly and heavenly treasure—this ambivalence, in fact, focused attention on contrasting values. After the introduction of the maiden who wears the pearl of price on her breast, however, the ambivalence of the symbol ceases to be felt, and the meaning widens and deepens. When the poet writes, late in his poem:

[1] On numerical symbolism, see Curtius, *European Literature and the Latin Middle Ages*, pp. 501 ff. The vision of the Earthly Paradise at the end of the *Purgatorio* uses colours symbolically, as does the description of Beatrice. For the *Pearl*-poet's use of symbolical colours, see below, p. 162. For the most important writings on the symbolism of *Pearl* before 1952, see Gordon, *Pearl*, p. lv, and add D. W. Robertson, Jr., 'The Pearl as a Symbol', *M.L.N.*, LXV (1950), pp. 155 ff. The most important articles to appear after 1952 are: M. R. Stern, 'An Approach to *Pearl*', *J.E.G.Ph.* (1955), pp. 684 ff.; 'The *Pearl*, Notes for an Interpretation', S. de Voren Hoffman, *M.P.* (1960), pp. 73 ff.; A. C. Spearing, 'Symbolic and Dramatic Development in *Pearl*', *M.P.* (1962), pp. 1 ff.; C. A. Luttrell, 'The Medieval Tradition of the Pearl Virginity', *M. Aev.* (1962), pp. 194 ff.

Symbols of Perfection

'O maskeleʒ perle in perleʒ pure,
Þat bereʒ,' quod I, 'þe perle of prys.'   (745–6)

he is able to draw on a complex of ideas by now established around the pearl—but he has excluded the idea of earthly treasure by his emphasis on other senses.

To understand how he could do this it is not necessary, even if it were possible, to give a complete history of the symbolism of the pearl. Such a history would throw little light on the *Pearl* itself. What is necessary is to understand what kind of symbol it was: what were the common ideas which underlie its separate manifestations, and how it was that an individual poet could ensure a particular effect through its use.

To understand the complex of ideas and feelings which, for a medieval poet, clustered round the pearl, we have to remember that all symbols of this type tend to link up with others which have something in common with them. Thus, the pearl could be linked to the dew or teardrop, because of an obvious physical analogy, and also because of its supposed origin in the coagulation of drops of dew received into the open oyster shell.[2] Manna, which was round and white and was also a coagulation of dew, is a part of this complex.[3] Although we need not assume that all the possible elements in a group are present in the forefront of a given poet's mind, it is still often necessary to remember them when we try to understand his imagery. For example, as we shall see, although the *Pearl*-poet does not use the image of the dew and the sun, he does, at the climax of his poem, relate the pearl to the Heavenly Lamp which, for the Blessed, replaces Sun and Moon.[4] Moreover, it is often necessary to use one part of the complex to illustrate another. Marvell's poem on *The Dew Drop*, for example, illustrates most aspects of the symbolism of the pearl, although pearls are not, in fact, mentioned in it.[5]

---

[2] This piece of natural history was handed down through the encyclopedic tradition. It is included, e.g., in Vincent of Beauvais' *Speculum Naturale*, and in Brunetto Latini's *Livre dou Trésor*. It is also in *Mandeville's Travels*.

[3] See above, p. 58.   [4] 1045–50, see below, p. 144.
[5] See below, Þ. 142–3.

The Dream

Alchemical writings, too, often provide illuminating examples of this nexus of symbolism. Their authors were concerned, above all, with the idea of perfection and completeness, since their whole system depended on the idea of perfecting the nature of substances. They described their process, too, in terms of death, putrefaction, and resurrection.[6] When we draw on such sources, however, we need to remember the curious phenomenon which Jung aptly called 'a melting down of images'.[7] Alchemical symbolism, in fact, takes on something of the fluidity of the mixtures in the retorts, and the result is often strangeness without the discipline and integration brought with it by the poetic imagination. Anyone who reads through, for example, Ripley's *Cantilena* and compares it with other texts in which the same imagery is subordinated to a different purpose will appreciate this point.[8] The alchemical writings, therefore, must be used with care, and there is little evidence that they influenced poets in the fourteenth century. From another point of view, however, they do throw light on an imagery derived from mineral substances, since they contain generally accepted scientific information about the properties of matter.

[6] See F. Sherwood Taylor, *The Alchemists* (London, 1951), p. 57.
[7] *Mysterium Coniunctionis* (translated R. F. C. Hull, *The Collected Works*, vol. 14, London, 1963), pp. 324–5.
[8] The crowned Queen of Ripley's *Cantilena*—

> Upon her head a Diadem she did weare,
> With fiery Feet sh'Advanced into the Aire;
> And glittering Bravely in her Golden Robes
> She took her Place amidst the Starry Globes—

nurses the bleeding green lion which is fed by the eagle. Compare, e.g., the Middle English lyric, *Quia Amore Langueo*:

> In a tabernacle of a toure,
> As I stode musyng on the mone,
> A crouned quene, most of honoure,
> Apered in gostly syght ful sone.

This also is Mother, who laments both her Son and 'man my brother' (*Cantilena* 34, the sixteenth-century English translation, quoted and adapted to bring it nearer the Latin in *Mysterium Coniunctionis*, p. 323; Carleton Brown, *Religious Lyrics of the Fourteenth Century*, no. 132, p. 234).

Symbols of Perfection

Historically speaking, there are at least two main strands of tradition to be distinguished in the development of the symbolism of the pearl. One is biblical, the other Eastern: because of its roundness, and its lack of facets, the pearl, like the egg, is a symbol of perfection, of wholeness, and of eternity.[9]

An excellent, though late, example of the Eastern type of 'world-pearl', parallel to the 'world-egg', the wholeness from which comes multiplicity, is provided by Thomas Burnet who says that he is drawing on Arabian sources:

> The *Arabians* tell us, that the great and good God being about to create all Things, first formed a large Table and Pen that he might write upon it all future Events to the End of the World. When this was done he created a white Pearl, and having viewed it with the Eye of his Majesty, it dissolved into Waters, whence arose the Abyss. Then followed the Production of the Air; then that of Animals and Angels. When God designed to make the other Creatures, he produced a white Jewel, which was immediately melted by the divine Aspect, and began violently to bubble and cast its Froth upwards. Which being done, God formed seven Earths from the Froth of it, together with Rivers and Mountains. And from the Smoke he raised as many Heavens. And thus Heaven and Earth were finished according to the Tradition of the Arabians.
>
> The *Mahometan* Creation is yet more absurd; as we find it in a Treatise concerning the Knowledge of subtil Truths, it runs thus: 'God first of all created the Light for *Mahomet* having the Nature and Shape of a Peacock: This he put in a lovely Pearl, and hung it on a most beautiful Tree where for about a Thousand Years it celebrated the Praises of its Creator. When this Light was viewed by Mahomet, he fell into a prodigious Sweat, and God made the Angels out of the Sweat of his Head, and from the Sweat of his Face a Throne, Table, Quill, Sun, Moon,

[9] St. Ephraem uses the pearl in this sense: 'And since I have wandered in thee, pearl, I will gather up my mind, and by having contemplated thee, would become like thee, in that thou art all gathered up into thyself, and as thou in all times art one, one let me become by thee' (Morris, p. 98). On the 'treasure hard to obtain' for which pearl, egg, flower, etc., are interchangeable symbols, see Jung, The *Archetypes and the Collective Unconscious* (translated R. F. C. Hull, *The Collected Works*, vol. 9), p. 160.

Heaven, Stars, and whatsoever is in the Heavens. Lastly, to pass by other Absurdities, he formed the whole Earth out of the Sweat of his Feet, and whatsoever is thereon.'[10]

The first account shows the connection between the pearl and the waters of the abyss and also, if the 'white jewel' can be taken as a pearl, with another important association, that with the smoke and spume from which the Universe is created. The second shows yet another symbol of wholeness in the peacock. The peacock's tail, as light, put in the white pearl, no doubt stands for the colours of the spectrum which make up white light and also for multiplicity arising from the monad. In the same way, the *Cauda pavonis* was used in Alchemy as a term for the colours which appeared, at a certain stage, on the surface of the retort, and also as a symbol of the achievement of the work.[11]

There is, obviously, no strict need in Christian tradition for the pearl as an equivalent to the 'world-egg'. Nevertheless, this concept seems to have left its mark, in that the pearl does stand for the perfect, all-including sphere. I have already quoted the lines from both *Pearl* and *Purity* in which, because of its endless, seamless nature the pearl becomes a symbol of wholeness.[12] In *Pearl* it is, further, 'lyke þe reme of heuenesse clere' (735). For the Kingdom of Heaven as a perfect sphere the poet might have gone to Albertus Magnus who had said: 'Heaven is a pure body . . . of the most pure matter, in the form of a sphere.'[13] For the pearl as by nature a perfect round he need have gone no farther than Mandeville, where it is stated that 'the perl of his owne kynde taketh roundness'.[14]

[10] *Archeologiae Philosophicae: or the Ancient Doctrine Concerning the Originals of Things*, (translated Foxton, London, 1736), I p. 60. I owe this reference to the kindness of Miss Valerie Barnes.

[11] See *Mysterium Coniunctionis*, pp. 285 ff. On the potential colours contained in light, see Aristotle, *de Anima*, III, 5.

[12] See above, p. 14.

[13] *Compendium Theolog. Veritatis*, 2, 4 (*Opera*, ed. Borgnet, 34, 42). The idea is Aristotelean. See *de Caelo*, II, 286b, 10: 'The shape of the heaven is of necessity spherical, for that is the shape most appropriate to its substance, and also by nature primary.' *The Works of Aristotle Translated into English*, by W. D. Ross, II (Oxford, 1930).

[14] *Mandeville's Travels*, from Cotton Titus C, xvi, ed. Hamelius, p. 105. The spherical drop of the dew/pearl remains an important

Symbols of Perfection

The tradition of the pearl = liquid drop, associated with whiteness and silver, but, by union with the sun, becoming gold, is an ancient alchemical one. A poem by the Greek poet Stephanos (seventh century A.D.) provides a good example, though it lacks the lucidity of the seventeenth-century poems:

> O wisdom of teaching such a preparation, displaying the work,
> O moon clad in white and vehemently shining abroad whiteness,
> let us learn what is the lunar radiance, that we may not miss what
> is doubtful. . . . What is this emanation of the same Moon? I
> will not conceal it, but will display visibly the sought-for beauty.
> For the emanation of it is the mystery hidden in it, the most
> worthy pearl, the flame-bearing moonstone . . . the food of the
> liquor of gold. . . . For it is white as seen, but yellow as appren-
> hended, the bridegroom to the allotted moon, the golden drop
> [falling] from it, the glorious emanation from it, the unchange-
> able embrace, the indelible orbit, the god-given work, the
> marvellous making of gold.[15]

In this passage the pearl is associated with the moon, which, as a rule, stands for silver, just as the sun stands for gold. However, it is clear, that in such contexts the pearl means whiteness, and so silver, and is therefore also assigned to the moon. In fact, Roger Bacon, writing of the technical terms of alchemy warns us to expect this equation (and at the same time reminds us of the dew):

> Silver is also called margarita on account of its white colour
> and is called unio, because margarita and unio are the same,
> as Solinus informs us in the book *de Mirabilibus Mundi*. For

[15] Translated by Sherwood Taylor. See E. J. Holmyard, *Alchemy* (Pelican Books, London, 1957), pp. 28–9. The passage as a whole is concerned with 'magnesia'—an unidentified substance. According to Chaucer it is 'a water that is maad, I seye, of elementes foure', and its exact composition is a secret of the philosophers (*Canon's Yoeman's Tale*, G. 1459 ff.). See Sherwood Taylor, op. cit., p. 4.

image for seventeenth-century poets. Marvell's 'On a drop of Dew' is an outstanding example. Thomas and Henry Vaughan are even more explicit. For Thomas Vaughan's Alchemical poem 'Hyanthe' (*Magia Adamica*, 1650, pp. 93 ff.), see Sherwood Taylor, *The Alchemists*, pp. 93 ff. Henry Vaughan used the same imagery in 'Isaacs Marriage', ll. 53 ff. (*Works*, p. 409).

margarita is called unio because never more than one at a time is generated in the marine shell. For shells naturally open to receive the dew of heaven and, a single drop of dew received, (the shell) shuts again and by its power solidifies the drop into a margarita or unio.[16]

That this is not an exclusively alchemical conception is suggested by Dante, who calls the moon 'l' etterna margarita' (*Paradiso*, ii, 34).

It may be felt that these writings are all very far in method and intention from the Middle English poem, the *Pearl*. Nevertheless, there is one passage, where the poet is describing the climax of his vision of heaven in which the symbolism is, I think, not fully intelligible unless we remember some at any rate of these ideas.

Section xviii of the *Pearl* is dominated by the idea of the displacement of the earthly sun and moon by a light which combines the radiance of both, and which can never know eclipse. Section xix carries this idea farther, and works it out in terms of the marriage of the Lamb, the Sun of Heaven, whose brides are pearls, which rise like the moon.

Stanzas 87–8 explain that the sun and moon we see from the earth have no place in heaven:

> Hem nedde nawþer sunne ne mone.
> Of sunne ne mone had þay no nede.   (1044–5)

These lights are replaced by what the alchemists would have called 'our Sun' and 'our Moon'. The sun is replaced by the Lamb:

> Þe self God watȝ her lombe-lyȝt,
> Þe Lombe her lantyrne, wythouten drede;
> Þurȝ hym blysned þe borȝ al bryȝt.   (1046–8)

---

[16] *Part of the Opus Tertium*, ed. A. G. Little (Aberdeen, 1912), pp. 83 ff. See J. M. Stillman, *The Story of Alchemy and Early Chemistry* (reprinted by Dover Publications, New York, 1960), pp. 268 ff., whose translation I quote. This dew corresponds to Ben Jonson's *ros-marine*, from which beauty is born. (*Masque of Blacknesse*, 340. *Ben Jonson*, ed. C. H. Herford, Percy and Evelyn Simpson, VII (Oxford, 1941), p. 180.)

Symbols of Perfection

The Lamb is associated with gold by an expansion of the Apocalyptic description:

> Wyth horneȝ seuen of red golde cler   (1111)

and, his garments are like pearls:

> As praysed perleȝ his wedeȝ wasse   (1112)

The procession of the Virgins approaches

> Ryȝt as þe maynful mone con rys
> Er þenne þe day-glem dryue al doun.   (1093–4)

Each one is

> Depaynt in perleȝ and wedeȝ qwyte;
> In vchoneȝ breste watȝ bounden boun
> Þe blysful perle wyth gret delyt.   (1102–4)

I do not think that, in this passage of extremely complex symbolism, the poet writes 'alchemically'. I would merely suggest that he would not have used the symbols in quite this way if he had been unaware of the fact that the equations pearl-moon and gold-sun played an important part in traditional descriptions of a process leading, through 'death' and 'putrefaction' to 'resurrection' and perfection.[17]

[17] There are two reasons for extreme caution in identifying imagery as alchemical. One is that the alchemists used Christian symbolism with perfect freedom—there was an alchemical crucifixion, resurrection, assumption, etc. (The chapter on 'Alchemical Symbolism' in Sherwood Taylor's book *The Alchemists* gives a particularly balanced and helpful account of this aspect of alchemical writing.) The other is that the alchemists believed that they were imitating the work of nature—one of the arguments in favour of the truth of alchemy was that since metals increase (i.e. grow, like plants) in nature there is no reason why the alchemist should not use gold like seed and make it 'grow' more gold. In nature gold grows through the heat of the sun, by a process of coagulation, just as other substances do under the influence of other planets. Thus not all references of this kind are in fact metaphorical—or if they imply comparison it is to the natural world, not to the alchemical process. (See F. D. Adams, *The Birth and Development of the Geological Sciences* (reprinted by Dover Publications, New York, 1954), chapters III–V for an account of medieval minerology. For its influence on the alchemists, see Stilman, op. cit., e.g., p. 243 ff., and the references there given.)

The Dream

In so far as the pearl is a stone beyond price, such alchemical associations are appropriate enough. But at this point in the poem the pearl is also a human soul, one of a company of souls who participate in the heavenly marriage. In this context the sun and moon belong to an equally ancient, but non-alchemical, tradition. In this symbolism the sun, the *Helios Pater* of pagan belief and mysticism, stands for God, and the moon, which Philo Judaeus called both feminine and dew-bearing, for the Christian Church. Origen already tells us that this is 'in a figurative sense spoken of as the moon'.[18] Through the marriage of God and His Church the divine light is reflected to the world. This imagery, however, became commonly used in a yet more specific sense when it was linked to the incarnation, and the Blessed Virgin took the place of the Church as the moon-bride. A good example of this usage is provided by the thirteenth-century hymn, *In rosa vernat lilium*. This is not too far removed from *Pearl* in time, and has recently been the subject of an interesting discussion by Peter Dronke, whose text and transla-tion I quote:[19]

> Ex luna solis emicat
>> radius elucescens:
> mundanis solem indicat
>> luna nunquam decrescens.
> Hic sol dum lune iungitur,
>> neuter eclypsum patitur,
>> sed est plus quam nitescens.

(From the moon shines forth the dawning ray of the sun, the moon that never wanes shows the sun to mankind. When this sun is united to its moon, neither suffers eclipse, but each is more than radiant.)

As Dronke points out, the dominant use of the sun–moon symbolism in the later Middle Ages was 'as figura of God and

[18] Philo, *De Providentia*, II, 77; Origen, *Commentary on St. John*, VI, 55. See Rahner, *Greek Myths and Christian Mystery*, p. 90. I am much indebted to the very full discussion of 'The Christian Mystery of Sun and Moon' in chapter IV of this book.

[19] See *Medieval Latin and the Rise of European Love Lyric*, I, pp. 128 ff. The full text of this hymn is printed in *Analecta Hymnica*, xx, p. 69.

the Virgin Mary'. But, as he also states, as early as apostolic times, the moon could also stand for man. Theophilus of Antioch said that 'the sun is a type of God, the moon of man' (*Ad Autolicum*, II, 15). The basic idea is, however, always of the moon as receiving and making something of the light of the divine sun, whether in mediation, as in the case of the Blessed Virgin / Church, or, as in the case of the individual soul, in the realization and fulfilment of its own blessedness, either on earth or, as in the case of the Pearl, in heaven.

That the pearl is something to be sought in the depths of the sea is a fact of natural history, and it is not surprising to find it repeatedly stressed. Nevertheless, especially in the East, it is often the danger and immensity of the depths which is emphasized, in a way which has nothing in common with the encyclopedists. Although this idea does not seem to have been directly transmitted to the West it seems worth mentioning, since it influences, as I believe, the conception of the pearl in the mire which is important in Western tradition. In the Gnostic *Hymn of the Soul* the pearl is dropped from the King's crown and has to be recovered by his Son from the depths of the sea, where it is guarded by a dragon.[20] St. Ephraem, in a strikingly beautiful passage, also emphasizes the unsearchable depths, and the danger. The pearl speaks:

> It answered me and said, 'The daughter of the sea am I, the illimitable sea! And from that sea whence I came up it is that there is a mighty treasury of mysteries in my bosom! Search thou out the sea, but search not out the Lord of the sea! I have seen the divers who came down after me, when astonied, so that from the midst of the sea they returned to the dry ground; for a few moments they sustained it not. Who would linger and be searching on into the depths of the Godhead? The waves of the Son are full of blessings and with mischiefs too.'[21]

The association of the pearl with impurity, with a mire which its brightness can survive untarnished, also seems to come from the East, though here too, as we shall see, biblical imagery was

[20] M. R. James *The Apocryphal New Testament* (Oxford, 1945), pp. 411 ff. See Gollancz, *Pearl*, p. xvii.
[21] Morris, *Select Works of St. Ephrem*, p. 87.

easily blended with the idea. In a Manichean treatise from China seven pearls are hidden 'in the labyrinth of the impure city of the demon of lust'. As Gollancz pointed out, Rabbinical literature, too, had the idea of the pearl as the soul enclosed in the flesh, through which it must not be defiled.[22]

In the Gospels, the pearl features in two important parables. It is not to be cast before swine (Matt. 7, 6), and it is of great price, to be exchanged for all that a man has (Matt. 13, 45–6). This pearl is associated with the treasure hidden in the field, and with the nets cast into the sea. In fact, the three parables, taken together, can imply all the different aspects of the pearl symbolism, and, as we shall find, the passage tended to be remembered as a whole:

> Simile est regnum caelorum thesauro abscondito in agro; quem qui invenit homo abscondit et prae gaudio illius vadit et vendit universa quae habet et emit agrum illum. Iterum simile est regnum caelorum homini negotiatori quaerenti bonas margaritas; inventa autem una pretiosa margarita, abiit et vendidit omnia quae habuit et emit eam. Iterum simile est regnum caelorum sagenae missae in mare et ex omni genere piscium congreganti.

> (The kingdom of heaven is like unto a treasure hidden in a field. Which a man having found, hid it; and for joy thereof goeth and selleth all that he hath and buyeth that field. Again the kingdom of heaven is like to a merchant seeking good pearls. Who, when he had found one pearl of great price, went his way and sold all that he had and bought it. Again the kingdom of heaven is like to a net cast into the sea and gathering together of all kind of fishes.   (Matt. 13, 44–7))

St. Bonaventura, for example, writes without comment or explanation of the pearl as the treasure in the field,[23] and other writers associate it with the nets going down into the sea.

---

[22] See Gollancz, *Pearl*, pp. xvii–xviii, and the references there given. The connection between Chinese and Western Alchemy is still an open question. See Sherwood Taylor, op. cit., chapter vi.

[23] *Vitis Mystica* III, 3 (*Decem Opuscula*, Ad Claras Aquas, 1926), p. 417.

As these strands twist together, and now one aspect, now another, is prominent, we can see a kind of semantic development which is very like that of the symbolism of the flower. As earthly treasure, the pearl can stand for what is transitory, as does the fading flower of the field: as symbolic treasure it stands, like the unfading flower, for the eternal treasure of heaven.[24] Just as the flower of the virtues is related to this eternal flower, since it was their cultivation in the soil of the soul which led to heaven, so the pearl tends also to stand for virtue. The flowers were often given special meanings according to colour, as we have seen. The pearl symbolizes specific virtues under the influence of its associations with perfection and wholeness. It often means purity. A Homily attributed to St. Bernard speaks of 'the holy religious (i.e. monastic) life, pure and unspotted', as like the pearl.[25] For Hugh of St. Victor the gates of the Heavenly Jerusalem are pearls because the just enter heaven through unity and purity of faith.[26] Sometimes it is seen as pure maidenhood, especially in association with St. Margaret.[27] For Albertus Magnus it stands for 'those who enter faith in all the virtues, or who are distinguished by one'.[28]

The pearl is also, from an early period, associated with the knowledge which leads to salvation. This was inevitable since the pearl which was not to be cast before swine was easily thought of as the full Christian revelation, not to be put inadvisedly before the profane. It is thus for St. Augustine the

[24] For the pearl as the bliss of heaven, see Gregory the Great, *Hom. in Evangelia*, I, 11, 2 (*P.L.*, 76, 1115).

[25] *P.L.*, 184, 1131. This Homily on Matt. 13, 45, has the same cluster of images as the *de Conversione*. The *margarita praefulgida* of the religious life is also a paradise 'ubi sunt rosae charitatis quae semper flammescunt, quae semper in sancto odore vivunt' (1133).

[26] *P.L.*, 176, 1159.

[27] See below, p. 152. As F. Mack points out (*Seinte Marherete*, *E.E.T.S.*, 193 (1934), p. xxxi) the symbolism of the pearl does not become an integral part of her legend before the *Legenda Aurea*. The *зimston* of the *Love Ron* also stands for virginity (Carleton Brown, *English Lyrics of the Thirteenth Century*, p. 68 ff.). Herrick can still use the pearl as an image of maidenhead ('His Daughter's Dowrye,' *Poetical Works*, p. 409).

[28] *Comm. in Apoc.*, 21, 21 (*Opera*, ed. Borgnet, 38, 778).

supreme knowledge of the Word 'pure and solid and nowhere contradicting itself'[29]; for St. Jerome it is the knowledge of the Saviour, the sacrament of the Passion and the mystery of the resurrection; and for St. Gregory the evangelical teaching.[30]

Again, like the flower, the pearl can stand for Christ Himself and, like most symbols of this type, on occasion for His Mother.[31] For St. Ephraem the pearl is 'in its brightness Christ; in its pureness His body; in its undividedness the truth' and for St. Augustine the pearl can also represent Christ.[32]

Both flower and pearl can also stand for the blessed souls, reclaimed by grace and the exercise of the virtues, who have gained, or will gain Heaven. Thus for Rupert of Deutz the pearls of the Heavenly gates are the saints of the church.[33] Dante describes the spirits of the blessed as spheres, which he calls pearls;[34] the Knight of La Tour Landry has the same conceit: 'The sowle is the precious marguarite vnto God',[35] and in *Pearl* itself, the poet's final prayer is:

> He gef vus to be his homly hyne
> Ande precious perleȝ vnto his pay.   (1211–12)

As a regeneration symbol, the pearl probably owes most to the idea of its reclamation from the dangerous depths of the sea or from the mire. These ideas come originally, no doubt, from

[29] *Quaest 17 in Matt.* I, 2, 13 (*P.L.*, 35, 1371).

[30] *Comm. in Matt.* I, 2, 13, 45 (*P.L.*, 27, 94); *Hom. in Evangelia*, I, 11, 2 (*P.L.*, 76, 1115).

[31] E.g. St. Bernard, *P.L.*, 184, 1069; Mone, *Hymni Latini* II, no. 508, p. 276. Here the pearl is associated with eternal life, not purity: salve mira margarita / duc nos ad superna sita / ubi est aeterna vita / tempestate carens (ll. 72–5).

[32] Morris, op. cit. p. 84. *P.L.*, 35, 1371. Cf. Mone, *Hymni Latini*, II, p. 350, no. 262, ll. 547–8, 'Jesu . . . mei cordis margarita.'

[33] *P.L.*, 169, 1202.

[34] *Paradiso*, xxii, 22–30. But in his description of the spheres Dante seems to echo Albertus Magnus' description of heaven as 'a pure body, . . . the inhabitation of blessed spirits', *Compend. Theolog. Veritatis*, 2, 4 (*Opera ed. Borgnet*, 34, 42).

[35] *The Book of the Knight of La Tour Landry*, E.E.T.S., 33 (1868), p. 158. Cf. Mone, *Hymni Latini*, II, p. 429, no. 302, ll. 64–6, where the *patientes* are shining pearls in heaven.

the non-biblical strand in its semantic development, but they enter into Christian imagery early in association with the nets cast into the sea of the Gospel and the mire naturally associated with swine. Psalm 68, 3, 'Infixus sum in limo profundi, et non est substantia; veni in altitudinem maris, et tempestas demersit me' (I stick fast in the mire of the deep: and there is no sure standing. I am come into the depth of the sea: and a tempest hath overwhelmed me) may also have been influential. It could certainly have helped to bring together the pearl in the mire and the pearl in the sea.[36]

Epiphanius interpreted 'the mire of the deep' as 'miry reflections and muddy thoughts of sin',[37] and we can see a strong tendency in much later writers to regard the pearl as something which emerges with its brightness unimpaired from the 'limo profundi' of man's fallen nature. St. Ephraem used the idea of the stainless Pearl which takes away the stains of sin:

[36] This verse certainly played a part in the development of alchemical imagery. See Jung, *Mysterium Coniunctionis*, p. 333, and *Psychology and Alchemy*, p. 313 f. In the passage quoted from the *Aurora consurgens*, the 'mire of the deep' and the 'abyss of the earth' are equated, and both refer to the earthy *prima materia*, the black mass to which the materials are reduced by heat at the beginning of the work. This was called 'putrefaction'. The Stone is often thought of as having to be reclaimed from a state of *vilitas*, and, in the *Philosophia Reformata* of Mylius (p. 199), this actually results in the production of the 'pearl of great price' (see Jung, *Mysterium Coniunctionis*, p. 235, and *Psychology and Alchemy*, p. 311). One of the most influential treatises of the fourteenth century was entitled the *Pretiosa Margarita Novella* (by Petrus Bonus, written 1330. Word-play may, of course, have influenced the choice of title, i.e., the good stone = the precious pearl). A curiously close parallel to the alchemical way of thinking is to be found in William of St. Thierry's *Expositio Altera in Cant.*, *P.L.*, 180, 494C: 'O imago Dei . . . tu tibi vilis es, sed pretiosa res est.' The image of God in the soul is exhorted to shine forth (from its obscurity) and to show itself in its true brilliance. This is a good illustration of the near impossibility of distinguishing alchemical and non-alchemical imagery within the Christian tradition. The pearl thrown before swine, and so into the mire, naturally linked itself to the pearl beyond price of the wise merchant. Cf., e.g., *Piers Plowman*, A xi, 9 ff.

[37] *Panarium*, 36, 4, ed. K. Holl, *Griechische christliche Schriftsteller* (Leipzig, 1915–33), I. See Jung, *Mysterium Coniunctionis*, p. 333.

Pearls have I gathered together that I might make a crown for the Son in the place of stains which are in my members. Receive my offering, not that Thou art shortcoming; it is because of mine own shortcoming that I have offered it to Thee. Whiten my stains! This crown is all spiritual pearls, which instead of gold are set in love, and instead of ouches in faith; and instead of hands, let praise offer it up to the Highest![38]

He also writes more directly of the pearl and the mire: 'It were a great disgrace if thou shouldest throw thy pearl away into the mire for nought'.[39] Here he is obviously thinking of the parable of the pearl cast before swine, for which he automatically substitutes the mire of another tradition.

The Latin life of St. Margareta shows a trace of the same idea. St. Margaret prays 'non proiciatur margarita mea in lutum'.[40] The context shows that the sense of 'pearl' is here quite general—'virtue', 'virtuous state'. But in the English versions this pearl is taken to mean virginity in a literal sense—the West Midland version edited by F. Mack even adds the parallel image of the flower in a passage quite without ambiguity:

> Ich habbe a deore ʒimstan, & ich hit habbe iʒeue
> þe, mi meiðhad i mene, blostme brihtest i bodi
> þe hit bereð & biwit wel; ne let tu neauer þe
> unwhit warpen hit i wurðinc . . .[41]

It is notable that here the pearl becomes the more general 'ʒimstan', which suggests that there was no very close or rigid equation of the pearl with virginity in the mind of the writer.

The idea of the pearl shining in spite of the mire plays an important part in *Purity*:

[38] Morris, op. cit., p. 98. By a natural transition the pearl also denotes the purity brought up from the water of baptism. See *Hymns for the Feast of Epiphany*, vi, 17, and vii, 18 (*The Nicene and Post-Nicene Fathers*, Series II, xiii, p. 274, 275).

[39] Morris, p. 94.

[40] F. Mack, *Seinte Marherete*, p. 129, l. 26.

[41] Ibid., p. 6, ll. 28–31.

3is, þat Mayster is mercyable, þaȝ þou be man fenny
And al tomarred in myre, whyl þou on molde lyvyes;
Þou may schyne þurȝ schryfte, þaȝ þou haf schome served,
And pure þe with penaunce tyl þou a perle worþe.
Perle praysed is prys þer perre is schewed,
Þaȝ hym not derrest be demed to dele for penies.
Quat may þe cause be called bot for hir clene hwes,
Þat wynnes worschyp abof alle whyte stones?
For ho schynes so schyr þat is of schap rounde,
Wythouten faut oþer fylþe, ȝif ho fyn were
And wax ever in þe worlde in weryng so olde,
3et þe perle payres not whyle ho in pyese lasttes.   (1113–24)

It is also present in *Pearl*, with its insistence on the supposed
ruin of the pearl's lustre by the clay:

> To þenke hir color so clad in clot!
> O moul, þou marreȝ a myry iuele,
> My priuy perle wythouten spotte.   (22–4)

and its brilliance when it is found again:

> Blysnande whyt watȝ hyr bleaunt . . .
> As glysnande golde þat man con schere,
> So schon þat schene an-vnder shore.   (163, 165–6)

While of the pearl on the Maiden's breast it is said:

> So watȝ hit clene and cler and pure,
> Þat precios perle þer hit watȝ pyȝt.   (227–8)

In this poem, especially in the proem, the buried pearl whose
lustre is not, after all, diminished, suggests, as well as the pearl's
power to shine unimpaired through the mire of the fall, a more
literal meaning. We may remember Bacon's note that 'There
hath beene a Tradition that *Pearle*, and *Corall*, and *Turchois-
Stone*, that have lost their Colours, may be recovered by
Burying in the *Earth*' (*Silva Silvarum*, §380). Here, as so often,
the development of symbolism and of what is claimed as
scientific observation are not to be distinguished, and it would
be impossible to say which influenced the other.[42]

[42] The tradition that the pearl shines out of darkness and decay
survives into the seventeenth century. Vaughan uses it in the elegiac
poem 'Silence and stealth of dayes' (*Works*, p. 426, ll. 18–31). L. L.
Martz identifies the 'one pearle' of this poem with 'the indestructible

The Dream

We have already discussed the close linking of the pearl with the idea of mortality. In the *Pearl* itself and in Herrick's poem *Jephthah's Daughter*, it is associated in elegy with the death of a particular person. There are signs elsewhere of the pearl as a symbol for something which survives death, and martyrdom, to the advantage of mankind. A Latin hymn to St. Barbara has this idea:

> Ave fulgens margarita
> in corona Jesu sita,
> tam in morte quam in vita
> sis nobis propitia.

(Hail shining pearl set in the crown of Jesus, in death, as in life, look on us with kindness.[43])

[43] Mone, *Hymni Latini*, III, p. 212, no. 824.

---

image of God' in the soul, and this is, no doubt, one of its meanings. But, since the main image in the poem is the lamp in the tomb, the pearl seems to stand also, as it does in the Middle English poem, in a more general sense for a regeneration which brings immortality out of mortality. There is also, I think, a glance at the alchemical stone, the perfect and perfecting substance. (See Martz, *The Paradise Within, Studies in Vaughan, Traherne, and Milton* (New Haven and London, 1964), p. 28.) The association of the pearl with dust, obscuring darkness or clouds is not uncommon. Sir Thomas Browne contrasts it with the dust and rubbish of mortality (*Christian Morals*, III, xi). Usk's *Testament of Love* repeatedly uses the image of cloud and smoke which obscures the light of the pearl (Skeat, *The Works of Geoffrey Chaucer*, VII, e.g., pp. 5, 7–8, 144). Usk is, however, drawing on Boethius, and may be thinking of the cloud which obscures the light of reason (*de Consolatione*, e.g., V, m. 3). Nevertheless, he finds it easy to combine this idea with the pearl. St. Ephraem also associated the pearl with clouds. See *Rhythms on the Pearl*, I, 1 (Morris, p. 85), 'The cloud was the likeness of her that bare Him'.

Two passages, one from St. Augustine and one from St. Gregory the Great, may also have been important in the formation of this tradition. St. Augustine (*Quaestionum septemdecim in Matthaeum*, I, xiii (*P.L.*, 35, 1371), associates the finding of the pearl 'in tegumentis mortalitatis, quasi concharum obstaculo, in profundis hujus saeculo', with dying to the flesh with Christ. St. Gregory (*Homiliarum in Evangelia*, I, xi, *P. L.*, 76, 1115), writes of the precious pearl in comparison with which 'vilescunt omnia'. The love of this pearl causes a kind of death towards all earthly things: 'sicut mors corpus interimit, sic ab amore rerum corporalium aeternae vitae charitas occidit.'

Symbols of Perfection

Lydgate in his *Life of St. Margaret* compares the saint to the jewel in her conquest of death:

> This stone in vertu is a cordyal,
>   To the spirit a grete confortatyf;
> Right so hir herte was imperyal
>   I mene, in vertu duryng al hir lyf:
>   For she venquesshed with al hir mortal stryf
> The deuel, the worlde, her storye dothe devyse,
> And of hir flesshe she made a sacryfice.[44]

And for St. Bonaventura the pearl is found in the ploughed-up field of Christ's body through His passion and death.[45]

From the pearl of the Gospels comes another group of ideas which are of great importance to the understanding of the symbol in *Pearl*. These are that, paradoxically, although it is a precious treasure, the pearl is a small object, easily hidden and easily overlooked. It is also, although it is of supreme value to those who understand it rightly, of little value to the world, which is apt to pass it over. How these ideas developed from the Gospels is clear: the pearl is something not to be cast before swine, that is something to be kept hidden from the incredulous or uninitiated, and, therefore, something normally undervalued in the world. In the parable of the pearl beyond price, the Merchant sells all that he has, that is all that is normally esteemed in the world, for the one pearl, and this implies an exchange of values. The pearl is also associated, in Matt. 7, with the hidden treasure kept from profane eyes, through the parable of the treasure in the field which comes in the verse before (Matt. 7, 44). The pearl before swine and the pearl beyond price thus fall together: both imply values not of this world; something normally overlooked, and to be kept secret from the profane. Chrysostom, in a passage transmitted in the *Catena Aurea* sums up this aspect well:

[44] *Minor Poems*, I, p. 175, ll. 43–9.
[45] *Vitis Mystica*, iii, 3 (*Decem Opuscula*, p. 417): Bonus thesaurus, pretiosa margarita cor tuum, optime Iesu, quam, fosso agro corporis tui, invenimus. Quis hanc margaritam abiiciat?

Et sicut qui margaritam habet, ipse quidem novit quod dives est, aliis vero non est cognitus, multoties eam manu detinens propter ejus parvitatem.

(and thus, he who has the pearl knows that he is rich, but other people often do not know it since because of its smallness he keeps it hidden in his hand.[46])

Alchemists frequently spoke in very similar terms of their treasure. For example:

> This is the stone, poor and of little price,
> Spurned by the fool, but honoured by the wise.[47]

The idea of the smallness of the Pearl makes it especially appropriate to the paradoxical *topos* of earthly and heavenly riches. St. Ephraem elaborates it:

> It is thou who art great in thy littleness, O pearl! Small is thy measure and little thy compass with thy weight, but great is thy glory: to that crown alone in which thou art placed, there is none like. And who hath not perceived of thy littleness, how great it is; if one despiseth thee and throweth thee away, he would blame himself for his clownishness, for when he saw thee in a king's crown he would be attracted to thee.[48]

St. Bernard, too, uses the pearl as a symbol for something appreciated by those who despise the world, and who value a 'counsel sacred and secret which is hidden from the wise and the prudent and is only revealed to the little ones'.[49]

Lydgate, in his *Life of St. Margaret*, takes over the symbol of the pearl as standing for Margaret's lowliness as well as for her virginity and other virtues:

[46] *Catena Aurea*, ed. P. A. Guarienti (Rome, 1953), I, p. 222.

[47] *Ros. Phil. in Art. Aurif.*, I, p. 120. See Jung, *The Archetypes and the Collective Unconscious* (*Collected Works*, 9, part 1), p. 141. See also *Mysterium Coniunctionis*, II, 'The Paradoxa'.

[48] Morris, p. 97. Cf. p. 94.

[49] *de Conversione ad Clericos*, xiv, 26 (*P.L.*, 182, 848C). St. Bernard brings together the pearl and Matt. 11, 25: 'Thou hast hid these things from the wise and prudent, and hast revealed them to little ones.'

Symbols of Perfection

For of nature perlys echone ben white,
Right vertuous of kynde, rounde and small—
Whiche propurtees resemblen hir at alle.

She was first white by virginyte,
    In al hir lyvyng preuyde vertuous;
And smal she was by humylite.[50]

In *Purity* the pearl is 'not derrest . . . to dele for penies' and
in *Pearl* it is 'smal'—an epithet which seems fairly constant in
pearl descriptions. This suggests the theme of the 'small, foolish,
weak things', which yet symbolise a great mystery.[51] Thus, in
Pearl the reference to Jesus calling the little children to him
(717–20) is immediately followed by the paraphrase, in ll. 729 ff.
of the parable of the Pearl of great Price. The pearl, in fact, is a
fitting symbol for the little ones, who, in turn, become all those
who are fit to inherit the kingdom of heaven:

And sayde hys ryche no wyȝ myȝt wynne
Bot he com þyder ryȝt as a chylde   (722–3)

It is clear that the poet, when he makes the pearl the main
symbol of his work does not depend on any simple equation. He
is using for a complex purpose, a symbol which traditionally
brings with it complexity of meaning. An important function of
the pearl-symbol for this poem is to fill out and elaborate the
two figures of Dreamer and Maiden. For the Jeweller, the pearl
is a symbol designed, in its double sense of the treasure of the
world and the apparently insignificant, easily missed, treasure
of heaven, to clarify and elaborate his state of mind and his
whole problem in the face of mortality and the workings of
God's laws. For the Maiden the pearl is a fit symbol because of
its association with the little ones, those who actually are, or

[50] *Minor poems*, I, p. 174–5. The source is the *Legenda Aurea* (see
Vitae Sanctorum, Coloniae Aggrippinae, III, 242).
[51] St. Paul's words greatly influenced the development of Christian
imagery. See Rahner, *Greek Myths and Christian Mystery*, p. 48 ff.,
p. 57, etc. So, for St. Ephraem, pearls as well as being associated with
'little ones' in the sense of simple fishermen, were also children in the
heavenly diadem (see *Select Hymns and Homilies*, H. Burgess, p. 14).

who become like, children, and with the perfection and bliss of heaven.

These ideas are developed from the opening in which, as we have seen, the conventional motif of the pearl set in gold establishes the ambivalence of the symbolism. In sections ii and iii the pearl-motif is kept before us by the gravel of pearls underfoot, but this belongs, as we have seen, to the Earthly Paradise description and has no symbolical or even metaphorical meaning. Section iv, with the appearance of the maiden, takes up and develops the symbolism. First there is the careful reversal of phrasing which, just as the opening leads us to suspect the maiden in the pearl, now leads us to suspect the pearl in the maiden. The motif of the gold setting, in which the gold, like the pearls, has undergone a heavenly transformation is also repeated here. Then come the pearls which ornament the maiden's white robe and form her crown. These are suggestive of the pearl as the virtues which are the means whereby the heavenly reward is won, as well as that crowning reward itself.

The climax of this section is the pearl on the maiden's breast:

> Bot a wonder perle wythouten wemme
> Inmyddeȝ hyr breste watȝ sette so sure;
> A manneȝ dom moȝt dryȝly demme,
> Er mynde moȝt malte in hit mesure.
> I hope no tong moȝt endure
> No sauerly saghe say of þat syȝt,
> So watȝ hit clene and cler and pure,
> Þat precios perle þer hit watȝ pyȝt. (221–8)

Finally, the Dreamer sums up this section with a *repetitio* which, besides giving fit expression to the intensity of his feeling, emphasizes the complexity of meaning of the pearl:

> 'O perle,' quod I, 'in perleȝ pyȝt,
> Art þou my perle þat I haf playned,
> Regretted by myn one on nyȝte?' (241–3)

This ends the statement of the pearl-theme. The maiden's exposition follows.

First, she takes up the theme of the two treasures, and links

them to that of mortality and of destiny. This is done through
the motif of the jewel in the cabinet, or coffer, which, as we have
already seen, can still be used by Donne to support an argument
on the resurrection. The theme of mortality leads into the long
argument of the central section, and when the maiden returns
to the exposition of the pearl-symbolism it is to define the Pearl
of Price in a way which shows that it is thought of primarily as
a symbol of perfection, of unity and wholeness, and of eternity.

> Þer is þe blys þat con not blynne
> Þat þe jueler soȝte þurȝ perré pres,
> And solde alle hys goud, boþe wolen and lynne,
> To bye hym a perle watȝ mascelleȝ.
>
> This makelleȝ perle, þat boȝt is dere,
> Þe joueler gef fore alle hys god,
> Is lyke þe reme of heuenesse clere:
> So sayde þe Fader of folde and flode;
> For hit is wemleȝ, clene, and clere,
> And endeleȝ rounde and blyþe of mode,
> And commune to alle þat ryȝtwys were.
> Lo, euen inmyddeȝ my breste hit stode.
> My Lorde þe Lombe, þat schede hys blode,
> He pyȝt hit þere in token of pes.
> I rede þe forsake þe worlde wode
> And porchace þy perle maskelles.   (729–44)

The Dreamer closes the section by a repetition, with significant
differences, of the words with which he ended the first section
on the Pearl. There,

> 'O perle,' quod I, 'in perleȝ pyȝt,
> Art þou my perle þat I haf playned?'   (241–2)

Now he abandons his claim to ownership:

> 'O maskeleȝ perle in perleȝ pure,
> Þat bereȝ,' quod I, 'þe perle of prys.'   (745–6)

With this stanza there is a transition from the symbolic pearl on
the maiden's breast, which the Dreamer is advised to substitute
for the pearl he had wrongly claimed, back to the pearl as the
Maiden. The Dreamer asks:

'Breue me, bry3t, quat kyn offys
Bere3 þe perle so maskelle3?' (755–6)

This introduces the section on the marriage of the Lamb, and it
is only here that the pearl is in any way associated with virginity.
Even here, it is 'spotlessness' in a general sense, which is in
question, while at 853 ff. the pearl stands for the unity of
heaven:

'Lasse of blysse may non vus bryng
Þat beren þys perle vpon oure bereste,
For þay of mote couþe neuer mynge
Of spotle3 perle3 þat beren þe creste.' (853–6)

At the end of section xv the Dreamer makes an end to a passage
of exposition. He does so by recalling an earlier passage. The
Pearl, in her explanation of mortality had used the images of
jewel and rose:

'For þat þou leste3 wat3 bot a rose
Þat flowred and fayled as kynde hyt gef.
Now þur3 kynde of þe kyste þat hyt con close
To a perle of prys hit is put in pref.' (269–72)

Now, the Dreamer marks his understanding of her teaching by
repeating her images in a different sense:

Quod I, 'My perle, þa3 I appose;
I schulde not tempte þy wyt so wlonc,
To Kryste3 chambre þat art ichose.
I am bot mokke and mul among,
And þou so ryche a reken rose,
And byde3 here by þys blysful bonc
Þer lyue3 lyste may neuer lose.' (902–8)

The imagery of the pearl is dropped for a while after this
conclusion. Pearls themselves recur in the gates of the heavenly
Jerusalem, in a way which balances the pearls of the description in the earlier account of the Earthly Paradise. The
last hundred lines of the poem finally reintroduce the pearl
under all its important aspects, and combine it, as we have
seen, with the symbolism of the sun and moon. The virgins
following the lamb are described in the same terms as the

maiden had been in ll. 193 ff. With the Dreamer's awakening there is a return to the mortal pearl:

> Þen wakned I in þat erber wlonk;
> My hede vpon þat hylle watȝ layde
> Þer as my perle to grounde strayd. (1171–3)

This, he at once acknowledges, is also the pearl transformed:

> 'O perle,' quod I, 'of rych renoun,
> So watȝ hit me dere þat þou con deme
> In þis veray avysyoun!
> If hit be ueray and soth sermoun
> Þat þou so stykeȝ in garlande gay,
> So wel is me in þys doel-doungoun
> Þat þou art to þat Prynseȝ paye.' (1182–9)

Finally, the closing lines return to the pearl as symbol of the blessed, repeating, but with an opposite sense, the phrasing of the opening:

> He gef vus to be his homly hyne
> Ande precious perleȝ vnto his pay. (1211–12)

2

The opening lines of the poem, as we have already seen, established the connection of the pearl both with the crown of the king and with gold. At that point the primary meaning was the earthly treasure not the heavenly one, but the dual nature of the symbolism is already apparent in the proem. In the Vision section, the heavenly treasure, with all its implications, naturally comes into the foreground. The description of the Pearl-Maiden, as well as developing the symbolism of the pearl, emphasises both crown and gold; and the crown, moreover, is presented in a way which links the imagery of treasure to the imagery of flowers, for it is both crown and garland:

> As glysnande golde þat man con schere,
> So schon þat schene an-vnder shore . . .
> A pyȝt coroune ȝet wer þat gyrle
> Of mariorys and non oþer ston,
> Hiȝe pynakled of cler quyt perle,

Wyth flurted flowreȝ perfet vpon.
To hed hade ho non oþer werle;
Her here leke, al hyr vmbegon,
Her semblaunt sade for doc oþer erle,
Her ble more blaȝt þen whalleȝ bon.
As schorne golde schyr her fax þenne schon,
On schyldereȝ þat leghe vnlapped lyȝte.

(165–6, 205–14)

Both gold and crown are symbols which have much in
common with the pearl itself. Both can stand for perfection. As
far as the Middle English poet is concerned, however, these two
are always subordinate to the main symbol of the pearl. They
appear as part of the description—they do not explicitly stand
for anything else. Nevertheless, to a contemporary reader their
use as constantly recurring minor themes would have helped to
amplify and enrich the symbolism of the pearl as well as adding
to the richness of the description, and helping to establish a
colour scheme which is carefully worked into the texture of the
poem. J. A. Burrow has recently suggested that red, green, and
gold provide a significant and deliberately maintained colour
scheme in *Sir Gawain and the Green Knight*.[52] We can certainly
see a similar choice of colour scheme in *Pearl*, worked out in
terms of gold-sun / white–pearl–moon. This scheme is exemplified in the figures of the Maiden and of the Lamb. After the
blaze of light and colour of the description of the jewels of the
Earthly Paradise, there are only the briefest references to anything but white, pearl, or gold until the balancing description of
the jewels of the Heavenly Jerusalem at the end of the poem.
After the initial brilliance, indeed, colour words are carefully
avoided even when the Earthly Paradise, or the Heavenly Kingdom are mentioned. The Earthly Paradise becomes merely,
'Paradys erde' (248)—þis gardyn gracios gaye' (260)—'schyr
wodschaweȝ' (284). The avoidance of colour is most striking in
the descriptions of the Lamb. In all the references to His blood
the word red is never used. At line 705 He is merely 'blody',

[52] See *A Reading of* Sir Gawain and the Green Knight, pp. 14–16,
39–40.

and at 646, where an epithet is used, it is chosen to convey an idea, not a visual effect:

> Ryche blod ran on rode so roghe.

It would seem, in fact, that the poet is to be taken seriously when he says:

> Thys Jerusalem Lombe hade neuer pechche
> Of oþer huee bot quyt jolyf. (841–2)

It is only in the final scene, when the idea of colour is re-established, that we are even told that the horns of the Lamb were of gold.

The two exceptions to this avoidance of colour in the central part of the poem reinforce the impression that the poet thought of it as something to convey ideas rather than visual effects. When the Dreamer expresses his outrage at what he imagines to be the Maiden's presumption, he says:

> 'Art þou þe quene of heueneȝ blwe,
> Þat al þys worlde schal do honour?' (423–4)

Blwe is appropriate here not only as the obvious colour-word for the sky, but as the traditional colour of the Virgin Mary. Its use early in the speech helps to make effective the climax of indignation achieved by the holding over of the actual name Mary to a later line. The only other colour word to occur in this section is *broun*, dark, dusky, at l. 537:

> Sone þe worlde bycom wel broun.

Evening in the vineyard, brought by the setting sun, is placed in a much more telling contrast to the brilliance and unfailing light of the blissful country and of the New Jerusalem than would be possible if the use of colour words was not so sparing.

Gold, therefore, is of great importance in the poem as a part of a carefully worked out colour scheme, in which its symbolical meanings contribute to the effect without undue insistence on the poet's part. As was the case with the Pearl, the symbolical meanings are linked to the physical characteristics of the metal. It is, above all, the perfect form of matter—just as the pearl was thought of as a perfect sphere, owing nothing to human manipulation of its material. It was this natural perfection which the Alchemists tried to achieve by art. By ridding other substances of their imperfections they could be turned to gold. Pseudo-Zosimos, to give an early example, expressed this view of gold:

> Gold is a substance of well proportioned native and perfect mixture. Soul, spirit, and body have become one in it, therefore it does not change by any happening, nor does it decay.[53]

Petrus Bonus, in the *Pretiosa Margarita Novella* expresses the same idea—indeed, it is this natural property of gold which is the basis, according to him, of the whole alchemical work:

> The difference between ordinary leaven and our ferment (the alchemical Stone) is that common leaven loses nothing of its substance in the digestive process, while digestion removes from our ferment all that is superfluous, impure, and corruptive, as is done by Nature in the preparation of gold.[54]

Gold thus owes its perfection to nature, and it is through this innate characteristic that it is linked, on biblical authority, to virtue. Because it is unaffected by fire, as a substance which cannot be purified any further, it stands for the virtuous man who survives every trial. For example, in Mal. 3, 2–3:

> Et quis poterit cogitare diem adventus eius? Et quis stabit ad videndum eium? Ipse enim quasi ignis conflans et quasi herba fullonum, et sedebit conflans et emundans argentum et purgabit filios Levi et colabit eos quasi aurum et quasi argentum.

> (And who shall be able to think of the day of his coming? And who shall stand to see him? For he is like a refining fire and like the fuller's herb. And he shall sit refining and cleansing the silver, and he shall purify the sons of Levi and shall refine them as gold and silver.[55])

[53] Quoted by Stillman, *The Story of Alchemy*, p. 215.

[54] Quoted, from the translation by Waites, by E. J. Holmyard, *Alchemy*, p. 143. The perfection of gold, as it exists in nature is not, however, a purely alchemical idea. It was an accepted principle of minerology. See Stillman, op. cit., p. 241, and F. D. Adams, *The Birth and Development of the Geological Sciences*, p. 297.

[55] This is, of course, a biblical commonplace, cf. Ecclus. 2. 5; Prov. 17, 3; Prov. 27, 21, etc.

Gold could also stand for the Divine image in the soul, and in such a context it becomes an alternative to the seed, the spark or, as we have seen, the pearl itself. It even, under the influence of Lamentations 4, 1 'How is the gold become dim, the finest colour is changed!', takes on the associations with the obscuring mire or dust which are so important in the symbolism of the *Pearl*. St Bernard's comment on Lam. 4.1 emphasizes that the gold, like the pearl, has the ability to remain essentially unchanged whatever defilement it is exposed to:

> *Obscuratum est insipiens cor illorum*, ait Apostolus; et propheta: *Quomodo obscuratum est aurum, mutatus est color optimus?* Obscuratum aurum plangit, sed aurum tamen; mutatum colorem optimum, sed non fundamentum coloris evulsum. Manet in fundamento prorsus inconcussa simplicitas, sed mimime apparet duplicitate operta humanae dolositatis, simulationis, hypocrisis.

> (Thus, the apostle says, 'Their foolish heart was darkened,' or, as the prophet puts it, 'How is the gold become dim, the finest colour changed!' The gold bewails its tarnished state; but it is still gold. The perfect colour may be changed; but the base on which it is made up remains the same. The soul's essential simplicity is unshaken; but it is hidden out of sight beneath a thick cloak of duplicity—that is to say of human fraud, hypocrisy, and sham.[56])

Gold is associated not only with the Sun (in alchemy, as we have seen *sol* is an alternative term) but also with kingship, in a way which links it naturally to the crown. The *Catena Aurea* gives this association in its comment on the gifts of the three Kings.[57] The crown, however, is more than an emblem of

---

[56] *In Cant.*, xxxii, 2 (*P.L.*, 183, 1178). R. A. Durr, *On the Mystical Poetry of Henry Vaughan*, compares Vaughan's 'Corruption', where the images of the spark and the gold seem to merge: '. . . Man in those early days / Was not all stone, and Earth, / He shin'd a little, and by those weak Rays / Had some glimpse of his birth' (*Works*, p. 440). The citation from Boehme which Durr gives on p. 146, note 16, is interesting as an illustration of the ease with which alchemical imagery merges with this tradition. Here man is 'as the gross Ore in *Saturn*, wherin the Gold is couched and shut up' (*Signatura Rerum*, viii, 47).

[57] *Catena Aurea*, ed. Guarienti, p. 38.

royalty—it also means, through a very common biblical usage, the highest thing of its kind. In 1 Thess. 2, 19, for example, St. Paul speaks of 'Our hope, or joy, or crown of glory.' Ps. 20, 4, has 'thou hast set on his head a crown of precious stones', and this is equated in the next two verses with eternal life and 'glory . . . in thy salvation'. In Isa. 28, 5, the crown is, as it is in *Pearl*, linked to the garland:

> In die illa erit Dominus exercituum corona gloriae et sertum exsultationis residuo populi sui.

> (In that day, the Lord of hosts shall be a crown of glory and a garland of joy to the residue of his people.)

Examples of the use of the crown in medieval Latin and vernacular literature are so common that they do not need further illustration. Several of the passages already quoted, especially those from St. Ephraem, link it to the pearl, as well as to gold.

The pearl is specifically associated with the crown, not only as a mortal treasure, but also in its symbolical senses. This seems to be an ancient tradition. In the Gnostic *Hymn of the Soul*, the pearl which is to be sought in the depths of the water, has dropped from the king's crown, and the image is preserved in medieval Latin hymnography, for example, in a hymn to St. Margaret which is particularly interesting for its likeness to the opening lines of *Pearl*: 'Empta pridem margarita / sic probata, sic polita, / regis auro redimita.'[58] A hymn to St. Barbara also has the pearl and crown: 'Ave fulgens margarita / in corona Jesu sita.'[59] Like the Pearl of our poem, Barbara follows the Lamb as a Bride and she, too, shares the imagery of flowers 'as a rose blooming in paradise and a lily of chastity'. St. Margaret, too, is a 'glorious rose' as well as a 'shining pearl' in a hymn preserved in a 15th century manuscript.[60]

In general, the crown follows the same type of semantic development as the jewel and the flower, though it tends,

---

[58] Mone, *Hymni Latini*, III, no. 1050, pp. 411–12.

[59] Ibid., no. 824, p. 212. Barbara is also 'clara quasi luna plena' in this hymn.

[60] Ibid., no. 1049, p. 410.

perhaps because of its inevitable association with kingship as 'a crown of glory', to keep more closely to the sense of wholeness and perfection. Dante, in the *Paradiso*, uses the image of the crown of fire, 'the encircling melody of flame', in association with jewel imagery, to stand for angelic love. This crown, descending on the sapphire which symbolizes the Blessed Virgin 'makes the clearest heaven all one sapphire':

> per entro il cielo scese una facella,
>   formata in cerchio a guisa di corona,
>   e cinsela e girossi intorno ad ella.
> Qualunque melodia più dolce sona
>   qua giù, e più a sè l' anima tira
>   parrebbe nube che squarciata tona,
> comparata al sonar di quella lira
>   onde si coronava il bel zaffiro
>   del quale il ciel più chiaro s' inzaffira.

> (A fire descended out of heaven from far
>   Shaped in a circle like a coronal,
>   Which turned and turned as it engirdled her.
> Whatever music sounds most sweet of all
>   On earth, and draws the soul most in desire,
>   Would seem cloud crackling in the thunder's brawl
> Compared with the resounding of that lyre
>   Whereby the beautiful Sapphire was crowned
>   Which makes the clearest heaven all one sapphire.
>   (*Paradiso*, xxiii, 94–102))

Here, the symbolism of jewel and crown has much in common with that of the *Pearl*, especially with the 'endeleȝ rounde' of the pearl which symbolizes the Heavenly Kingdom.

In *Richard the Redeless*, the crown itself and its jewels symbolize virtue in a more particular sense—we have already seen that flowers and gems are interchangeable images of virtue in general, and of the specific virtues. The pearl comes first in the list:

> Ȝe come to ȝoure kyngdom er ȝe ȝoure-self knewe,
> Crouned with a croune that kyng vnder heuene
> Miȝte not a better haue bouȝte, as I trowe;
> So ffull was it ffilled with vertuous stones,

With perlis of pris to punnysshe the wrongis,
With rubies rede the riȝth for to deme,
With gemmes and Iuellis Ioyned to-gedir,
And pees amonge the peple ffor peyne of thi lawis.
It was fful goodeliche ygraue with gold al aboute;
The braunchis aboue boren grett charge;
With diamauntis derue y-doutid of all
That wrouȝte ony wrake within or withoute;
Withe lewte and loue yloke to thi peeris,
And sapheris swete that souȝte all wrongis,
Ypoudride wyth pete ther it be ouȝte,
And traylid with trouthe and treste al aboute;
ffor ony cristen kynge a croune well ymakyd.[61]

In the *Pearl* the crown is emphasized at each important point. In the first encounter it features in the account of the Marriage of the Lamb:

Bot my Lorde þe Lombe þurȝ hys godhede,
He toke myself to hys maryage,
Corounde me quene in blysse to brede
In lenghe of dayeȝ þat euer schal wage;   (413–16)

and it is also present in the final vision of the New Jerusalem:

Þis noble cité of ryche enpryse
Watȝ sodanly ful wythouten sommoun
Of such vergyneȝ in þe same gyse
Þat watȝ my blysful an-vnder croun:
And coronde wern alle of þe same fasoun.   (1097–101)

Finally, in his summing up, the Dreamer uses the image of the garland, as Dante does, for the circling dance of the blessed:[62]

If hit be ueray and soth sermoun
Þat þou so stykeȝ in garlande gay,
So wel is me in þys doel-doungoun
Þat þou art to þat Prynseȝ paye.   (1185–8)

[61] W. W. Skeat (ed.), *Piers the Plowman and Richard the Redeless* (Oxford, 1924), p. 607, ll. 32–48. The *Myroure of Oure Ladye* has the same figure (ed. Blunt, *E.E.T.S.*, E.S., XIX, p. 182–3). Elsewhere in this text the Blessed Virgin is 'arayed with the croune of vertues' (p. 181), and in the lesson which follows the crowns become God's acts of power in the creation (181 ff.).

[62] Cf. *Paradiso*, x, 91–3, and xii, 19–20.

3

We have already traced the use of the rose in *Pearl* as a part of the flower imagery. It remains only to note that it also can have the same meaning as the crown and pearl as a symbol of perfection. The rose as a symbol of the blessed in heaven is introduced once only, but at the climax of the poem where it signifies the Dreamer's final and full understanding of the lesson the maiden has to teach him:

> And þou so ryche a reken rose,
> And bydeȝ here by þys blysful bonc
> Þer lyueȝ lyste may neuer lose.   (906–8)

Dante had used the rose as an image of the heaven of heavens, but the *Pearl*-poet does not extend the meaning of the symbol to this point. We have already seen that it is used in devotional writing for Christ, for the Blessed Virgin, for the saints, for the blessed in heaven, and for the virtues which take them there; it follows, in fact, the same lines of development as the other symbols we have been considering.

As do the other symbols of perfection, pearl, crown, and gold, the rose plays a part in the symbolism of alchemy and it is here that its sense of wholeness emerges most clearly, since it stands for the completed and perfected work as an alternative to the pearl, the crown of glory, and the other commonly used symbols.[63]

St. Bonaventura, in a passage of great beauty, provides one of the best examples of the working out of the symbolism of the many-petalled rose in relation to redemption and salvation. In chapter xvi of the *Vitis Mystica* he begins by distinguishing the rose of love and the rose of the passion, and goes on (chapter xvii):

> Ecce, in expositione huius verbi necessarium habemus rosam passionis rosae caritatis coniungere, ut rosa caritatis in passione rubescat, et rosa passionis igne caritatis ardescat.

[63] See Jung, *Psychology and Alchemy*, Index, under Rose. On the Stone as crown, see also *Mysterium Coniunctionis*, Index, under Kether. It is probable that, in the case of this symbol, alchemical writers were influenced by rabbinical as well as biblical usage.

(Behold, to explain these words we must needs unite the rose of the passion and the rose of love, so that the rose of love may grow red through the passion, and the rose of the passion burn in the fire of love.[64])

Finally, in chapter xxiii, after the pains of the Passion have been described, the two roses are brought together again in a passage of great richness which combines the images of the wintry night of sin and the lost paradise of Adam, with the symbolism of the rose opening to the sun:

Intuere et respice rosam passionis sanguineae, quomodo rubet in indicium ardentissimae caritatis. Contendunt simul caritas et passio, illa, ut plus ardeat, ista, ut plus rubeat. Sed mirabiliter per ardorem caritatis fit passio rubea, quia, nisi diligeret, non pateretur; et in passione ac passionis rubore ardor maximae et incomparabilis ostenditur caritatis. Sicut enim rosa per frigus noctis clausa, solis ardore surgente, tota aperitur et foliis expansis in rubore demonstrat ardorem iucundum; ita flos caeli deliciosus, optimus Iesus, qui multo tempore a peccato primi hominis quasi in frigore noctis clausus fuit, peccatoribus nondum gratiae plenitudinem impendens, tandem plenitudine temporis accedente, radiis ardentis caritatis accensus, in omni corporis sui parte apertus est, et rosae caritatis ardor in rubore sanguinis effusi refulsit. . . . O quam multo numero foliorum multiplicata et exornata est rosa tua! Quis illa omnia enumerat? Numera guttas sanguinis effusi de dulcissimo latere et corpore amantissimi Iesu, et habebis rosae passionis caritatisque folia enumerata. Singulae enim guttae sanguinis singula folia sunt.

(Look, and see the rose of the bloody passion, how it reddens as a sign of the most ardent love. For love and the passion are contending, one to burn hotter, the other to become more red. But, in a marvellous way, the passion is reddened by the heat of love, for, unless He had loved He would not have suffered. And in the passion, in the redness of the passion, He showed the greatest ardour and an incomparable love. For, just as the rose closes during the cold night, but opens and spreads all its crimson petals in the heat of the rising sun, as a sign of its warm delight, so the glorious flower of heaven, Jesus, best of all flowers, which for a long time, through the sin of the first man

[64] *Decem Opuscula*, p. 454.

was closed, as it were in the cold of night—and still withholds the plenitude of grace from sinners—now, in the fullness of time, burning in the rays of ardent love, is laid open in every part of His body, and the fire of the rose of charity shines forth in the redness of flowing blood . . . O how manifold and intricate is this rose of yours, with its innumerable petals! Who could count them all? Number the drops of blood shed from the most sweet side and body of the most loving Jesus, and you will have counted the petals of the rose of love, for every separate drop of blood is a separate petal.[65])

In English, Lydgate's poem, 'Lat no man booste of konnyng nor vertu', provides an excellent example of the ambivalence of the symbol and succeeds, for a moment at least, in sounding a deeper note than this poet usually attains. From the mid-summer rose of transience and mortality he turns to the rose of the martyrs—'Ther bloody suffraunce was no somyr roose'—and then to the rose of the Passion:

> It was the Roose of the bloody feeld,
>   Roose of Iericho, that greuh in Beedlem;
> The five Roosys portrayed in the sheeld,
>   Splayed in the baneer at Ierusalem.
> The sonne was clips and dirk in euery rem
> Whan Christ Ihesu five wellys lyst vncloose,
>   Toward Paradys, callyd the rede strem,
> Off whos five woundys prent in your hert a roose.[66]

Lastly, the rose is a flower with a golden centre—'The rose within, in the midst of itself, has another flower, of a golden colour', as Petrus de Mora puts it.[67] This fact links it to the symbolism of gold, and of the golden flower which could also be a symbol of perfection in its own right.[68] Walter of Chatillon,

---

[65] *Decem Opuscula*, p. 463–4.

[66] *Minor Poems*, II, p. 785.

[67] *De Rosa*, ed. J. B. Pitra, *Spicilegium Solesmense*, iii, 493. I owe this and the following reference to Peter Dronke, *Medieval Latin and the Rise of European Love Lyric*, pp. 186 ff. His discussion of the symbolism of the rose is illuminating and should be read in full. It is, of course, orientated towards the love lyric, not to devotional writing.

[68] On the golden flower, a common symbol of the alchemists, see Jung, *Psychology and Alchemy*, Index, under Flower.

The Dream

in his poem *Ecce Nectar roseum*, calls the gold of the rose wisdom, and its colour, red (also the colour of gold, as we have seen), love.[69]

The rose, like pearl and crown, thus bears a natural relation to gold, and fits into the pattern of symbolical figures and colours which the *Pearl*-poet works out in his poem.

[69] K. Strecker (ed.), *Moralisch-satirische Gedichte Walters von Châtillon* (Heidelberg, 1929), pp. 128 ff. See Dronke, op. cit., p. 187. The golden crown (which in turn could be equated with the golden flower) was symbolical of the New Jerusalem when it was used in churches in the form of a Candelabrum (see the material collected by I. Bishop, 'The Significance of the "Garlande Gay" in the Allegory of *Pearl*', *R.E.S.* (1957), pp. 12 ff.). I do not think that this symbolism is, in fact, present in l. 1186 (see above, p. 168), but it is an interesting example of the nexus which is certainly present elsewhere in *Pearl*.

Part Three

THE REVELATION

I

LESS AND MORE

I

LIKE MANY OTHER guiding figures in Vision literature, the
Pearl-Maiden has two tasks to perform: through a dialogue of
question and answer she resolves a problem; and she leads the
Dreamer to a further vision, that of the New Jerusalem. This is
the whole purpose of the dream, and the whole reason for the
poet's choice of the form.

The dialogue is the heart of the poem, and it is here that the
poet develops the themes which he established in his proem.
To sum it up, as Gordon does, as 'an argument on salvation,
by which the father is at last convinced that his Pearl, as a
baptized infant and innocent, is undoubtedly saved'[1] is to over-
simplify. On the other hand, as we have seen, the elegiac tone is
always present and 'without . . . the sense of great personal
loss which pervades it, *Pearl* would indeed be the mere theo-
logical treatise on a special point, which some critics have called
it'.[2]

By reversing the normal order of events in significant dreams,
and causing the 'parent or other holy and grave person' to be
replaced by the child, the poet at once keeps the reality of his
grief in the foreground, and also develops his main theme of
'less and more'. He takes up, with a strong personal interest,
the case of the least possible acquired merit on man's side and
the greatest possible grace on God's.

If we follow out his argument in outline, it will become clear
that, in fact, he has nothing to say of an alternative fate for
baptized children, nor does he show any real anxiety on their

[1] Gordon, p. xviii.
[2] Ibid., loc. cit.

175

behalf.[3] His difficulties in this section are due to other causes. In his inability to understand the true place of death in the scheme of things, he believes, for a moment, that it has been cheated:

> I trawed my perle don out of dawe3.
> Now haf I fonde hyt, I schal ma feste,
> And wony wyth hyt in schyr wod-schawe3,
> And loue my Lorde and al his lawe3
> Þat hat3 me bro3t þys blys ner. (282–6)

His error is a double one: he joyfully concludes that she is alive 'in Paradys erde' (247–8), and that he can cross the water to join her. But the joyous lift of these lines is the last expression for some time to come of the purely lyric mood: the Maiden disabuses him of his errors in a firmer, more emphatic rhythm, the characteristic one of the discussion section. She is not, she says, in reality, in the Earthly Paradise at all. Even if she were, he could not cross the river alive, or live with her there:

> 'Jueler,' sayde þat gemme clene,
> 'Wy borde 3e men? So madde 3e be!
> Þre worde3 hat3 þou spoken at ene:
> Vnavysed, for soþe, wern alle þre.
> Þou ne woste in worlde quat on dot3 mene;
> Þy worde byfore þy wytte con fle.
> Þou says þou trawe3 me in þis dene,
> Bycawse þou may wyth y3en me se;
> Anoþer þou says, in þys countré
> Þyself schal won wyth me ry3t here;
> Þe þrydde, to passe þys water fre—
> Þat may no ioyfol jueler.' (289–300)

All this has nothing to do with salvation, but it has much to do with the Dreamer's personal, instinctive reaction to the fact of death.

His second difficulty is that he thinks of death, and of the destiny that brings it about, as a thief and a destroyer:

---

[3] For a discussion of this point, and for the justification of the Maiden's place among the Virgins who follow the Lamb, see Gordon, pp. xix ff. (especially xxv–xxvi) and the references there given.

What wyrde hat3 hyder my iuel vayned,
And don me in þys del and gret daunger?   (249–50)

The Pearl deals with this error on two counts. He has suffered not loss, but conservation:

> 'Sir, 3e haf your tale mysetente,
> To say your perle is al awaye,
> Þat is in cofer so comly clente
> As in þis gardyn gracios gaye,
> Hereinne to lenge for euer and play,
> Þer mys nee mornyng com neuer nere.
> Her were a forser for þe, in faye,
> If þou were a gentyl jueler.'   (257–64)

Moreover, the pearl is not merely preserved but also transformed, through the Destiny which, working in accord with the natural order, has brought death to it:

> 'For þat þou leste3 wat3 bot a rose
> Þat flowred and fayled as kynde hyt gef.
> Now þur3 kynde of þe kyste þat hyt con close
> To a perle of prys hit is put in pref.
> And þou hat3 called þy wyrde a þef,
> Þat o3t of no3t hat3 mad þe cler;
> Þou blame3 þe bote of þy meschef,
> Þou art no kynde jueler.'   (269–76)

This, again, shows no concern with the particular fate of the baptized infant; and, when this problem does arise, in ll. 469 ff., it is as a problem of degree and of justice and right, not of salvation as such. The poet, indeed, has much to say concerning degree throughout the argument, and sets God's plenitude of merciful love against man's limitations. The Maiden, in showing him his error, shows him in revolt against the whole system imposed on the world by God, and by developing the theme of legality, in which God's justice and God's law are contrasted with man's idea of legal right, proves him wrong.

2

The discussion divides into two parts. The first, in sections v to vii, turns on the immediate problem of the Dreamer's rebellious will. The second part, sections viii to xvi, is concerned with the question of the reconciliation of God's justice and mercy. This is discussed in terms of degree in acquired merit, as opposed to baptismal innocence; and, using the parable of the vineyard, of the amount of labour done, ranging from the full day's work to mere entry at the eleventh hour.

The whole passage is full of terms of comparison and degree. The actual words 'less' and 'more' are twice used in a refrain-phrase so carefully placed and balanced as to suggest very deliberate planning. In section x 'more' is the refrain word, combined with 'less' in the last verse of the stanza. In section xv 'less' is used for the refrain, and is combined with 'more' in the first stanza. In a scheme of twenty sections this positioning of the key words is significant.[4] The emphasis throughout the tenth section is on the abundance of God's grace and mercy and of the bliss of heaven, as against the smallness of man's desert. The climax, as far as this idea is concerned, is the great stanza on God's plenitude of grace which comes at the exact centre of the poem at the beginning of section xi.[5]

Section vi, to return to the first part of the discussion, uses *deme*, 'judge' (verb and noun), as its link word, and the idea of judgement with its inevitable implication of comparison and its legal associations, hardens in the last stanza to a clear statement by the Maiden about the all-embracing nature of God's judgement:

> Al lys in hym to dyȝt and deme.   (360)

The Dreamer only uses the word in the sense of human judgement or opinion, and finally, in the first line of the next section (361), implies his failure to comprehend the force of the Maiden's argument by weakening it still further to 'express an opinion', 'speak'. The Maiden uses it not only in the sense of man's judgement but also of God's, and never in a weakened sense.

---

[4] I have elsewhere discussed the poet's possible interest in and use of numerical structure (see 'Numerical Structure in *Pearl*,' *Notes and Queries*, N.S. 12, 2 (1965), pp. 49 ff.).

[5] Stanza 51, since the extra stanza brings the total to 101, is the middle one of the poem, and contains, as near its centre as the 12-line scheme allows, l. 606—half of the total of 1212.

Less and More

Section vi also reintroduces the theme of less and more:

> For dyne of doel of lureȝ lesse
> Ofte mony mon forgos þe mo.   (339–40)

The Maiden sets God's unchanging decree against man's wavering between extremes:

> And loue ay God, in wele and wo. . . .
> When þou no fyrre may, to ne fro,
> Þou moste abyde þat he schal deme.   (342, 347–8)

Section vii stresses the idea of abundance, both in earthly sorrow and heavenly bliss:

> 'Ne worþe no wrathþe vnto my Lorde,
> If rapely I raue, spornande in spelle.
> My herte watȝ al wyth mysse remorde,
> As wallande water gotȝ out of welle'.   (362–5)

> 'He toke myself to hys maryage,
> Corounde me quene in blysse to brede
> In lenghe of dayeȝ þat euer schal wage;
> And sesed in alle hyse herytage
> Hys lef is. I am holy hysse:
> Hys prese, hys prys, and hys parage
> Is rote and grounde of alle my blysse.'   (414–20)

The statement, which the Dreamer is to challenge, that the Pearl has been crowned a queen in the marriage of the Lamb takes the argument on to a further stage. The key-word of this section is *grounde*, 'foundation', that is, an irreducible basis, common to all, whatever their degree.

Section viii introduces the subject of degree again in the sense of 'rank', and follows out the idea of the crowning of the queen. The refrain deals with kings and queens and the fifth stanza links this rank to actual achievement in the world:

> Þyself in heuen ouer hyȝ þou heue,
> To make þe quen þat watȝ so ȝonge.
> What more honour moȝte he acheue
> Þat hade endured in worlde stronge,
> And lyued in penaunce hys lyueȝ longe
> Wyth bodyly bale hym blysse to byye?

179

What more worschyp moȝt he fonge
Þen corounde be kyng by cortaysé? (472–80)

The refrain word is *cortaysye* in the sense of a noble generosity in giving and receiving which leaves no room for comparison.[6]

Section ix turns on the idea of 'limit' with the refrain word *date*. The poet, indeed, draws on most of the possible senses of this word. At 528, 529, and 540:

> Welneȝ wyl day watȝ passed date.
> At þe date of day of euensonge . . .
> Þe day watȝ al apassed date . . .

it has the meaning 'the limit, term, or end of a period of time'.[7] Line 516, 'Ne knawe ȝe of þis day no date?', means 'Do you think the day will last for ever?', 'Do you not know that there is a limit, an inevitable termination to the day?'. At 517:

> 'Er date of daye hider arn we wonne'

the meaning must be 'limit' in the sense of 'the beginning of a period of time' (not in *O.E.D.*). 505, 'date of ȝere', means 'time', 'date' in the modern sense[8] and 503–4:

> Of tyme of ȝere þe terme watȝ tyȝt,
> To labor vyne watȝ dere þe date,

is the related 'season, right time'.[9] 492 'Bot a quene! Hit is to dere a date' is more difficult. If *date* means 'limit' we might have something like the modern phrase 'it really is the limit!' If it means 'end', 'final termination', then we could translate 'it is too high a consummation!' It is possible, however, that the real

---

[6] Dante also uses *cortese* of God, with particular reference to the abundance of his gifts:

> 'Benedetto sia tu', fu 'trino e uno,
> che nel mio seme se tanto cortese!'
> (*Paradiso*, xv, 47–8)

For the sense 'nobleness, generosity, benevolence, goodness' in English, see *O.E.D.*, Courtesy, sb. sense 2, and for its use in M.E. of the beneficence of God in a general sense (a common one), see *M.E.D.*, courteisie, n. 4.

[7] See *O.E.D.*, date, sb². 5.   [8] Ibid., date, sb². 2a.

[9] Ibid., date, sb². 2b.

meaning is 'decree'. The title to the rank of queen would then be thought of as conferred by statute, and the usage is a legal one, reflecting the Medieval Latin use of *datum* for *statutum, decretum.*[10]

Another important idea which is emphasized in this section is that of God's justice as co-extensive with his limitless goodness:

> 'Þer is no date of hys godnesse,'
> Þen sayde to me þat worþy wyȝte,
> 'For al is trawþe þat he con dresse.
> And he may do noþynk bot ryȝt.' (493–6)

Section x reintroduces the idea of degree and comparison with the refrain of 'more', combined, in the last stanza, with 'less'. 'More', alone, is used of God, and of the bliss of heaven:

> Þe merci of God is much þe more.
> More haf I of ioye and blysse hereinne. (576–7)

This is contrasted with the poverty, littleness, and helplessness of man:

> Þus pore men her part ay pykeȝ,
> Þaȝ þay com late and lyttel wore;
> And þaȝ her sweng wyth lyttel atslykeȝ,
> Þe merci of God is much þe more. (573–6)

The Dreamer reverses this, by speaking of man as capable of achievement—'he þat stod þe long day stable' (597)—and claiming that the 'more' of God's reward corresponds to a very different human 'less':

> 'And þou to payment com hym byfore,
> Þenne þe lasse in werke to take more able,
> And euer þe lenger þe lasse, þe more.' (598–600)

The first lines of the next section use the refrain phrase in flat contradiction of his assertion:

> 'Of more and lasse in Godeȝ ryche,'
> Þat gentyl sayde, 'lys no joparde,
> For þer is vch mon payed inlyche,
> Wheþer lyttel oþer much be hys rewarde;' (601–4)

[10] See ibid., date, sb². 6. This sense is rare, and *M.E.D.* records no instance before *c.* 1470.

The Revelation

Section xi has the idea of sufficiency as its key one. The sufficiency (*inoghe*) of God's grace eliminates degree and comparison through its abundance, expressed through the imagery of flowing water. Line 606, the middle line of the poem, falls in the centre of the stanza, and at the climax of the argument:

> For þe gentyl Cheuentayn is no chyche,
> Queþer-so-euer he dele nesch oþer harde:
> He lauez hys gyftez as water of dyche.   (605–7)

This stanza drives home the argument with its expressions of contrast or degree, *more and lasse*; *lyttel oþer much*; *nesch oþer harde*; all of which are cancelled out by expressions like *no joparde*; *inlyche*; *gret inoghe*. The use of *Cheuentayn* is also significant—like the other forms of degree, human rank, the theme of an earlier section, is swallowed up in the overwhelming majesty of God. The next stanza, however, introduces a fresh turn in the discussion:

> 'Bot now þou motez, me for to mate,
> Þat I my peny haf wrang tan here;
> Þou sayz þat I þat come to late
> Am not worþy so gret fere.'   (613–16)

This, with the words *wrang tan*, brings in the idea of just or unjust action, uncompromisingly stated at the end of the stanza:

> Þay laften ryzt and wrozten woghe.   (622)

After this, the poet turns again to his favourite image of abundantly flowing water to express the concept of an 'enough' which leaves no room for any comparison:

> Bot þeron com a bote astyt.
> Ryche blod ran on rode so roghe,
> And wynne water þen at þat plyt:
> Þe grace of God wex gret innoghe.
>
> Innoghe þer wax out of þat welle,
> Blod and water of brode wounde.
> Þe blod vus bozt fro bale of helle
> And delyuered vus of þe deth secounde;
> Þe water is baptem, þe soþe to telle,

> Þat folȝed þe glayue so grymly grounde,
> Þat wascheȝ away þe gylteȝ felle
> Þat Adam wyth inne deth vus drounde.   (645–56)

Section xii turns on the idea of right and the righteous man as contrasted with the innocent: that is of justice and desert, The first stanza sums up:

> Grace innogh þe mon may haue
> Þat synneȝ þenne new, ȝif him repente,
> Bot wyth sorȝ and syt he mot hit craue,
> And byde þe payne þerto is bent.
> Bot resoun of ryȝt þat con noȝt raue
> Saueȝ euermore þe innossent;
> Hit is a dom þat neuer God gaue,
> Þat euer þe gyltleȝ schulde be schente.
> Þe gyltyf may contryssyoun hente
> And be þurȝ mercy to grace þryȝt;
> Bot he to gyle þat neuer glente
> And inoscente is saf and ryȝte.   (661–72)

The last stanza but one of this section contains a grim warning:

> Anende ryȝtwys men ȝet saytȝ a gome,
> Dauid in Sauter, if euer ȝe syȝ hit:
> 'Lorde, þy seruaunt draȝ neuer to dome,
> For non lyuyande to þe is justyfyet.'
> Forþy to corte quen þou schal com
> Þer alle oure causeȝ schal be tryed,
> Alegge þe ryȝt, þou may be innome,
> By þys ilke spech I haue asspyed:
> Bot he on rode þat blody dyed,
> Delfully þurȝ hondeȝ þryȝt,
> Gyue þe to passe, when þou arte tryed,
> By innocens and not by ryȝte.   (697–708)

Section xiii is built round the pearl of great price, and the theme of abundance is developed with expressions like *endeleȝ* and *commune to alle* in stanza two. The link-word is *maskelleȝ*, 'without blemish', 'perfect', but *makeleȝ*, 'without match', or 'without comparison' is used in ll. 733, 757, and 780, and in the opening stanza of the next section, the Maiden uses both words to make her point:

'Maskelles,' quod þat myry quene,
'Vnblemyst I am, wythouten blot,
And þat may I wyth mensk menteene;
Bot "makeleȝ quene" þenne sade I not.' (781–4)

The idea of comparison is also introduced in l. 759 with *make* =
'bride' and 'match', and *vnmete* = 'unfit', 'not comparable'.
This idea proves a stumbling block to the Dreamer at the end of
the stanza, when he thinks of the Marriage as involving displacement, and so degree:

And þou con alle þo dere out dryf
And fro þat maryag al oþer depres,
Al only þyself so stout and styf,
A makeleȝ may and maskelleȝ. (777–80)

Section xiv has Jerusalem as its refrain-word, and it deals with
the death of the Lamb who takes away the sins of the world:

Lo, Godeȝ Lombe as trwe as ston,
Þat dotȝ away þe synneȝ dryȝe
Þat alle þys worlde hatȝ wroȝt vpon.
Hymself ne wroȝt neuer ȝet non;
Wheþer on hymself he con al clem.
Hys generacyoun quo recen con,
Þat dyȝed for vus in Jerusalem? (822–8)

Section xv has as its refrain-phrase *neuer the lesse*, and it deals
with an abundance which has no comparative degree: a 'more',
in fact, without a 'less':

Þe mo þe myryer, so God me blesse.
In compayny gret our luf con þryf
In honour more and neuer þe lesse. (850–2)

Words and phrases for number and quantity abound: *a store*
(847), *the mo þe myryer* (850), *compayny gret* (851); the apocalyptic 144,000 (869–70). The imagery of water in flood is once
more used, following the Book of Revelations, in ll. 873–6:

A hue from heuen I herde þoo,
Lyk flodeȝ fele laden runnen on resse,
And as þunder þroweȝ in torreȝ blo,
Þat lote, I leue, watȝ neuer þe les. (873–6)

184

This section, in fact, repeats the argument and imagery of section xi, in such a way as to bring final conviction to the Dreamer. The elimination of degree in abundance concludes the argument proper, and section xvi leads on to the description of the New Jerusalem. Nevertheless, its refrain-word *mote*, used in two senses, 'spot', 'blemish' and 'castle', 'city', links it to what has gone before by recalling the earlier use of *maskelleʒ* as a refrain-word. *Mote* may also bear the sense dispute[11]—certainly the absence of discord in heaven, as a result of the elimination of degree, is constantly stressed.

Such, in bare outline, is the scheme according to which the argument is developed. To fill out this outline we must now look more closely at the idea which, next to that of degree, plays the chief part in it. This is the idea of justice and of legality. We must also look closely at the terminology by means of which it is expressed.

3

The ideas associated with law in action, of the trial of a cause, the weighing up of right and wrong and the passing of judgement between parties, are necessarily not far from the ideas of comparison and degree. It is not, therefore, surprising that the poet works out his argument in legal terms, as well as in terms of 'less and more'. Moreover, in doing so, he is able to develop the same paradox: just as degree vanishes in the superabundance of heaven, so the emphasis on exact measurement of merit, which is an inescapable part of human justice, vanishes in the plenitude of God's justice and mercy.

In order to trace out the poet's argument we must look closely at the words he uses: many of them have a more precise and technical sense than the editors and translators have allowed, and it is only when they are understood in these senses that the argument becomes clear. The poet of *Pearl* is not alone in this liking for technical legal language. Dante used it, and, in

[11] Ibid., mote, sb[1]. 2; sb[2]. b, and moot, sb[1]. 4.

England, Langland developed some of his most important themes in legal terms.[12]

In the proem the Dreamer has suffered a simple loss. This, however, soon comes to be seen in terms of right to property and its forfeit. He comes to think of his misfortune as an assault on his property by Destiny—as the Maiden says, 'þou hatȝ called þy wyrde a þef'. *Wyrd,* according to l. 249, has conveyed away his jewel, and by doing so has placed him in 'þys del and gret daunger'. This phrase is usually taken as 'sorrow and great harm', that is as a vague summary of the regret and longing described in the first part of the stanza. But the last two lines are emphatic:

> Fro we in twynne wern towen and twayned,
> I haf ben a joyleȝ juelere. (251–2)

They refer to separation. Line 250 would be more effective in its context if we took *daunger* in a more precise sense, as 'having incurred a liability', 'under jurisdiction', especially as forfeiting goods to the law, e.g. as a debtor.[13] Thus, we could translate: 'What fate has conveyed away my Pearl to this place and caused me this sorrow and made me liable to so terrible a forfeit?' It may well be that other senses are also implied: *daunger* may carry overtones from its common use for separation or unhappiness in love.

In l. 285 the Dreamer makes appeal to 'my Lorde and al his laweȝ' in support of his belief that he has recovered the Maiden and will be able to live with her. The phrase is ironical in the extreme, as she hastens to point out, since the law of God, as exemplified in his actual promise to man (305–6), and also, in

---

[12] On Langland's knowledge and use of technical legal terminology, see Rudolph Kirk, 'References to the Law in *Piers Plowman*', *P.M.L.A.*, XLVIII (1933), pp. 322 ff. For the importance of legal-political ideas and terms, especially in the *Visio*, see my article 'Love, Law and *Lewte* in *Piers Plowman*', *R.E.S.*, N.S., XV (1964), pp. 241 ff. J. A. Burrow has recently pointed out the importance of the poet's use of legal terms in *Sir Gawain* (*A Reading of* Sir Gawain and the Green Knight, pp. 22 f.).

[13] See *O.E.D.*, Danger, sb. 1d, and the citations there given. The phrase 'out of debt out of danger' (1e) is also relevant.

the laws of Nature (265 ff.), give him the lie. In answering him, the Maiden uses a number of words which have legal or feudal overtones: *tryȝe* (311), 'to test' and also 'to try a case', and *deme*, 'judge', verb and noun, the link-word in this section. *Bayly* in line 315, means the outer court, and so the first line of defence in a feudal castle—to penetrate it would imply a right of conquest, ownership, or permission. *Graunt* (317), means 'permission' in a general sense, but also an authoritative, legal assignment. It can have another legal sense which would fit the context, although this is not recorded before the sixteenth century; that is, 'a conveyance of property by deed'.[14] *Forgarte*, in l. 321, means 'forfeited'.[15]

Some of these words, it is true, are ambiguous: they can have a general as well as a more technical meaning, and the poet certainly plays on more than one sense. Nevertheless the idea of law, in the widest sense, has been invoked, and the idea of legal right and legal limitation is being gradually strengthened. When the Pearl describes her actual position in Heaven in the marriage of the Lamb she returns to legal phraseology, this time of an unambiguous sort—'And sesed in alle hys herytage / Hys lef is' (417–18). This assertion becomes the basis of the argument, and legal terminology now becomes more frequent and more technical. *Sesed in*, 'seized in', means 'to be the legal possessor of a thing'.[16] It relates especially to a feudal holding, or to an office or dignity.[17] *Herytage* has several shades of meaning which are appropriate to the context, and on which the poet probably plays. It can mean, and this sense fits in well with *sesed in*, 'anything given or received to be a proper and legally

[14] See ibid., grant, sb¹. 3, 'an authoritative bestowal or conferment of a privilege, right, or possession', supported by a quotation from Wycliffe. For 'conveyance by deed', see sense 4; the earliest instance is from Spenser.

[15] There seems to be no evidence for the sense 'ruined', 'made corruptible' (Gordon, glossary). *O.E.D.*, forgar, v, is glossed 'to destroy', 'corrupt', but the quotations do not support this. All the instances except one concern man's (or the fallen angels') forfeiture of Paradise.

[16] *O.E.D.*, Seize, v. I, 1b.

[17] Ibid., I, 1.

held possession'.[18] It was also almost a technicality for the position allotted in the life to come.[19] It means, too, 'heritable property to which the heir has a right', as distinct from property gained by conquest or purchase.[20] The Pearl, indeed, as innocent, *inherits* her property in heaven, she is distinct from those who 'porchaseʒ and fongeʒ pray' in l. 439.

Section viii makes its point through the continued use of terms which are associated with the obtaining of property, and the right to it. In ll. 439–40—

> 'Sir, fele here porchaseʒ and fongeʒ pray,
> Bot supplantoreʒ none wythinne þys place'—

porchaseʒ and *fongeʒ pray* are usually understood as 'strive' or 'contend' and 'get the prize', and this common biblical metaphor may well be implied.[21] But *supplantoreʒ* seems to demand another sense. It meant in the fourteenth century, with more force than the modern equivalent, to get what belongs to someone else by wrongful means.[22] If *porchaseʒ* here means, as it can do, 'to get a title to property otherwise than by inheritance' (as a rule by conquest in war)[23] and *pray* 'what is taken in war or by violence',[24] then *supplantoreʒ* would help to enforce the paradox, which is implicit throughout the whole section, of the opposition of earthly and heavenly justice. The Kingdom of Heaven may be won by violence—and this may seem unjust. But this violence is not the unlawful activity of

[18] *O.E.D.*, heritage, sb. 3. Examples are from the fourteenth century.

[19] Ibid., 1c. This usage, of course, implies, in accordance with St. Paul, that all Christians are, in fact, possible inheritors of heaven. The *Pearl*-poet is not unaware of this. His argument presently widens to include all those who become as 'innocents' with the Maiden (see below, p. 195).

[20] Ibid., 1 and 1b.

[21] See Gordon, note on l. 439, p. 61.

[22] See *O.E.D.*, supplanter, 1, and supplant, v. 3.

[23] See ibid., purchase, v. II, 5.

[24] See ibid., prey, sb. I, 1. Wycliffe uses the phrase 'toke prayes' (1 Macc., i, 33); the quotation from the *Faytes of Armes* is also interesting, since it concerns the permanent acquisition of property, 'Where as byfore he was a powere knyght he was becom ryche by the proyes that he had goten and taken' (III, xi, 191).

'supplanters'. *Erytage* in l. 443 carries the idea farther: to take violent possession of something to which someone else has a proper legal right, by inheritance or other means, must always be an unjustifiable act.

Property in l. 446—

> 'The court of þe kyndom of God alyue
> Hatȝ a property in hytself beyng'—

certainly means 'quality' 'attribute', a common sense in the fourteenth century. There may, however, be a suggestion of another common and more technical sense: 'the condition of belonging to a person'—'appropriation to'.[25] The kingdom of heaven is, thus, in its very nature, through its distinctive quality, common property, in which all the just have inalienable rights.

The whole section is full of feudal terms—'King', 'Queen', 'Empress', 'court', 'kingdom', 'realm', 'bayly'—and these make natural the use of *cortaysye* as a refrain-word. For the poet here, and in *Sir Gawain*, 'courtesy' has wide connotations. It stands for nobility and generosity of conduct, and for goodness. It is not, in fact, restricted to either fine manners or to the code of behaviour associated with Courtly Love—though, in *Gawain* at least, the poet shows awareness of these senses.[26] He is not, of course, alone, in using the word with these wider meanings. A glance at the illustrative material collected in *O.E.D.* and *M.E.D.* will show that they were, even, the more usual ones in the fourteenth century. As far as *Pearl* is concerned, the most important element in the idea of courtesy seems to be generosity —freedom from limitation, abundance in goodness and in loving-kindness. Limitation could be imposed on generosity of

[25] For the fourteenth century the quality or attribute indicated by 'property' would probably be a distinctive or essential one (*O.E.D.*, property, sb. 5). For the sense of 'appropriation to', see sense 1, and, especially, the citation from Wycliffe 'þe cite of Beedleem was Daviþis bi sum propirte' (*Serm., Sel. Works*, I, 317).

[26] See Gervase Mathew, 'Ideals of Knighthood in Late Fourteenth Century England', *Studies in Medieval History Presented to F. M. Powicke* (Oxford, 1948), pp. 354 ff.; J. A. Burrow, *A Reading of* Sir Gawain and the Green Knight, pp. 46–7.

this kind by a strict interpretation of the concept of human law. So it is that, through the repeated use of the word 'courtesy', the idea of a fundamental difference between earthly legality and the Justice of Heaven is further built up.

'Courtesy' is the word that the Dreamer picks up in his protest in section ix—this, he says, is a courtesy outside law and reason—'to fre of dede' (481). The idea of just, legal title is reinforced by *halde asstate* (490) and, *date* (492), if, as I have suggested, it bears the sense of 'statute'. By the play on the meanings of *date*, too, the implications of *cortaysye* are further developed, and, once again, the idea of contract is insisted on through the terms used of the work in the vineyard—for example, *acorde* (509), *made hit toȝt* (522), *couenaunt* (562), *louyly* (565). Line 580, *By þe way of ryȝt to aske dome*, by apparently contradicting ll. 563–4, maintains the double sense of law. The Maiden does, in fact, enjoy a greater reward than anyone could demand of strict justice.

In stanza 50 the Dreamer sums up his objections, and in doing so points up even more emphatically this fundamental ambiguity by the use of further words with legal implications. He speaks of *Goddes ryȝt* as something which cannot be *vnresounable*; he uses *determynable*; *quyteȝ . . . desserte*; *stable*; all words which help to establish the idea of finality and incontrovertibility. Lastly, he apostrophises the Just God as '*þou hyȝe kyng ay partermynable*'. This is a phrase which has caused difficulty and at which we must pause. But, first, if we read these lines beside the psalm which they purport to paraphrase we shall see that their chief function is to maintain the ironic ambiguity of the two conceptions of justice and law which runs through the passage. Ps. 61, 12–13 reads: 'Semel locutus est Deus; duo haec audivi: quia potestas Dei est, et tibi, Domine, misericordia; quia tu reddes unicuique iuxta opera sua.' (God hath spoken once. These two things have I heard: that power belongeth to God, and mercy to thee, O Lord: for thou wilt render to every man according to his works.) This psalm, which brings together God's retributive justice and His mercy, is thus particularly appropriate to the argument. The Dreamer bases his case on the first of the 'two things', the *potestas Dei*, which he interprets in relation to judgement. The Maiden, in her refutation of him, takes up the psalmist's second thing: the mercy of God. The idea contained in *partermynable*, therefore, must correspond to the *potestas Dei*, exercised in the judgement of man according to his works.

The actual form of the word is difficult to establish. The MS. has for the first syllable the abbreviation which normally stands for *per-* or *par-*. All the editors, however, adopt *pre-* in the text.[27] This is a particularly unfortunate reading since *pretermynable* would presumably mean 'preordaining' and would refer to an idea, that of predestination, which is not otherwise present in the passage, and which does not fit. *Per-*, or *partermynable*, on the other hand would mean 'who above all others givest just judgement'[28] and, this would fit in well with the legal associations of the passage. *Determynable* would bear much the same sense, but without the intensification, and a *poynt determynable* would be 'an argument capable of settling the case', 'of leading to a just, incontrovertible verdict'. The Dreamer, in fact, uses terms which can bear a legal meaning to define God's power of doing strict justice, and uses them with perfect correctness; but his understanding of what he says is, as usual, at fault.

The Maiden's reply, in st. 51, is in two parts: she first returns to the idea of degree and comparison—this is an ineradicable part of the concept of human justice, but has no place in that of God. Secondly, she goes back to the psalm which has been quoted against her. Now, Ps. 61 is built round the idea that God rewards the man who makes submission to Him:

Nonne Deo subiecta erit anima mea? ab ipso enim salutare meum; . . .
Veruntamen Deo subiecta esto, anima mea, quoniam ab ipso patientia mea.
Quia ipse Deus meus et salvator meus, adiutor meus: non emigrabo.

[27] Gordon, however, suggests in his note to l. 596 (p. 65–6) that the MS. '*per-*' can be interpreted and need not be emended. I am greatly indebted to Father E. J. Stormon, S. J., for placing his notes on the form and meaning of *per-/par-termynable* at my disposal and what follows on this word is largely based on his work.

[28] Stormon points out that *par-* in such a thoroughly French formation is more likely than *per-*, and compares '*paradmirable*', etc.

In Deo salutare meum et gloria mea; Deus auxilii mei, et spes mea in Deo est.

(Shall not my soul be subject to God? For from him is my salvation: . . .
But be thou, O my soul, subject to God: for from him is my patience.
For he is my God and my saviour: he is my helper, I shall not be moved.
In God is my salvation and my glory: he is the God of my help, and my hope is in God. (2, 6–8)

The second part of the Maiden's reply in stanza 51 runs:

> Hys fraunchyse is large þat euer dard
> To Hym þat matȝ in synne rescoghe;
> No blysse betȝ fro hem reparde,
> For þe grace of God is gret inoghe. (609–12)

These lines have been variously interpreted, but, if we take *dard to* as corresponding to *subjecta erit*,[29] they suggest a free paraphrase of the relevant verses of psalm 61; and they effectively reintroduce the idea of mercy which had been left out of the Dreamer's version. To balance the Dreamer's technical use of *determynable* and *partermynable*, the Maiden uses three expressions to develop her argument, all of which can bear a special legal sense: these are *fraunchyse* (609); *matȝ . . . rescoghe* and *forfeted* (619), *forfete* (639). If these are understood in their legal, as well as in their more general senses, the argument becomes clear. 'Forfeit' in its legal sense means 'to lose one's right to property by a crime', or 'to incur a fine by a crime';[30] in fact, to come within the jurisdiction of a court and to lose by its action something which one had before. So Adam, and after him mankind, lost the right to Paradise before the court of

[29] *Dard* would then derive from O.E. *darian* 'lurk, lie low, in fear'. It has been objected that this verb should not in M.E. be followed by *to*, but Gordon points out that the poet, hard-pressed for a rhyme-word, could have been influenced by such phrases as *bowed to, louted to*, etc. See his note to ll. 609–10, p. 67–8, and the references there given.

[30] *O.E.D.*, Forfeit, v. 2, especially 2a. The poet, of course, is also aware of the more general meaning 'to sin', and this is important in these lines.

God's Justice. The other two terms refer to limitations of the action of a court of justice. *Fraunchyse* means 'legal immunity', especially from a particular exaction or tribunal;[31] 'to make rescue' means 'to recover forcibly a person or goods out of legal custody'.[32]

Thus, the Maiden's contention is that those who subject themselves to God's will gain immunity from the exaction to which the forfeit of original sin exposed them through the operation of God's justice, and are, by His act of Redemption, forcibly recovered from the legal penalty they, and all mankind, have incurred.[33]

The imagery of water pouring out which the poet uses to emphasize the abundance of God's 'gifts' in salvation is made vivid by the use of the concrete, probably localized, words *gotez* and *golf*.[34] Nevertheless, as in so many striking passages in *Pearl*, the model is a biblical one. In John 4, 10–14, God's gift, the *donum dei*, for which the Samaritan woman might have asked, is like 'a fountain of water, springing up into life everlasting'—*fons aquae salientis in vitam aeternam*. 'Source' would be a better translation of *fons* than 'fountain', and *gotez of golf*— 'streams from a deep source'—would thus correspond closely to *fons aquae*, while 'that neuer chard' carries out the idea of *salientis in vitam aeternam*.

Section xi, as a whole, deals with the terms on which the innocent are saved. Stanza 53 shows that, although

[31] *O.E.D.*, franchise, sb. I, 2. The more general senses 'freedom as opposed to servitude' (I, 1) and 'moral freedom' (I, 1b) must also be borne in mind.

[32] Ibid., rescue, sb. 2.

[33] Lines 609–12 could thus be translated: 'His immunity from punishment is great, who subjects himself to the One Who makes forcible recovery from the power of the law.' Discussion of Redemption in terms of law is a commonplace. It is an essential part of the popular Debate of Justice and Mercy. This is well exemplified in *Piers Plowman*, B. XVIII, 112 ff. (see especially, 189 ff.). It can also play a part in the Harrowing of Hell, where the Devil can use arguments similar to those of the Dreamer (cf. *Piers Plowman*, B. XVIII, 260 ff., or the York Play of the Harrowing of Hell, 253 ff.).

[34] See Gordon, p. 67, note to ll. 607–8 and the references there given.

> . . . innoghe of grace hatȝ innocent,
> As sone as þay arn borne, by lyne,[35]

even the innocent are not saved by grace alone. With baptism:

> Þen arne þay boroȝt into þe vyne.
> Anon þe day, wyth derk endente,
> Þe niyȝt of deth dotȝ to enclyne:
> Þat wroȝt neuer wrang er þenne þay wente,
> Þe gentyle Lorde þenne payeȝ hys hyne.
> Þay dyden hys heste, þay wern þereine;
> Why schulde he not her labour alow,
> Ȝys, and pay hem at þe fyrst fyne? (628–35)

The point is given a three-fold emphasis. The innocent are 'brought into the vineyard'. They 'did the Lord's command'. 'Why should he not pay them for their *labour*?' Thus, the Maiden is able to claim reason and justice, as well as mercy, on their behalf—

> Bot resoun of ryȝt þat con noȝt raue
> Saueȝ euermore þe innossent;
> Hit is a dom þat neuer God gaue,
> Þat euer þe gyltleȝ schulde be schente—(665–8)

and section xii has as its triumphant refrain 'þe innosent is ay saue by ryȝte'.

A variation of this refrain, however, comes in stanza 59:

> Bot he on rode þat blody dyed,
> Delfully þurȝ hondeȝ þryȝt,
> Gyue þe to passe, when þou arte tryed,
> By innocens and not by ryȝte. (705–8)

[35] 625–6. This punctuation seems to me to be required by the sense. Children are not normally baptized 'as soon as they are born' (though a fourteenth-century child would have been baptized as soon as possible). The poet, however, certainly does not mean to assert the salvation of unbaptized children. His thought would seem to be that the innocent are endowed by right of inheritance (i.e. as members of the human race) with the ability to receive grace, realized in baptism. Baptism itself, since he equates it with entry into the vineyard, he seems to account as a 'work'—as indeed it is since the sponsors act in it on behalf of the child.

That is, the argument for the justice of the merciful salvation of the innocent is now extended to all Christians, who must become as children.[36] The first part of this stanza, once more in technical legal terms, states the idea of a justice which is overcome by grace, not coincident with it:

> Anende ryȝtwys men ȝet saytȝ a gome,
> Dauid in Sauter, if euer ȝe syȝ hit:
> 'Lorde, þy seruaunt draȝ neuer to dome,
> For non lyuyande to þe is justyfyet.'
> Forþy to corte quen þou schal com
> Þer alle oure causeȝ schal be tryed,
> Alegge þe ryȝt, þou may be innome,
> By þys ilke spech I haue asspyed.   (697–704)

'*Corte*', '*causeȝ*', '*tryed*' all have a legal sense here, and Dorothy Everett and Naomi Hurnard convincingly argued that *alegge þe ryȝt* and *innome* are also legal terms meaning 'if you base your plea on the assumption of legal right' and 'trapped', 'refuted in argument'.[37] The paradoxical double meaning of justice which runs through the section is brought out sharply in the closing lines, through the contrast with the death on the Cross and the safe passage of the innocent, and through the triumphant statement of the further paradox that, though justice untempered by mercy condemns all mankind, it is nevertheless by justice (*ryȝt*) that the innocent (now thought of as all those who gain heaven) are saved.

The argument based on legality ends with this section, but the poet gives us one more reminder of the disparate natures of earthly and heavenly justice, and makes a last use of legal terminology, when he speaks of the fate of the Lamb, to Whose bloody death he has already referred. He paraphrases Isa. 53, 4–9:

> Þat gloryous gyltleȝ þat mon con quelle
> Wythouten any sake of felonye,
> As a schep to þe slaȝt þer lad watȝ he;

[36] Cf. ll. 721–4.
[37] 'Legal Phraseology in a passage in *Pearl*', *M. Aev.* XVI (1947), pp. 9 ff.

And, as lombe þat clypper in hande nem,
So closed he hys mouth fro vch query,
Quen Jueȝ hym iugged in Jerusalem.   (799–804)

The phrases, which the poet did not find in Isaiah, 'wythouten any sake of felonye', 'gyltleȝ', used of one subjected to the machinery of human justice, and 'iugged', provide a poignant comment on the whole argument.

What, then, is the conclusion to the long discussion? Briefly, that no man could earn salvation in strict justice, excepting those who have preserved baptismal innocence in their short period of 'work' in the vineyard. Yet, that God's justice is unlike human justice, and is ultimately coincident with that mercy which made it possible for fallen man to become as a child again; that in its overwhelming sufficiency all question of degree of desert is made meaningless. This does not imply, of course, that the poet did not believe in differing rewards in heaven nor in differing merit on earth. He merely states the case for the insufficiency of man and the all-sufficiency of God, as far as salvation is concerned.[38]

4

For the whole of the long argument the poet uses a style which is sharply contrasted with the earlier part of the poem. It is much sparser—imagery, and even description, are kept to a minimum, and the effect depends almost entirely on the accurate placing of the theme words, both in the refrain phrases and in the repetitions within the stanzas, and in the subtle play on different possible meanings.

The demands of the stanza-form are never allowed to stand in the way of the simple direct style, with short sentences which build up into clear, logical exposition, and a near-natural

[38] Hilton, for example, expresses a similar view of the all-sufficiency of God's grace and love and the little that man can do to deserve it or cooperate with it. See *Scale of Perfection*, Bk. II, chapter 34 (translated G. Sitwell, Orchard Books), especially p. 251. Cf. also Sitwell's note, pp. 249–50.

word-order. The passage, based on St. Paul, explaining how we
are all members of Christ is a good example:

> 'Of courtaysye, as sayt3 Saynt Poule,
> Al arn we membre3 of Jesu Kryst.
> As heued and arme and legg and naule
> Temen to hys body ful trwe and tryste.
> Ry3t so is vch a Krysten sawle
> A longande lym to þe Mayster of myste.
> Þenne loke what hate oþer any gawle
> Is tached oþer ty3ed þy lymme3 bytwyste.
> Þy heued hat3 nauþer greme ne gryste,
> On arme oþer fynger þa3 þou ber by3e.
> So fare we alle wyth luf and lyste
> To kyng and quene by cortaysye.'[39]

The tone is that of the spoken voice: inversion (*al arn we . . . is
vch a . . . fare we . . .*) corresponds to its emphasis, not to the
exigencies of the verse. The placing of the refrain phrase *by
cortaysye* is perhaps an exception, but its position suggests a
useful ambiguity: king and queen owe their rank to 'courtesy',
which also governs the behaviour of the blessed.

The same emphatic, conversational style is used for narrative
in the paraphrase of the parable of the vineyard:

> Þat date of 3ere wel knawe þys hyne.
> Þe lorde ful erly vp he ros
> To hyre werkmen to hys vyne,
> And fynde3 þer summe to hys porpos.
> Into accorde þay con declyne
> For a pené on a day, and forth þay got3,
> Wryþen and worchen and don gret pyne,
> Keruen and caggen and man hit clos.
> Aboute vnder þe lorde to marked tot3,
> And ydel men stande he fynde3 þerate.
> 'Why stande 3e ydel?' he sayde to þos.
> 'Ne knawe 3e of þis day no date?   (505–616)

---

[39] Lines 457–68: The punctuation usually given to this stanza
makes the sentences more complex and misses the earnest, forceful
ticking off of the points of the argument in short, rhythmically simple
sentences.

What imagery there is, is all the more striking. The imagery of
flowing water is a recurring theme; and the imagery of day and
night symbolizes life and death in the exposition of the parable:

> Anon þe day, wyth derk endente,
> Þe niy3t of deth dot3 to enclyne:
> Þat wro3t neuer wrang er þenne þay wente,
> Þe gentyle Lorde þenne paye3 hys hyne. (629–32)

The lyrical address to the Virgin introduces the image of the
phoenix:

> Now, for synglerty o hyr dousour,
> We calle hyr Fenyx of Arraby,
> Þat freles fle3e of hyr fasor,
> Lyk to þe Quen of cortaysye . . .[40]

and, as the argument comes to its conclusion, the apocalyptic
symbolism of the lamb and the lamp is brought together in
the punning lines:

> Of sunne ne mone had þay no nede;
> Þe self God wat3 her lombe-ly3t,
> Þe Lombe her lantyrne, wythouten drede;
> Þur3 hym blysned þe bor3 al bry3t.
> Þur3 wo3e and won my lokyng 3ede,
> For sotyle cler no3t lette no ly3t. (1045–50)

This leads straight into the final great description of the golden
city of Jerusalem.

There is yet another aspect of the central part of the poem
which must not be forgotten. In spite of the fact that in it father
and child are briefly reunited, and in spite of the underlying
tenderness which never allows the relationship to be forgotten,
it is, in fact, an externalization of the warring, discordant voices
of the proem. The Dreamer speaks with the voice of his own
'wreched wylle', the Maiden with that of Reason; and as more
than Reason, with something of the divine authority on which

---

[40] Lines 429–32: 'Now, because her sweetness is unequalled, we
call her the Arabian Phoenix, that bird of peerless form, like the Queen
of Courtesy.' On the difficulties of *fle3e* and *fasor*, see the notes to the
various editions. D. Everett's version is followed here.

reason depends. It is this which accounts for the sharpness of much of the dialogue—for flat contradiction on the Dreamer's part, abruptly phrased—

> 'I may not traw, so God me spede,
> Þat God wolde wryȝe so wrange away.
> Of countes, damysel, par ma fay,
> Wer fayr in heuen to halde asstate,' (487–90)
> 'Me þynk þy tale vnresounable. . . .' (590)

and for severity in taking him up on the Maiden's.

The situation—the reunion of two beings who hold each other in affection—makes it necessary that this note should not be sounded too strongly. The poet gets over this difficulty by establishing the theme of angry words in the earlier part of the debate section by other means. He does this by constant use of suggestive words and phrases. Line 314, 'As man to God wordeȝ schulde heue', suggest impious, defiant speech. Line 343 refers to anger, and 346 'Braundysch and bray þy braþeȝ breme,' implies raging words, as does 363 'If rapely I raue, spornande in spelle.' Lines 378–9:

> 'And, quen we departed, we wern at on;
> God forbede we be now wroþe. . . .'

and 390:

> 'I wolde bysech, wythouten debate,'

imply that a quarrel has been taking place—and give a stronger impression than the actual dialogue justifies. The Maiden's words in ll. 400–2—

> 'For now þy speche is to me dere.
> Maysterful mod and hyȝe pryde,
> I hete þe, arn heterly hated here—'

reinforce this impression. The theme of warring voices is, in fact, established in this part of the poem by an accumulation of oblique references, rather than by the actual tone of the dialogue. Of necessity the discussion becomes more peaceable as it goes on, but as the poet handles it, we have, increasingly, the impression of numerous voices raised in a great debate. This effect is achieved by constant quotation, introduced as direct speech. In Section ix, for example, stanza 42 introduces the parable with a curious effect of three speakers. First, the Maiden—

> Þen sayde to me þat worþy wyȝte, (494)

then the Gospel writer—

> As Mathew meleȝ in your messe, (497)

with a suggestion in 'messe' of voices raised in the church service—and then the Lord himself. 'My regne,' he saytȝ, . . . (501). The characters in the parable argue—and argue in surly tones:

> And þenne þe fyrst bygonne to pleny
> And sayden þat þay hade trauayled sore:
> 'Þese bot on oure hem con streny;
> Vus þynk vus oȝe to take more.

> 'More haf we serued, vus þynk so,
> Þat suffred han þe dayeȝ hete,
> Þenn þyse þat wroȝt not houreȝ two,
> And þou dotȝ hem vus to counterfete.' (549–56)

The psalm quotation in stanza 57 is introduced as question and answer:

> 'Þe Sauter hyt satȝ þus in a pace:
> "Lorde, quo schal klymbe þy hyȝ hylle,
> Oþer rest wythinne þy holy place?"
> Hymself to onsware he is not dylle:
> "Hondelyngeȝ harme þat dyt not ille . . ."' (677–81)

This technique is constantly used for biblical quotation and reference. For example:

> As quo says, 'Lo, ȝon louely yle!
> Þou may hit wynne if þou be wyȝte. . . .'
> Anende ryȝtwys men ȝet saytȝ a gome,
> Dauid in Sauter, if euer ȝe syȝ hit:
> 'Lorde, þy seruaunt draȝ neuer to dome,
> For non lyuyande to þe is justyfyet.' (693–5, 697–700)

All this has the effect of making the debate seem more contentious than are the actual words exchanged between Maiden and Dreamer.

The lyric mood which characterizes the description of the Earthly Paradise is not, however, allowed to disappear entirely. The Pearl had described her actual state in lines which even surpass those which expressed the Dreamer's ill-founded joy:

> 'Sir, ȝe haf your tale mysetente,
> To say your perle is al awaye,
> Þat is in cofer so comly clente
> As in þis gardyn gracios gaye,
> Hereinne to lenge for euer and play,
> Þer mys nee mornyng com neuer nere.' (257–62)

The lines in which she addresses the Blessed Virgin sound the same blissful note:

> 'Cortayse Quen', þenne sayde þat gaye,
> Knelande to grounde, folde vp hyr face,
> 'Makeleȝ Moder and myryest May,
> Blessed bygynner of vch a grace!' (433–6)

and it is heard again whenever the Lamb is mentioned:

> 'My makeleȝ Lambe þat all may bete,'
> Quod scho, 'my dere destyné. . . .'
> My Lombe, my Lorde, my dere juelle,
> My ioy, my blys, my lemman fre. . . . (757–8, 795–6)

The warring voices of the mind are finally stilled by the united utterance of heaven, which has all the terror of the apocalyptic vision, but which changes to a gentler music. The Apocalypse thus describes the sound:

Et audivi vocem de caelo tanquam vocem aquarum multarum et tanquam vocem tonitrui magni; et vocem, quam audivi, sicut citharoedorum citharizantium in citharis suis.

(And I heard a voice from heaven, as the noise of many waters and as the voice of great thunder. And the voice which I heard was as the voice of harpers, harping on their harps. (14, 2)

The Poet renders this, putting the description into the mouth of the Apostle John, in the usual form of direct speech:

> 'A hue from heuen I herde þoo,
> Lyk flodeȝ fele laden runnen on resse,
> And as þunder þroweȝ in torreȝ blo,
> Þat lote, I leue, watȝ neuer þe les.
>
> Nauþeles, þaȝ hit schowted scharpe,
> And ledden loude alþaȝ hit were,
> A note ful nwe I herde hem warpe,
> To lysten þat watȝ ful lufly dere.
> As harporeȝ harpen in her harpe,
> Þat nwe songe þay songen ful cler,
> In sounande noteȝ a gentyl carpe;
> Ful fayre þe modeȝ þay fonge in fere (873–84)

The harps of Revelations here become 'a gentyl carpe', and the song of heaven is conducted in accordance with the best musical tradition.

II

THE HEAVENLY CITY

I

WHEN THE DREAMER first found himself beside the river in the blissful country of his dream, he thought, so he tells us:

> þat Paradyse
> Watȝ þer ouer gayn þo bonkeȝ brade.   (137–8)

After this, both he and his audience might reasonably expect that a sight of the elusive stronghold of the Earthly Paradise would be vouchsafed them. At this point in the poem, indeed, such a sight would have been the crowning marvel of a series of marvellous descriptions, and a fitting conclusion to the idyllic mood of the lyrical lines which stand just before the opening of the debate section, and which are rudely interrupted by it. When we actually come to the vision which concludes the poem, however, the interruption has been made. The long debate, with all its seriousness and urgency has taken place, and it has brought both Dreamer and audience to a point where the mere completion of the description of the Earthly Paradise would come as an anticlimax. It would, moreover, add nothing to the development of the work. The Dreamer's problem of a will at variance with reason, with its reasonable Creator, and with the laws of His world has been examined literally *sub specie aeternitatis*. It is fitting that the final revelation should be of the eternal city.

The transition from the Earthly Paradise to the Heavenly Kingdom is not abrupt. The vision has been carefully prepared within the debate section. Every reference to the Maiden's way of life suggests a setting quite other than 'þys countré' (297), where the Dreamer, rashly believing the evidence of his eyes, thinks she lives. The Maiden, for example, speaks, in a sounding phrase, of 'The court of þe kyndom of God alyue' (445), or of 'Godeȝ ryche' (601); and, as we have seen, the symbolism of the pearl itself is turned to account to elaborate the idea of 'þe reme of heuenesse clere' (735). Moreover, section xiv is built round the two Jerusalems, which provide its link word. Stanza 66 states unequivocally that Jerusalem is the place of the marriage, and anticipates what the Dreamer is actually to see later on:

> Þe Lambeȝ vyueȝ in blysse we bene,
> A hondred and forty fowre þowsande flot,
> As in þe Apocalyppeȝ hit is sene;
>
> Sant John hem syȝ al in a knot.
> On þe hyl of Syon, þat semly clot,
> Þe apostel hem segh in gostly drem
> Arayed to þe weddyng in þat hyl-coppe,
> Þe nwe cyté o Jerusalem.   (785–92)

Stanzas 67, 68, and 69 tell of the Earthly Jerusalem as the scene of the Passion. Stanza 70 links the two cities, and returns to the material of the Apocalypse:

> In Ierusalem þus my lemman swete
> Twyeȝ for lombe watȝ taken þare,
> By trw recorde of ayþer prophete,
> For mode so meke and al hys fare.
> Þe þryde tyme is þerto ful mete,
> In Apokalypeȝ wryten ful ȝare;
> Inmydeȝ þe trone, þere saynteȝ sete,
> Þe apostel John hym saȝ as bare,
> Lesande þe boke with leueȝ sware
> Þere seuen syngnetteȝ wern sette in seme;
> And at þat syȝt vche douth con dare
> In helle, in erþe and Jerusalem.

Moreover, the description of the Heavenly Paradise is linked to that of the Earthly one by the use of the same epithets and phrases. These echoes make us feel, when we come to the vision of Heaven, that we are not in entirely unfamiliar country, and that the earlier marvels were a foreshadowing of, and a preparation for, what was to come. Thus, the New Jerusalem 'schyrrer þen sunne wyth schafteȝ schon'; and

> What schulde þe mone þer compas clym
> And to euen wyth þat worþly lyȝt
> Þat schyneȝ vpon þe brokeȝ brym?
> Þe planeteȝ arn in to pouer a plyȝt,
> And þe self sunne ful fer to dym.   (1072–6)

The surroundings of the Earthly Paradise had been similarly described:

> Þe sunnebemeȝ bot blo and blynde
> In respecte of þat adubbement.   (83–4)

The river of the New Jerusalem is compared to the Sun and Moon:

> Sunne ne mone schon neuer so swete
> As þat foysoun flode out of þat flet;
> Swyþe hit swange þurȝ vch a strete.   (1057–9)

In the Earthly Paradise the light came from the precious stones, but:

> Swangeande swete þe water con swepe   (111)

In l. 141 the word *mereȝ* (if we accept the reading of the manu-script) is used of the river which forms an impassable barrier between the Dreamer and the Earthly Paradise. The same word is used in l. 1166 of the river which bars him from the Kingdom of Heaven. Indeed, in the manner of a dream, we hardly know which river the Dreamer is looking at, as he finds himself 'kaste of kytheȝ þat lasteȝ aye', and then, excluded even from the Earthly Paradise, awake again 'in þat erber wlonk'.

In spite of all the careful preparation for the vision of Heaven, the Dreamer's mind still clings to the beauty that is actually before his eyes. Even in the lines which, by picking up the earlier image of the rose, show comprehension at last of the problem of mortality, he can still make statements which con-tradict each other, and show how slight his understanding really is:

> 'To Krysteȝ chambre þat art ichose . . .
> And bydeȝ here by þys blysful bonc,'   (904, 907)

and he goes on to urge that David's royal city 'by þyse holteȝ hit con not hone'.

The Maiden answers him by returning to the theme of the two Jerusalems:

> 'Of motes two to carpe clene,
> And Jerusalem hyȝt boþe nawþeles—
> Þat nys to yow no more to mene
> Bot "ceté of God", oþer "syȝt of pes":
> In þat on oure pes watȝ mad at ene;
> Wyth payne to suffer þe Lombe hit chese;
> In þat oþer is noȝt bot pes to glene
> Þat ay schal laste wythouten reles.' (949–56)

The Dreamer, however, is still unable to shake off his preconceived ideas. Just as his first thought on recognizing the Pearl had been to get to her—

> Now were I at yow byȝonde þise waweȝ,
> I were a ioyful jueler— (287–8)

so, now, he still demands to be taken to the place where she is:

> Þen sayde I to þat lufly flor,
> 'Bryng me to þat bygly bylde
> And let me se þy blysful bor.' (962–4)

There is nothing here to soften the arrogance of the demand, and the stern tone of the Maiden's reproof is understandable:

> Þat schene sayde: 'Þat God wyl schylde;
> Þou may not enter wythinne hys tor.
> Bot of þe Lombe I haue þe aquylde
> For a syȝt þerof þurȝ gret fauor.
> Vtwyth to se þat clene cloystor
> Þou may, bot inwyth not a fote;
> To strech in þe strete þou hatȝ no vygour,
> Bot þou wer clene wythouten mote.' (965–72)

As we have seen, there is no question—and this passage alone would be enough to prove the point—of a maiden guide who can raise the man who loves her to a full participation in the heavenly vision.[1]

---

[1] See above, pp. 130–1.

The Heavenly City

The exclusion of the Dreamer from 'þat clene cloystor', and his continued reluctance, even now, to pass beyond the immediate and easily comprehended experience of the dream, the blissful country in which he longed to dwell for ever, is emphasized by the way in which the vision is finally introduced. The Maiden issues directions which relate to the place in which the Dreamer actually is:

> 'If I þis mote þe schal vnhyde,
> Bow vp towarde þys borneȝ heued,
> And I anendeȝ þe on þys syde
> Schal sve, tyl þou to a hil be veued.'   (973–6)

The Dreamer's account of his obedience to this command is given in terms of a return to the lyrical mood which preceded the debate—it gives us our last glimpse of the blissful country in all its beauty:

> Þen wolde I no lenger byde,
> Bot lurked by launceȝ so lufly leued,
> Tyl on a hyl þat I asspyed
> And blusched on þe burghe, as I forth dreued.   (977–80)

By this means the vision of the New Jerusalem is established as something which happens within the landscape setting of the poem as a whole. It cannot transport the Dreamer to fresh realms, and he remains outside.

The transition from the beautiful landscape of the country of the dream to the apocalyptic description of the Heavenly City is made within two lines. The City is, by a special dispensation, brought down from heaven and placed in the country of the dream, where it is seen shining across the water like the sun. We accept the comparison as a naturalistic one here, while we are still thinking in terms of landscape, but it also points forward to the symbolical sun which, with its companion moon, dominates the description of the Heavenly Host. The Dreamer sees the city:

> Byȝonde þe brok, fro me warde keued,
> Þat schyrrer þen sunne wyth schafteȝ schon.   (981–2)

The Revelation

Here he speaks as an eyewitness, but the last two lines of the stanza are an appeal to the authority on which the detailed description of the city is based:

> In þe Apokalypce is þe fasoun preued,
> As deuyseȝ hit þe apostel Jhon. (983–4)

The introduction to the vision is, thus, carefully contrived. It is especially successful in keeping constantly before us the figures of Dreamer and Maiden, with their differing points of view. Through its interweaving of references to the place of the dream and the place of the vision, too, we are never allowed to forget that, with all its beauty, the blissful country is still a place of exile, as far as the Eternal City is concerned. All this arises out of the plan and meets the special needs of this particular poem. Nevertheless, this is a passage in which we may once more suspect the influence of the *Divina Commedia*. If the poet did turn to the Italian work, however, it was not to borrow actual material, or for the main plan of this section, but for a guide as to the management of a technically difficult transition passage.

In the *Purgatorio*, as in *Pearl* an encounter with a Maiden guide, seen on the opposite bank of a river, leads to a striking vision. This vision, like that in *Pearl* is based on a biblical source, in this case the first chapter of Ezechiel. To reach the place of this appearance Dante follows Mathilda as she passes on through the shady wood—the 'launceȝ so lufly leued' of *Pearl*—until, turning towards the East, the direction of the sunrise, he sees a splendour of light which dazzles him:

> E come ninfe che si givan sole
> per le salvatiche ombre, disïando,
> qual di veder, qual di fuggir lo sole,
> Allor si mosse contra il fiume, andando
> su per la riva; e io paru di lei,
> picciol passo con picciol seguitando.
> Non eran cento tra' suoi passi e' miei,
> quando le ripe igualmente dier volta,
> per modo ch' a levante mi rendei.
> Nè ancor fu così nostra via molta,
> quando la donna tutta a me si torse,
> dicendo: 'Frate mio, guarda e ascolta.'

The Heavenly City

Ed ecco un lustro subito trascorse
    da tutte parti per la gran foresta,
    tal, che di balenar mi mise in forse.

(Like nymphs that used to wander, each alone,
    Amid the shadowing green from tree to tree,
    One seeking, and one hiding from, the sun,
Against the motion of the stream moved she
    Upon the bank; and I with her abreast
    Made little step with little step agree.
Not to a hundred had our steps increased
    When both the banks so curved as to compel
    My feet to turn aside unto the East.
Thus went we, and were not far when it befell
    The Lady towards me turning full about
    Said: 'Now, my brother, look and listen well!'
And lo! a sudden splendour dazzled out
    From all sides of the forest through the trees,
    So that, if it were lightning, I made doubt.
                         (xxix, 4–18))

The two passages are alike in the sequence of events described, and, allowing always for the difference in scale between the two poems, in mood. It is too, a little surprising to find the Dreamer of *Pearl* moving through a wood, since in the earlier description of the dream country, out of all the features he mentions 'of doun and daleȝ / Of wod and water and wlonk playneȝ', he appeared to be in the open meadow beside the stream. This point, however, cannot be pressed—the description is vague, and the poet tends to fix on the detail that suits the mood at any given moment.

Dante compares the light to lightning, presumably following Ezechiel 1, 14, 'And the living creatures ran and returned like flashes of lightning'. He does not follow Ezechiel in his comparison of the vision to fire, or to a lamp (Ezechiel 1, 4 and 13). The *Pearl*-poet compares his vision to the sun, which, as we have seen is appropriate to his plan and purpose. It is not, of course, necessarily the case that he drew on the *Divina Commedia* for this light-simile. Visions are commonly associated with a blaze of light, and his main source, the Apocalypse has the same motif, though it compares the brilliance of the city to a jewel, not to the sun.

2

The vision which has been so carefully prepared is, as far as its content goes, a sublime one. It concerns the Heavenly City, the Lamb, and the Hosts of the Blessed. It corresponds, in fact, not to the vision of the *Purgatorio*, which introduces the figure of Beatrice, but to the final vision of the *Paradiso*. No one could doubt that Dante's vision of the Heavenly Rose is one of the greatest passages of the *Paradiso*, and that it is entirely suited to its position at the triumphal climax of the whole work. It does not seem to me obvious that the vision of the Heavenly City in *Pearl* is as successful. The close biblical paraphrase, the rapid shift of interest from the Lamb to the Dreamer's personal mood, the failure at the climax of the experience to maintain the ecstacy, all make for a passage which is by no means easy to grasp. When the Dreamer sees the Lamb's wound—and describes it in prosaic terms:

> Bot a wounde ful wyde and weete con wyse
> Anende hys hert, þurȝ hyde torente— (1135–6)

his reaction is expressed in almost the tone of the Dreamer of the *Book of the Duchess*. His question, 'Alas, þoȝt I, who did þat spyt?' (1138), is followed by a brief, impersonal comment:

> Ani brest for bale aȝt haf forbrent
> Er he perto hade had delyt. (1139–40)

Chaucer's Dreamer shows the same lack of comprehension, and the same economy of comment—in his case dictated by good manners:

> 'Allas, sir, how? What may that be? . . .
> Is that your los? Be God hyt ys routhe!' (1308, 1310)

What is appropriate to a courtly poem addressed to a patron, seems oddly at variance with a moment which, we feel, would normally call for a much higher emotional tension.

The poet's reasons for this playing down of the supreme

moment of the vision become clear when we consider the plan of his poem as a whole. Within that plan, the glimpse of the New Jerusalem and its triumphant host cannot be a personal triumph for the Dreamer. We have seen how carefully the linking passage was organized to emphasize his exclusion from what he sees. Nor is the moment one of illumination for him. On the contrary his misunderstanding continues, unmitigated by the sight of the Lamb, and is the cause of his awakening. All this means that, while the vision must be sufficiently worked up to convince the reader of its truth and importance, it must not lead to an emotional climax which would destroy the pattern of the closing sections of the poem. If we examine the description in detail we shall see how this delicate balance was achieved, not by any comment on the poet's part—any explicit leading of his reader— but through the ordering of the material itself.

After his reaction to the blaze of sunlight which illuminates the wood, the Dreamer interposes between his direct experience of what he sees and his audience the figure of the apostle John, with a persistence which, in spite of the repeated 'I saws', gives the description the effect of a second-hand report. Stanza 82 ends, and each succeeding stanza up to stanza 86 both begins and ends, with a reference to the source: 'As John þe apostel hit syȝ wyth syȝt . . . As derely deuyseȝ þis ilk toun / In Apocalyppeȝ þe apostel John'; 'As John þise stoneȝ in writ con nemne . . . he con hit wale / In þe Apocalyppce, þe apostel John', and so on, to make one of the most elaborately end- and beginning-linked sets of stanzas in the poem.

The source, moreover, is followed closely as far as the content and details of the description are concerned. There are changes in order and organization, but there is little or no additional detail, and no attempt either to make a fuller appeal to the senses, or to exploit the symbolical possibilities of the material in the manner of the numerous commentaries.[2] The result of

[2] It is difficult to be sure whether the poet used a commentary on the Apocalypse. Most of the details which he could have got from one could also have been taken from a lapidary or encyclopedia. (See Gordon's notes to ll. 1007, 1012, 1015 for details.) He must, however, have known and used some exegetical work. His introduction of the

this illusion of reported speech and of close dependence on a familiar biblical text, while it certainly does nothing to diminish the magnificence of a splendid passage, is to present it at a distance—almost as a lesson read in church, a retelling, recognizably at some remove, of an impressive and meaningful story. This, as well as greatly decreasing the immediacy of the Dreamer's experience, helps to bring about the *dimminuendo* of the ending, and also to make effective the sudden shift of focus from the glories of the City and of the Lamb to the Dreamer's personal feeling for the Maiden, and the sudden uprush of unregenerate emotion which brings the dream to an end.

The impression of close dependence on the source throughout the description of the New Jerusalem is so great that it comes as a surprise when closer examination shows how much re-ordering of the material actually takes place. As it stands in the Apocalypse the order of presentation does not suit the poet's usual way of handling visual description in accordance with the natural passage of the eye over the scene. Some details, too, are inappropriate to this theme, others need more emphasis to make their effect. For the description of the City given in sections xvii and xviii, the poet draws on chapter 21 of the Apocalypse. We have already noticed his first major change. Where Rev. 21, 11 compares the light of the city to 'a precious stone', he compares it to the sun with its beams. This, as we have said, enables him to link the vision to the landscape into which it descends, and to keep before the reader the theme of sun and moon.

Other changes, this time by omission, alter the character of the vision so as to fit it better for its new context. There is no reference in *Pearl* to the City as the Bride of Christ—as, for example, in 21, 2:

---

rybé for the sardius of his source, proves, as Gordon points out, that he related this passage to Exod. xxviii, 17, the description of the High Priest's ephod—from which he also takes the detail of the names of the children of Israel in the order of their birth. Further, he is aware of the exegetical tradition which alters the sex of the Virgins of Revelations, and that which includes the innocents among them (see further, Gordon, note to l. 869). Again, though he makes little use of possible symbolical interpretations of the City, he does know of etymological speculations concerning its name (see Gordon, note to ll. 950–2).

The Heavenly City

And I, John, saw the holy city, the New Jerusalem, coming
down out of heaven from God, prepared as a bride adorned for
her husband,

and again, at the beginning of the passage on which the *Pearl*
draws most heavily:

Come, and I will show thee the bride, the wife of the Lamb.
(21, 9)

The reason for this change is obvious. It is the Virgin company,
described in terms of the moon, who are the brides of the sun-
like Lamb, and the marriage itself is treated in terms of this
symbolism.[3] The effect, however, is, necessarily, to reduce the
symbolical content of the vision itself at this point; and it is in
keeping with the poet's refusal to exploit the possibilities for
detailed symbolical meaning in the whole passage on the
jewels. Also in keeping with this change, is the omission of any
reference to the very beautiful passages in the original which
justify the conception, put into the mouth of the Maiden earlier,
of the City as 'syȝt of pes'. A verse like 21, 4:

Et absterget Deus omnem lacrimam ab oculis eorum, et mors
ultra non erit, neque luctus neque clamor neque dolor erit ultra,
quia prima abierunt.

(And God shall wipe away all tears from their eyes; and death
shall be no more; nor mourning, nor crying, nor sorrow shall be
any more; for the former things are passed away,)

would be inappropriate in *Pearl*, where the vision is, in fact,
interrupted by the return of sorrow, and by the Dreamer's
failure to find peace in it. On the other hand, the poet could
justifiably assume that his reader's familiarity with the passage
would remind him of the main theme of a consolation always at
hand, and only kept from the sufferer by a will at odds with
reason.

The second stanza of section xvii gives a general view of the
City and its most important parts, in which each detail corresponds exactly to the source, but in which all are reorganized

[3] Lines 785–92 equate the Bride with the Virgin host, not with the
City. This change is made without comment, and with the usual
appeal to the authority of the Apostle John.

into a single coherent picture. First comes the City as a whole, with the emphasis on its salient characteristic, its golden brightness:

> I syȝe þat cyty of gret renoun,
> Jerusalem so nwe and ryally dyȝt,
> As hit was lyȝt fro þe heuen adoun.
> Þe borȝ watȝ al of brende golde bryȝt
> As glemande glas burnist broun . . .   (986–90)

This, by bringing together details from Rev. 21, 1–2, 10, and 21, gives the first impression of the onlooker. Next come the first details to strike him. His eyes focus first on the lowest point: the city is 'Wyth gentyl gemmeȝ an-vnder pyȝt' (991). This was the method used in the description of the castle in *Sir Gawain*. There, after the first general view, Gawain's eye passes to the lowest point where:

> Þe walle wod in þe water wonderly depe.   (787)

From here it travels upwards so as to get a comprehensive picture of the whole, following the wall as 'eft a ful huge heȝt hit haled vp on lofte' (788). The same movement from lowest to highest point is, I think, followed out in *Pearl*. After mentioning the foundation gems the poet says that the City is

> Wyth banteleȝ twelue on basyng boun.

If, as I think, the *banteleȝ* are the highest parts of the fortification—the projecting outworks, which bible illustrators often gave to the walls of the city,[4] then the first general impression is

---

[4] W. W. Skeat's explanation of *banteleȝ* as 'outworks'—i.e. three-cornered projections from the main battlements, standing higher than the rest of the fortification, seems to me to be etymologically more convincing than their identification with the *fundamenta duodecim* of Rev. 21, 14 (see *Transactions of the Philological Society* (1905–6), pp. 359 f.; for the alternative view, see C. T. Onions, *M. Aev.* II, 184 f., and Gordon, p. 78, note to l. 992). It is true that there is no mention of towers of any kind in the description of the City in the Apocalypse, but a fourteenth-century writer who was familiar with the work of its illustrators would not hesitate to bring them in. For good examples, see plates 55b (Trinity College, Cambridge, MS. R. 16. 2) and 59b (Eton College MS. 177), in *English Art 1216–1307*, by Peter Brieger. These plates show the position of the projecting

followed, as in *Sir Gawain*, by an overall view, working from bottom to top, leading to a concentration on details—in the case of *Pearl* on the most striking and important part of the description as it stands in the Bible, that of the jewel-foundations.

For the foundations the poet combines 21, 14, and 19. In the detailed description he follows the order of Revelations, since there is no reason to alter it, using verses 18, 19, and 20 in the order in which they stand. Verses 19 and 20 are expanded over two stanzas to provide an impressive set-piece. The jewels need this emphasis, partly because they carry out the theme of treasure, and partly because they balance earlier passages of elaborate description. The arrangement is a simple one: six jewels are given to each stanza (the division between the two verses in Revelations of four and eight does not suit the poet's feeling for symmetry) and each is fitted into one or more lines by the addition of suitable descriptive phrases. These sometimes add to the visual effect, though never in an especially striking way. Of the jasper, for example, it is said that 'He glente grene' (1001); of the emerald that it is 'so grene of scale' (1005). The beryl is 'cler and quyt' (1011); the amethyst is 'purpre wyth ynde blente' (1016). Sometimes the addition merely indicates the number and position of the gem: 'Saffer helde þe secounde stale' (1002); 'þe sardonyse þe fyfþe ston' (1006). At times epithets seem to be carelessly applied. For example, in l. 1014, the jacynth is 'þe enleuenþe gent', while in the next line the amethyst is 'þe gentyleste in vch a plyt'. This refers, no doubt to the 'virtue' of the amethyst—one of the poet's few excursions into lapidary lore—but it is weakened by the repetition. Again, the comparison to the brightness of glass loses force on its third appearance in thirty-five lines (ll. 990, 1018, 1025). Necessary as an effective set piece is to the plan of the poem, it does not, in fact, seem to engage the poet's concentrated attention; and he seems to depend on his reader's reaction to the general effect, and to recognition of a familiar context, rather than on his usual technical skill.

---

turrets in an overall view of the city. The illustration in MS. Cotton Nero A, x, shows, as well as a kind of hall inside the walls, a tower projecting above the battlements. It appears, however, to be inside them.

After the jewel description the focus shifts from the foundations to the wall of the City—once again, I think, causing the
eye to travel from the bottom, the foundations, to the *banteleȝ*
as the topmost point:

> Þe wal abof þe bantels bent
> O jasporye, as glas þat glysnande schon;
> I knew hit by his deuysement
> In þe Apocalyppeȝ, þe apostel John.   (1017–20)

The next stanza gives another general view of the City, repeating yet again the movement from bottom to top. The purpose
this time is to introduce the measurements of the source, so that
the emphasis is on the three-dimensional shape rather than on
the façade:

> As John deuysed ȝet saȝ I þare:
> Þise twelue degres wern brode and stayre;
> Þe cité stod abof ful sware,
> As longe as brode as hyȝe ful fayre.   (1021–4)

This corresponds to Rev. 21, 16, but before giving us the
actual measurements contained in this verse, the poet allows
our eyes to stray inward, to the streets and houses which lie
within the wall:

> Þe streteȝ of golde as glasse al bare,
> Þe wal of jasper þat glente as glayre;
> Þe woneȝ wythinne enurned ware
> Wyth alle kynneȝ perré þat moȝt repayre.   (1025–8)

The streets are from Rev. 21, 21, but the houses of precious
stones are the poet's own addition. They provide an answer to
the Dreamer's question 'Haf ȝe no woneȝ in castel-walle?'
(917), and they are described in the conventional manner of the
many mansions of Paradise.[5] The last four lines of the stanza

[5] Heavenly mansions shining with precious stones are mentioned in
Arabic eschatological sources (see M. Manzalaoui, 'English Analogues
to the *Liber Scalae*', *M. Aev.*, XXXIV, pp. 27–8). There is no need,
however, to go beyond the main stream of homiletic tradition. Aelfric,
for example, wrote of 'scinende gebytlu mid wistum afyllede, and
mid ecum leohte' prepared for the blessed in heaven (*Homily on the
Assumption of St. John*).

give the measurements of the City, with the curious alteration of twelve thousand furlongs to only twelve:[6]

> Þenne helde vch sware of þis manayre
> Twelue forlonge space, er euer hit fon,
> Of heȝt, of brede, of lenþe to cayre,
> For meten hit syȝ þe apostel John.   (1029–32)

Finally, the description is completed by a paraphrase of Rev. 21, 21, combined with 21, 12, on the gates. These two verses, which contain the reference to the twelve tribes of Israel and to the twelve pearls, are welded together in a single stanza:

> As John hym wryteȝ ȝet more I syȝe:
> Vch pane of þat place had þre ȝateȝ;
> So twelue in poursent I con asspye,
> Þe portaleȝ pyked of rych plateȝ,
> And vch ȝate of a margyrye,
> A parfyt perle þat neuer fateȝ.
> Vchon in scrypture a name con plye
> Of Israel barneȝ, folewande her dateȝ,
> Þat is to say, as her byrþ-whateȝ:
> Þe aldest ay fyrst þeron watȝ done.   (1033–42)

The detail that the names of the children of Israel were given in the order of their birth does not come from Revelations. It is taken from the description of the jewels on the High Priest's ephod in Exodus xxviii, and shows, once again, the complex way in which the poet handles his source.[7] The whole passage, in fact, with its apparently rigid dependence on the frequently named original, proves to be very carefully organized to meet the poet's needs, and to fit the descriptive technique which he prefers.

[6] It is, again, possible that the alteration indicates use of a commentary (see Gordon, p. 81, note to l. 1029).

[7] Here, too, the poet may have found the two passages already brought together in a commentary (see Gordon, pp. 79–80, note to l. 1007, for details).

The Revelation

3

In section xviii, with its sun and moon refrain, and its concentration on the following of the Lamb, there is none of the carelessness of phrasing, or the dependence on the effectiveness of familiar material, which we found in the section before. The Apocalypse is still closely followed, but, after the first line of xviii which, according to custom links back to the section before, direct reference to the source is dropped, apart from a single reminder in l. 1053, and the figure of the Dreamer is given much greater prominence. He becomes, in fact, the immediate and only authority for the experience he describes.

At first the Apocalypse is followed in due order. After the description of the gates of pearl, the Lamb is described as the Lantern of Heaven (Rev. 21, 23), and as its Temple, (Rev. 21, 22). The river which flows from the throne of God is woven through the passage in a way which gives it greater prominence, and helps to balance the earlier description of the river of the Earthly Paradise. It is given the end of stanza 88, the beginning of 89, and the end of 90—in between comes the expanded description of the heavenly light. Stanza 91 has no counterpart in Revelations, and is entirely devoted to the Dreamer's feelings. The treatment of the source thus becomes more and more free as the section advances. The details taken from it, too, are all skilfully orientated towards the idea of the sun and moon, so that the half-verse (Rev. 21, 23), 'And the city hath no need of the sun, nor of the moon to shine upon it', comes to dominate the whole passage, and prepares for the climax in which the Virgin Host and the Lamb are brought together at the beginning of the next section. To appreciate how all this is done the passage must be read as a whole:

Such lyȝt þer lemed in alle þe strateȝ
Hem nedde nawþer sunne ne mone.

Of sunne ne mone had þay no nede;
Þe self God watȝ her lombe-lyȝt,
Þe Lombe her lantyrne, wythouten drede;
Þurȝ hym blysned þe borȝ al bryȝt.

The Heavenly City

Þurȝ woȝe and won my lokyng ȝede,
For sotyle cler noȝt lette no lyȝt.
Þe hyȝe trone þer moȝt ȝe hede
Wyth alle þe apparaylmente vmbepyȝte,
As John þe appostel in termeȝ tyȝte;
Þe hyȝe Godeȝ self hit set vpone.
A reuer of þe trone þer ran outryȝte
Watȝ bryȝter þen boþe þe sunne and mone.

Sunne ne mone schon neuer so swete
As þat foysoun flode out of þat flet;
Swyþe hit swange þurȝ vch a strete
Wythouten fylþe oþer galle oþer glet.
Kyrk þerinne watȝ non ȝete,
Chapel ne temple þat euer watȝ set;
Þe Almyȝty watȝ her mynster mete,
Þe Lombe her sakerfyse þer to refet.
Þe ȝateȝ stoken watȝ neuer ȝet,
Bot euermore vpen at vche a lone;
Þer entreȝ non to take reset
Þat bereȝ any spot an-vnder mone.

Þe mone may þerof acroche no myȝte;
To spotty ho is, of body to grym,
And also þer ne is neuer nyȝt.
What schulde þe mone þer compas clym
And to euen wyth þat worþly lyȝt
Þat schyneȝ vpon þe brokeȝ brym?
Þe planeteȝ arn in to pouer a plyȝt,
And þe self sunne ful fer to dym.
Aboute þat water arn tres ful schym,
Þat twelue fryteȝ of lyf con bere ful sone;
Twelue syþeȝ on ȝer þay beren ful frym,
And renowleȝ nwe in vche a mone.

An-vnder mone so great merwayle
No fleschly hert ne myȝt endeure,
As quen I blusched vpon þat bayle,
So ferly þerof watȝ þe fasure.
I stod as stylle as dased quayle
For ferly of þat frelich fygure,
Þat felde I nawþer reste ne trauayle,
So watȝ I rauyste wyth glymme pure.

For I dare say wyth conciens sure,
Hade bodyly burne abiden þat bone,
Þaȝ alle clerkeȝ hym hade in cure,
His lyf were loste an-vnder mone.   (1043–92)

The last stanza is the fullest expression in the poem of the visionary ecstacy, and even here we are set curiously at a distance from the figure of the Dreamer by the introduction in the last lines of a hypothetical 'bodyly burne' to share his experience.

Section xix develops and prolongs the ecstatic mood, and elaborates the symbolism of the marriage of sun and moon. The link-phrase is 'gret delyt', and words for joy and delight are repeated again and again within the stanzas. 'Blysful' is used both of the Maiden and of the symbolical pearl in ll. 1100 and 1104. In stanza 93 it is 'tor to knaw þe gladdest chere', and in stanza 94:

Þen glory and gle watȝ nwe abroched;
Al songe to loue þat gay juelle.
Þe steuen moȝt stryke þurȝ þe vrþe to helle
Þat þe Vertues of heuen of ioye endyte.   (1123–6)

Of the Lamb it is said:

Best watȝ he, blyþest, and moste to pryse,   (1131)

and:

So wern his glenteȝ gloryous glade.   (1144)

Between these two lines, however, comes the description of His wound, and this is utilized to fix our attention once more on the Dreamer and his feelings towards the Lamb, which are those of earth, not of heaven:

Bot a wounde ful wyde and weete con wyse
Anende hys hert, þurȝ hyde torente.
Of his quyte syde his blod outsprent.
Alas, þoȝt I, who did þat spyt?
Ani breste for bale aȝt haf forbrent
Er he þerto hade had delyt.   (1135–40)

The Lamb is not here described in apocalyptic terms, but, in keeping with the sensibility of the poet's own day, 'His lokeȝ

symple, hymself so gent' (1134). It is doubtful if he would have
been aware of the change. Visual art and homiletic and exegetical treatment had all tended to reduce the more terrifying
elements in the divine figures of the Revelation of John.

The Dreamer's eyes, however, soon leave the Lamb, to focus
on his following, and then on one particular figure—and it is
then, rather than at what would have been, from a mystic's
point of view, the supreme moment of the vision, that the
emotional climax is reached:

> I loked among his meyny schene
> How þay wyth lyf wern laste and lade;
> Þen saȝ I þer my lyttel quene
> Þat I wende had standen by me in sclade.
> Lorde, much of mirþe watȝ þat ho made
> Among her fereȝ þat watȝ so quyt!
> Þat syȝt me gart to þenk to wade
> For luf-longyng in gret delyt.   (1145–52)

This has been well prepared through the establishment of the
difference between the feelings and experience of the Dreamer,
and those of the heavenly host. The effect is now reinforced by
a certain colloquial tone—the affectionate 'lyttel quene', the
exclamation 'Lorde!' which sets us effectively at a distance from
the splendours of the heavenly assembly. There has, too, been
a gradual change in tempo in this section, which is indicative of
a rapidly changing mood, and of a work hastening to an inevitable conclusion. This is achieved by the sense of sweeping,
purposeful movement as the procession comes into view, and
by the repeated use of words for sudden, vigorous action.
Moon and sun 'con rys', and 'dryue al doun' in the first stanza:
the procession 'glod in fere' headed by the advancing Lamb who
'byfore con proudly passe'. Even verbs used figuratively have a
sense of motion—*encroched* in l. 1117, and *abroched*, l. 1123,
imply movement towards and away from something. And when
the united voice of heaven is heard, it, too, is described in terms
of movement:

> Þe steuen moȝt stryke þurȝ þe vrþe to helle.   (1125)

The Revelation

The description of the Lamb in stanza 95 provides a focal point for all this activity, and brings the movement of heaven to rest. But at the end of the section the dominant idea of motion is transferred to the Dreamer, and indicates his human inability to forget his loss, or to share in the tranquillity of the Heavenly Host—'þat syȝt me gart to þenk to wade'—and it is through this impulsive start into an activity which runs, as it were, counter to the heavenly pattern, that his awakening is brought about.

A section which was introduced by a transition passage built on the movement of the two main figures is thus ended in the same way. As the Dreamer's eyes focus on the figure of the Maiden—suddenly removed from his side and placed at an unattainable distance among the Lamb's following—his mood of hopeless longing returns, and with it a final attempt to disregard God's laws and to try to regain what he has lost:

> Delyt me drof in yȝe and ere,
> My maneȝ mynde to maddyng malte;
> Quen I seȝ my frely, I wolde be þere,
> Byȝonde þe water þaȝ ho were walte . . .
> Bot of þat munt I watȝ bitalt;
> When I schulde start in þe strem astraye,
> Out of þat caste I watȝ bycalt:
> Hit watȝ not at my Princeȝ paye.   (1153–6, 1161–4)

The phrasing recalls the rebellious mood of the beginning of the poem. 'My maneȝ mynde to maddyng malte', echoes the Maiden's reproofs: 'Me þynk þe put in a made porpose' (267); 'Wy borde ȝe men? So madde ȝe be!' (290). This brief return to the Dreamer's former mood ends his vision. He wakes to regret and repentance, and to a resignation which seems curiously partial:

> Þerfore my ioye watȝ sone toriuen,
> And I kaste of kytheȝ þat lasteȝ aye.
> Lorde, mad hit arn pat agayn þe stryuen,
> Oþer proferen þe oȝt agayn þy paye.   (1197–1200)

In this transition passage, as well as in the one which begins the section, it is once more tempting to compare a passage in the *Divina Commedia*. In the *Paradiso* Dante uses a similar pattern, though a different mood, to help to bring his vision to its end. In canto xxxi he contemplates the Rose of Paradise:

> La forma general di paradiso
> già tutta mïo sguardo avea compresa,
> in nulla parte ancor fermato fiso.

> (The general form of Paradise my sight
> Had apprehended in its ambience,
> But upon no part had it rested quite.   (xxxi, 52–4))

From this general view he turns back to Beatrice; to find that she has vanished from his side:

> credea vider Beatrice, e vidi un sene
> vestito con le genti glorïose.

> (I thought to have seen Beatrice, and behold!
> An elder, robed like to those glorified.   (xxxi, 59–60))

His new guide, St. Bernard, reassures him and points her out:

> . . . 'A terminar lo tuo disiro
> mosse Beatrice me del loco mio:
> e se riguardi su nel terzo giro
> dal sommo grado, tu la rivedrai
> nel trono che suoi merti le sortiro.'
> Sanza risponder, li occhi su levai,
> e vidi lei che si facea corona
> reflettendo da sè li etterni rai.

> ('To end thy longing, Beatrice was stirred,'
> He answered then, 'to bring me from my place.
> Her shalt thou see, if to the circle third
> From the highest rank thine eyes thou wilt up-raise.
> There on the throne whereto she hath been preferred.'
> Without reply, I lifted up my gaze
> And saw her making for herself a crown
> Of the reflection from the eternal rays.   (xxxi, 65–72))

Beatrice, 'sorrise e riguardommi' (92). The Pearl Maiden, is described in more familiar terms: 'Lorde, much of mirþe watȝ þat ho made.' Beatrice, in a magnificent image, plays the part of moon to the divine sun: she makes her crown from its reflected

223

rays. The Pearl-Maiden is one of the moon-like procession of Virgin Brides.

If the poet of *Pearl* did utilize the Italian poem here, once again, what strikes us most is the perfect adaptation of the material to the needs of his own work. What is sublime in the *Divina Commedia* is given a much more familiar tone; and the pattern which Dante uses to lead up to a triumphant climax is made a part of the downward curve with which the *Pearl* ends.

Part Four

CODA

THE POET OF *Pearl* used a single section of five stanzas to introduce his poem and to establish its themes. In the same way, his
final summing up, and his withdrawal from his dream and his
Dreamer, are contained in the last set of five stanzas. This whole
section is closely associated with the opening one, since the
words of the poem's first line 'to prynces paye' provide the link
phrases, while the last line 'Ande precious perleʒ vnto his pay' is
especially close to the first, 'Perle, plesaunte to prynces paye.'
Apart from these obvious echo-links, there are many reminders
of earlier passages within the stanzas—in fact, the method of the
coda is to recall the most important aspects of what has gone before, and to indicate the poet's final, unambiguous verdict on it.

In the first two stanzas the Dreamer's mood of rebellious
excitement is brought to its climax. This is expressed in terms of
the restless movement which we noticed as one of the main
themes of the previous section. The Dreamer describes his impulsive actions in words which recall the Maiden's earlier re-
bukes and warnings:

> Delyt me drof in yʒe and ere,
> My maneʒ mynde to maddyng malte;
> Quen I seʒ my frely, I wolde be þere,
> Byʒonde þe water þaʒ ho were walte.
> I þoʒt þat noþyng myʒt me dere
> To fech me bur and take me halte,
> And to start in þe strem schulde non me stere,
> To swymme þe remnaunt, þaʒ I þer swalte.
> Bot of þat munt I watʒ bitalt;
> When I schulde start in þe strem astraye,
> Out of þat caste I watʒ bycalt:
> Hit watʒ not at my Prynceʒ paye.
>
> Hit payed hym not þat I so flonc
> Ouer meruelous mereʒ, so mad arayde.
> Of raas þaʒ I were rasch and ronk,
> ʒet rapely þerinne I watʒ restayed.

> For, ry3t as I sparred vnto þe bonc,
> Þat brathþe out of my drem me brayde.
> Þen wakned I in þat erber wlonk;
> My hede vpon þat hylle wat3 layde
> Þer as my perle to grounde strayd.
> I raxled, and fel in gret affray,
> And, sykyng, to myself I sayd,
> 'Now al be to þat Prynce3 paye.' (1153–76)

Apart from the verbal echoes in 'my mane3 mynde to maddyng malte'; 'so mad arayde', which have already been pointed out, the whole passage recalls the Maiden's earlier prediction:

> 'Who nede3 schal þole, be not so pro.
> For þo3 þou daunce as any do,
> Braundysch and bray þy braþe3 breme,
> When þou no fyrre may, to ne fro,
> Þou moste abyde þat he schal deme.' (344–8)

The Dreamer, whom no words nor sights could convince, is now brought into precisely this position, where the force of circumstances compels him at last to acknowledge the truth. He is, at the same time, returned to the garden in which he first heard, but failed to attend to, the voice of reason.

The next stanza still gives expression to the Dreamer's grief and disappointment; but the note of resignation sounded in the refrain phrase, which at least acknowledged the importance of God's will, is somewhat deepened:

> Me payed ful ille to be outfleme
> So sodenly of þat fayre regioun,
> Fro alle þo sy3te3 so quyke and queme.
> A longeyng heuy me strok in swone,
> And rewfully þenne I con to reme:
> 'O perle,' quod I, 'of rych renoun,
> So wat3 hit me dere þat þou con deme
> In þis veray avysyoun!
> If hit be ueray and soth sermoun
> Þat þou so styke3 in garlande gay,
> So wel is me in þys doel-doungoun
> Þat þou art to þat Prynse3 paye.' (1177–88)

Coda

This description of violent, explosive physical action running parallel to a deep emotional disturbance on the part of the main character has effectively broken the thread of the narrative, and prepares us for the final twist which brings the conclusion. As we have said, *Pearl* is not a poem which builds up to a triumphal climax, but one which ends with the failure—the partial failure at least—of the main character to achieve what he sets out to do. By a final alteration of focus, however, even this is not seen as the last word: the poet disengages himself, as it were, from the Dreamer-figure and sets him at a distance—a process which enables us to take a more comprehensive view of his problem and to see where its true solution lies. The same technique is used for a very similar purpose in *Sir Gawain and the Green Knight*. This poem, like *Pearl*, does not end in triumph for the main character, but in a disillusionment and disappointment which leave the hero a wiser but sadder man. This twist in the plot is achieved much as it is in *Pearl*. There is the same explosion into violent action caused by sudden, overwhelming joy (Delyt me drof in y3e and ere), which quickly turns to another emotion when it is seen to be founded on a mistake. Gawain first realizes that he has fulfilled his promise, received the return blow from the Green Knight, and yet lives:

> And quen þe burne se3 þe blode blenk on þe snawe,
> He sprit forth spenne-fote more þen a spere lenþe,
> Hent heterly his helme, and on his hed cast,
> Schot with his schulder3 his fayre schelde vnder,
> Brayde3 out a bry3t sworde, and bremely he speke3—
> Neuer syn þat he wat3 burne borne of his moder
> Wat3 he neuer in þis worlde wy3e half so blyþe! (2315–21)

The Green Knight's words, however, show him that his whole view of himself and his situation has been a mistaken one, and his mood changes from joyful relief to an emotion which is vividly described:

> Þat oþer stif mon in study stod a gret whyle,
> So agreued for greme he gryed withinne;
> Alle þe blode of his brest blende in his face,
> Þat al he schrank for schome þat þe schalk talked. (2369–72)

Coda

Like the Dreamer of *Pearl*, Gawain blames past faults for present misery:

> 'Corsed worth cowarddyse and couetyse boþe!'   (2374)

In neither poem is the matter left here, with only the comments and reactions of the character concerned. In *Pearl* the author steps in and speaks in *propria persona*. In *Sir Gawain*, we are made to see Gawain's fault and his reaction to it in a different focus when he returns to the court and is among friends who take a more balanced view of his case. If evidence for common authorship was still needed, similarity of this kind, affecting narrative structure and the pattern in accordance with which an incident is worked out, would be more convincing than any similarities of diction.

After stanza 99 the Dreamer does not speak again in the person we have come to identify with him: the narrative 'I' is still kept, but it is used to give explanation and comment which could not come convincingly from one whose 'wreched wylle in wo ay wraȝte'. There is no indication that the solution to the moral problem of the opening is conceived in terms of the complete conversion of the Dreamer: he has stood so consistently as 'Will', and his reaction at every crisis of the poem has been so turbulent, that such a conversion would fail to satisfy. The poet therefore speaks, as the maker of a poem in which he has been giving expression to an aspect of himself through the Dreamer-mask, but from a standpoint undisturbed by the emotional involvement of this other self. In stanza 100 he defines this figure's failure. He has only thought in terms of personal loss and gain, not of God's plan and purpose for mankind, and has, therefore, failed to penetrate His mysteries. Even the vision of the Heavenly City has only brought his personal, earthly relationship to the Maiden more poignantly before him:

> To þat Prynceȝ paye hade I ay bente,
> And ȝerned no more þen watȝ me gyuen,
> And halden me per in trwe entent,
> As þe perle me prayed þat watȝ so þryuen,
> As helde, drawen to Goddeȝ present,
> To mo of his mysterys I hade ben dryuen;

Coda

Bot ay wolde man of happe more hente
Þen moȝte by ryȝt vpon hem clyuen,
Þerfore my ioye watȝ sone toriuen,
And I kaste of kytheȝ þat lasteȝ aye.
Lorde, mad hit arn þat agayn þe stryuen,
Oþer proferen þe oȝt agayn þy paye. (1189–1200)

Failure is defined through a return to the idea of 'ryȝt'—here both 'justice' and 'reason'—and also to the idea of less and more: by trying to grasp a 'more' to which he was not entitled by divine law and reason, the Dreamer has gained a 'less'. His attempt to enjoy once more what was most transitory and most selfish in his relationship with the Maiden has meant the loss of what could have made this relationship most permanent and valuable.

The final stanza explains these ideas in an even clearer way. First comes an uncompromising statement of the relationship with God which should form the basis of the Christian life:

To pay þe Prince oþer sete saȝte
Hit is ful eþe to þe god Krystyin;
For I haf founden hym, boþe day and naȝte,
A God, a Lorde, a frende ful fyin. (1201–4)

This simple, direct statement, in a sense repudiates the elaborate machinery of the Dream. *Veray avysyoun* as it was, there is no need for a special dispensation; a more direct form of consolation is at hand—and, indeed, was available in the beginning, in the garden. By this means the poet refocuses attention on the basic moral problem—that of the individual will in conflict with reason, and strips it once more, of the colourful devices with which he had surrounded it. These lines, too, eliminate the Dreamer's rebelliousness: the compulsion of 'Lorde, mad hit arn þat agayn þe stryuen', becomes a free submission in a treaty of peace (*sete saȝte*). This implies the consent of both parties, and it is, moreover, a treaty made with a friend, as well as with an all-powerful lord. This, finally, is the fortune (*lote*), which is gained in the garden, and through it, rebellious grief is changed to a gentler emotion—that of pity:

Ouer þis huyl þis lote I laȝte,
For pyty of my perle enclyin. (1205–6)

Coda

In this changed mood the pearl is entrusted to God, on whose redeeming sacrifice, figured forth daily in the mass, all hope of immortal blessedness depends:

> And syþen to God I hit bytaȝte,
> In Krysteȝ dere blessyng and myn,
> Þat in þe forme of bred and wyn
> Þe preste vus scheweȝ vch a daye.   (1207–10)

These lines give the logical basis for consolation in earthly loss, but they also increase the impression, which has been growing since the closing lines of the stanza before, of withdrawal from the Dreamer, and his special problems and failures, and of a shift from the exceptional experience of his dream to the firm foundations of the Christian faith which is the same in all circumstances for all men. The final prayer completes this process:

> He gef vus to be his homly hyne
> Ande precious perleȝ vnto his pay.   (1211–12)

The final reference to pearls has, as we have seen, the whole development of the symbolism of the poem behind it. The unusual phrase 'homly hyne', is, I believe, intended to recall words used by St. Paul in Gal. 6, 10, where he speaks of the 'domesticos fidei'. This is rendered 'those who are of the household of the faith' by the Douay and Authorized Versions, but Wycliffe translated it 'hem þat ben homliche of þe feith'. Verses 7 and 8 of the same chapter are especially appropriate to the theme of *Pearl*, and it seems likely that the poet intended his reminiscence of verse 10 to carry its context with it, and so to provide a final comment on his theme:

Nolite errare: Deus non irridetur. Quae enim seminaverit homo, haec et metet. Quoniam qui seminat in carne sua de carne et metet corruptionem; qui autem seminat in spiritu, de spiritu metet vitam aeternam.

(Be not deceived; God is not mocked. For what things a man shall sow, that also shall he reap. For he that soweth in his flesh of the flesh also shall reap corruption. But he that soweth in the spirit of the spirit shall reap life everlasting.)

232

Coda

In the coda, as I believe, it is the author who speaks the final word, through which the Dreamer's errors are defined and repudiated. But, if this is so, it will be necessary to define as closely as possible, just what the poet feels to be wrong in his Dreamer's attitude. It would, I think, be to introduce a false, and indeed, absurd emphasis if we were to suggest that the poet denies the validity of either love for a fellow human being or grief at their loss, or that he sees any virtue in submission to the proposition that death is inevitable and therefore grief is useless. The poet would hardly have found a good subject for a poem in the philosophical coolness of Sarah Gamp: 'He was born into a wale, and he lived in a wale; and he must take the consequences of such a sitiwation.' I think that the poet does, in fact, have more precise views about his Dreamer's situation.

At no time, in fact, does he state that grief is in itself wrong. He does say, in the proem, that the violence of the Dreamer's emotions have involved his will in a conflict, which makes it impossible for him to hear the voices of Reason, and of Nature, whose message comes from Christ.[1] He also implies, through the Maiden, that the Dreamer mourns for the wrong reasons.

It would, certainly, be difficult to find authority in the Middle Ages for the view that grief was in itself a sin. But its dangers were often, and authoritatively pointed out. St. Gregory the Great wrote of his personal distress at the deaths caused by the great pestilence at Carthage, and said:

Quia vero infirmitatis nostrae natura est ut non possimus de obeuntibus non dolere.

(The nature of our infirmity is such that we cannot but grieve for those who pass away.)

[1] For the meaning of the phrase *kynde of Kryst*, see above, p. 41. The Dreamer's sin has been discussed by Sister M. V. Hillman, 'Some Debatable Points in *Pearl* and its Theme', *M.L.N.* (1945), pp. 241 ff.; by S. de Voren Hoffman, 'The *Pearl*, Notes for an Interpretation', *M.P.* (1960), pp. 73 ff.; and by M. R. Stern, 'An Approach to *Pearl*,' *J.E.G.Ph.* (1955), pp. 686–7.

He is emphatic, however, in advising patience and submission to the will of God,

> ut tantae nobis percussionis favente eius gratia, non damnationis initium, sed beneficium purgationis existant.

> (so that such great smitings may be to us, by the favour of His grace, not the beginning of damnation, but a purgation for our good.[2])

St. Bernard, in the sermon on the death of his brother which interrupts the sequence of the *Sermons on the Song of Songs*, examined the case for and against those who mourn for the dead even more searchingly, but he is as clear as St. Gregory on the main issue. To feel grief is the inevitable lot of humankind. Sin enters in when it involves the mourner in rebellion against the divine will: 'Numquid quia sentio poenam, reprehendo sententiam? Humanum est illud, hoc impium' (To feel God's punishment is not to rebel against his decree. Grief is human, rebellion is impious.[3]) Earlier in the same homily he wrote, in words which could stand as a commentary on *Pearl*, of mourning for wrong reasons, of 'the dead lamenting their dead':

> Non culpamus affectum, nisi cum excedit modum; sed causam. Ille nimirum naturae est, et eius turbatio poena peccati: haec vanitas et peccatum. Etenim ibi sola (nisi fallor) plorantur damna gloriae carnis vitae praesentis incommoda. Et plorandi qui ita plorant.

> (We do not blame affection, unless it goes beyond measure, but we blame the cause of such grief. Truly, grief itself is natural, but the torment to which it gives rise is a penalty of sin, its cause, in such a case, vanity and sin. Indeed, unless I am much mistaken, they weep for the loss of the comforts of the flesh, and of the amenities of this present life. Those who weep thus deserve to be wept for themselves.[4]

Just so the Dreamer laments his *own* pearl,

> Þat wont watȝ whyle deuoyde my wrange
> And heuen my happe and al my hele.   (15–16)

[2] *Reg. Epist.*, XI, lxiii (*P.L.*, 77, 1115–16).
[3] *Sermones in Cantica*, xxvi, 10 (*P.L.*, 183, 910A).
[4] Ibid., 8, 909B.

Coda

This self-willed possessiveness is repudiated in the coda when the pearl is finally left 'In Kryste₃ dere blessyng and myn'. The idea of recovering the personal possession of the pearl, as it was once enjoyed on earth is set aside, but the words suggest a more permanent relationship in which it is shared with God. St. Bernard expresses a haunting doubt as to whether a blessed soul in heaven could still be aware of human love, or whether human relationships might not be utterly dissolved and lost in the contemplation of the God-head:

> Forte enim, etsi nosti nos secundum carnem, sed nunc iam non nosti: et quoniam introisti in potentias Domini memoraris iustitiae eius solius, immemor nostri.

> (Perhaps, although you knew us in the flesh, now you know us no more, and because you have entered into the glory of the Lord, you are mindful only of his justice, and have no further memory of us.[5])

Such doubts are quickly answered:

> Deus autem charitas est, et quanto quis conjunctior Deo, tanto plenior charitate. Porro impassibilis est Deus, sed non imcompassibilis, cui proprium est misereri semper et parcere. Ergo et te necesse est misericordem esse, qui inhaeres misericordi, quamvis iam minime miser sis: et qui non pateris, compateris tamen. Affectus proinde tuus non est imminutus, sed immutatus; nec quoniam Deum induisti, nostri cura te exuisti: et ipsi enim cura est de nobis. Quod infirmum est abjecisti, sed non quod pium. Charitas denique nunquam excidit: non obivisceris me in finem.

> (Now, God is charity, and therefore he who is united more closely to God is more full of charity. Truly, God is impassible, but not without compassion, since He is by definition one who pities and pardons. Therefore it follows that you too must feel pity, since you are united to one who pities. Even though you are far from grief and suffering you can still feel compassion. Your affections are not diminished but changed: you have not put off concern for us because you are clothed with God, because God himself is concerned for us. You are freed from what is worthless, not from what is good. For charity never falleth away, and therefore you will never forget me.[6])

[5] *Sermones in Cantica*, 5, 906C.　　[6] Ibid., loc. cit. 906D–907A.

235

Coda

In the same way Peter the Venerable envisages a relationship restored in the life of heaven through the love of God when he offers consolation in her loss to Heloise:

> Hunc, ergo, venerabilis et charissima in Domino soror, cui post carnalem copulam, tanto valdiore, quanto meliore, divinae charitatis vinculo adhaesisti, cum quo, et sub quo diu Domine deservisti, hunc, inquam, loco tui, vel ut te alteram in gremio suo confovet, et in adventu Domini, in voce archangeli, et in tuba Dei descendentis de caelo, tibi per ipsius gratiam restituendum reservat.

> (Venerable Sister, he to whom you were joined first in the flesh, and then by the stronger and more perfect bond of divine charity, he with whom and under whom you too have served the Saviour, is now sheltered in the bosom of Christ. Christ now protects him in your place, indeed, as a second you, and will restore him to you on that day when he returns from the heavens between the voice of the archangel and the sounding trumpet.[7])

Both St. Bernard and Peter the Venerable acknowledge the value and importance of the love of one human being for another.[8] Both see it as renewed and restored in heaven. But, for both, restoration can only take place through the love of God and in obedience to his will. It would be prevented by a weak and selfish clinging to 'the comforts of the flesh and the amenities of this present life'. This, as we have seen, is the position in which the Dreamer places himself, and it is to point this aspect of his error that the poet opens his poem with a treatment of the *topos* of the two treasures, that of earth and that of heaven. The poet also causes his Dreamer to accuse his destiny of robbing him of his treasure on earth; and it is, I believe, through the ideas which are associated with destiny that he elaborates another aspect of the Dreamer's failure: his lack of faith in and obedience to God's will. This, I think, is a theme which is of importance in other of his poems besides *Pearl*, and,

[7] *P.L.*, 179, 352.
[8] It is hardly necessary to point out that both have before them an ideal of *amicitia* rather than *amor*; the poet of *Pearl* was, obviously, not concerned with profane love.

by examining what he has to say elsewhere, we can define his thought with reasonable precision.

3

The *Pearl* poet uses the words *destiné*, *wyrd*, and *fortune* in his poem. In general he distinguishes between destiny (for which *wyrd* is usually a synonym) and fortune in accordance with the thought of Boethius, who was certainly the most influential writer on the subject. For Boethius *fortuna*, which would naturally be rendered *fortune* in Middle English—Chaucer does so in his translation—is the lesser power, further removed from the providence of God.[9] *Fatum*, on the other hand, was more closely related to the divine will, and was regarded as the executant of individual decrees of providence.[10] The word 'fate' was not available in Middle English to render this term, and Chaucer uses *destiné* for it. The *Pearl*-poet, although, as we shall see, he is, as always, ready to exploit the existence of different shades of meaning, agrees, on the whole, with this practice. For him *wyrd* and *destiné* are always very closely connected with the divine will, especially as it affects the life of the individual. His approach, in fact, to the problem of destiny is not a philosophical but a moral one, and in this he differs from Chaucer. He gives no general exposition of the subject and shows no interest in the kind of destinal forces—those inherent in the planets, for example—which often play a part in the development of the plot in Chaucer's poems.

Thus, in *Pearl*, *fortune* is used at ll. 98, 129, and 306 for the particular turn which events take in the world. No moral problem is posed by it, and it has no immediate reference to the working of God's will. At l. 306, for example, the 'fortune', the particular happening, which causes life to end is deliberately contrasted with the unalterable effect of God's promise to mankind:

'I halde þat iueler lyttel to prayse . . .
Þat leueʒ oure Lorde wolde make a lyʒe,

9 *De Consolatione Philosophiae*, II, especially pr. i–iv.
10 Ibid., IV, pr. vi.

Þat lelly hyȝte your lyf to rayse,
Þaȝ fortune dyd your flesch to dyȝe.' (301–6)

Destiny, on the other hand, at l. 758 means the fate prepared
for all mankind by God through the direct intervention of the
redemption—a sense it also bears in *Sir Gawain*. The maiden
apostrophises

'My makeleȝ Lambe þat al may bete,
. . . my dere destyne.' (757–8)

So, in *Gawain*, Christmas Day is the day on which 'dryȝtyn for
oure destyné to deȝe was borne' (996).

The Dreamer's individual destiny is referred to as *wyrd*. This
is God's providential decree as it affects him personally, and it
is a major part of the Maiden's arraignment of him that he is in
rebellion against it. At ll. 249–50 he speaks slightingly of *wyrd*
as a power which has done him harm, giving the word a sense
closer to fortune than to destiny:

'What wyrde hatȝ hyder my iuel vayned,
And don me in þis del and gret daunger?

The Maiden, in her reply takes up the term, but uses it un-
ambiguously in the sense of 'destiny'. Significantly she calls it
'þy wyrde', so that the Dreamer's 'what stroke of fortune' becomes '*your* destiny', 'God's will for you':

'And þou hatȝ called þy wyrde a þef,
Þat oȝt of noȝt hatȝ mad þe cler;
Þou blameȝ þe bote of þy meschef,
Þou art no kynde jueler.' (273–6)

With the phrase 'bote of þy meschef', she relates *wyrd* to the
idea of redemption, with which we have already seen destiny
associated in *Pearl*.

The idea of destiny is brought into even closer relation to the
idea of submission to God's will in *Patience*, in the prologue, in
which the poet speaks in his own person:

Thus Pouerte & Pacyence are nedes play-feres.
Syþen I am sette with hem samen, suffer me byhoues;
Þenne is me lyȝtloker hit lyke & her lotes prayse,
Þenne wyþer wyth & be wroth & þe werse haue.

Coda

З̇if me be dyзt a destyne due to haue,
What dowes me þe dedayn, oþer dispit make?
Oþer зif my lege Lorde lyst on lyue me to bidde,
Oþer to ryde oþer to renne, to rome in his ernde,
What grayþed me þe grychchyng bot grame more seche?

(45-53)

As in *Pearl*, l. 1205, the poet uses the word *lote* for the result of
the destinal decree, which, coming as it does from Poverty and
Patience, is thought of as essentially a part of the moral life. So,
in *Pearl*, the Dreamer's *lote* is a change of moral attitude, from
rebellious grief to a compassion which is not incompatible with
faith in God.

In *Sir Gawain* the terms *destiné* or *wyrd* are used a number of
times in relation to the end of his quest. When Gawain bids
farewell to Arthur he equates *destiné* with the pattern of
events which shapes his life, with particular reference to its end:

Of destinés derf and dere
What may mon do bot fonde? (564-5)

This, however, has something of the ambiguity of the Dreamer's
first reference to *wyrd*. It could mean no more than the events
brought about by fortune. When the poet describes Gawain's
troubled dreams during his stay at Sir Bertilak's castle, *destiné*
is more precisely used. Gawain is disturbed by

. . . mony þro þoзtes,
How þat destiné schulde þat day dele hym his wyrde. (1751-2)

Here destiny corresponds to *fatum*, its particular ordinance for
Gawain is called *wyrde*. In this sense destiny is, for this poet, so
closely linked to God's will that when Gawain speaks to Sir
Bertilak he substitutes 'God' for the 'destiny' of the earlier
passage: he asks for a guide,

. . . 'to teche as зe hyзt,
Þe gate to þe grene chapel, as God wyl me suffer
To dele on Nw зereз day þe dome of my wyrdes.' (1966-8)

After the final temptation by the servant, when he is urged to
turn back from the encounter, he once more expresses submission to his destiny in the form of God's will:

239

Coda

'Bot I wyl to þe chapel, for chaunce þat may falle,
And talk wyth þat ilk tulk þe tale þat me lyste,
Worþe hit wele oþer wo, as þe wyrde lyke3
　　　hit hafe
Þa3e he be a sturn knape
To sti3tel, and stad with staue,
Ful wel con dry3tyn schape
His seruaunte3 for to saue.'　(2132–9)

There is, however, a subtle difference in this speech. Gawain's submission is not that of entirely untroubled faith: he hopes that God will bring it out right.

Much has been written about Gawain's sin of recent years, but it seems to me that one important aspect of it has been forgotten: that is the failure in faith implied by his questioning of God's destiny for him.[11] When he accepts a talisman from the Lady in the form of her green girdle, he embarks on a course whose aim is to change the order of events; he is no longer prepared to accept, in perfect confidence, the trials that God sends as they come.

There is, I think, a subtle change in the words which Gawain uses to refer to his quest at the point at which he brings himself to accept the girdle. He reflects that:

Hit were a juel for the jopardé þat hym iugged were,
When he acheued to þe chapel his chek for to fech;
My3t he haf slypped to be vnslayn, þe sle3t were noble.

(1856–8)

Gawain here speaks of his quest in much less serious terms than usual. It is no longer his destiny, God's decree for him, but *jopardé*, a divided issue which fortune will decide,[12] and a *chek*, a piece of bad luck. Such things might be 'slipped out of' by a trick which, with unconscious irony he refers to as 'noble' (i.e.

---

[11] See J. A. Burrow, *A Reading of* Sir Gawain and the Green Knight, especially pp. 104 ff., and the same author's 'The Two Confession Scenes in *Sir Gawain and the Green Knight*', *M.P.*, LVII (1959), pp. 73 ff.; D. F. Hills, 'Gawain's Fault in *Sir Gawain and the Green Knight, R.E.S.*, N.S. (1963), pp. 124 ff.

[12] Cf. *Sir Gawain*, ll. 97–9, where *jopardé* is explicitly related to fortune.

'fine', as used in modern colloquial English). In the same way Jonah, horrified by the dangers of the quest on which God has sent him, hopes to slip away and get out of it:

> 'I wyl me sum oþer waye þat he ne wayte after;
> I schal tee into Tarce & tary þere a whyle,
> &, lyȝtly, when I am lest he letes me alone.'   (86–8)

The subject of *Patience* is Jonah's attemps to evade the destiny which God has ordained for him, and he laments his fault in terms which are very similar to those in which Gawain accuses himself. Jonah addresses God:

> 'Now prynce, of þy prophete pité þou haue!
> Þaȝ I be fol and fykel, and falce of my hert.'   (282–3)

Gawain says:

> 'Now I am fawty and falce, and ferde haf ben euer
> Of trecherye and vntrawþe: boþe bityde sorȝe
>   and care!'   (2382–4)

Gawain has been false to his pledged word, and to his host, and these are certainly faults. But I think that he also expresses regret for a failure to be true to his destiny, and to the God who was the only friend to accompany him on his quest.[13] In all three poems, *Pearl*, *Patience*, and *Gawain*, the attempt to evade a destiny which is seen as the expression of God's will is, it seems to me, an important theme, and, for this poet, the full and un-questioning acceptance of and co-operation with God's plan is an especially important aspect of the Christian moral life.[14]

The old controversy as to whether the *Pearl* was auto-biographical or allegorical cannot, I believe, now be seen as relevant to the real problems of the poem. Whatever the core of

---

[13] Gawain travelled through the realm of Logres with 'no gome bot God bi gate wyth to karp' (696).

[14] For a somewhat different view of the significance of destiny in *Sir Gawain*, see T. McAlindon, 'Magic, Fate and Providence in Medieval Narrative and *Sir Gawain and the Green Knight*', *R.E.S.*, N.S., XVI (1965), pp. 121 ff. The author associates destiny with a fatalism which is opposed to God's providence. I am not convinced that the poet uses the term in this sense in *Sir Gawain*, and he certainly does not do so in *Pearl* or in *Patience*.

personal experience on which the poet built may have been, there can be no doubt that he expresses his deepest feeling in the lines near the close:

> For I haf founden hym, boþe day and naȝte,
> A God, a Lorde, a frende ful fyin.

He is, essentially, a Christian poet, and, in all the works we associate with him he examines problems of Christian morality. In *Pearl*, with its wide theme of the meaning of mortality, its place in the divine scheme, and the moral problems it sets the individual who experiences its sorrows, he comes nearest to qualifying as a devotional poet. Like Langland, however, he never loses his firm grasp on actuality. He writes, above all, of the facts and difficulties of the Christian life as they present themselves to imperfect individuals—good men who yet sin seven times daily.[15] His poem begins with a generalization concerning the value of the pearl considered as an earthly treasure; it ends with the widest possible reference to the good life in the service of God which leads to the blessed life in heaven. The personal and particular issue is set aside, and, even though the limitations of the Dreamer are never wholly overcome, the poet himself ends on a note of Christian faith and affirmation.

[15] Cf. *Piers Plowman*, B. VIII, 28.

INDEX

Aelfric, 62 *n.*, 216 *n.*
Alain de Lille, 6, 108–9, 115–16
Albertus Magnus, 142, 149
Alchemy, 142, 154 *n.*, 156; gold, 164, 165; imagery of, 140, 151 *n.*; pearl—silver—moon, 143–5
Alexander Romances, 92 *ff.*; *Epistola ad Aristotelem*, 111 *n.*; *Iter ad Paradisum*, 93, 98, 105, 111 *n.*; *Wars of Alexander*, 98–9, 103, 104 *n.*, 113
'An Autumn Song', 63
Annot and Johon, 18 *n.*
Aristotle, 142 *n.*
Audelay, John, 16, 57–8
Augustine, St., 44, 62, 77, 79 *n.*, 149–50, 154 *n.*

Bacon, Francis, 24, 74, 153
Bacon, Roger, 143–4
Barbara, St., hymns to, 154, 166
Bede, 44
Bernard, St., of Clairvaux, 36 *n.*, 66, 150 *n.*; on grief, 234–5; uses gold as symbol, 165; uses pearl as symbol: of wisdom, 156; in doubtful homily, 149; uses *topos* of Seasons of Year, 49–51, 61; of treasure, 56–7; of garden, 37–41, 42
Bernadus Silvestris, 106 *n.*
Beryl, symbolical, 14
Bible, 6–7, 30, 35, 90, 141; Genesis, 27, 35–9, 42, 44–5, 52, 54, 75; Exodus, 42, 75 *n.*, 212 *n.*, 217; 1 Kings, 27; Job, 63 *n.*; Psalms, 72 *n.*, 108, 109, 151, 166, 190–2; Proverbs, 164 *n.*; Ecclesiastes, 55 *n.*; Song of Songs, 16–18, 19,

21, 26, 33–4, 35–9, 42, 43, 52, 55; Wisdom, 57, 61; Ecclesiasticus, 164 *n.*; Isaiah, 62, 63 *n.*, 91 *n.*, 166, 196; Lamentations, 165; Ezechiel, 55–6, 209; Malachai, 164; Matthew, 19, 75, 148, 155, 156 *n.*; Mark, 75; Luke, 75; John, 77, 81, 193; 1 Corinthians, 77, 81; Galatians, 232; Apocalypse, 7, 19–21, 28, 30, 35–9, 42, 51–2, 54–5, 134 *n.*, 201–2, 211 ff.
Bible-paraphrase, 6–7
Boehme, Jacob, 165 *n.*
Boethius, *de Consolatione Philosophiae*, 3–4, 6, 62, 115, 117, 118, 154 *n.*, 237
Bonaventura, St.: *Arbor Vitae*, 109–1; *Stimulus Amoris*, 57; *Vitis Mystica*, 69, 148, 155, 169–71; expanded version, 70
Browne, Sir Thomas, 154 *n.*
Brunetto Latini, 139 *n.*
Bruno Astensis, 70
Burnet, Thomas, 141–2

Calendar illustrations, 51–2
Catena Aurea, 155–6, 165
Carols: on the Root of Jesse, 80; of the Eucharist, 80–1
Chaucer, Geoffrey, 5–6, 237; *Book of the Duchess*, 210; *Canterbury Tales*, 78; *House of Fame*, 4, 5, 29, 96, 130; *Legend of Good Women*, 15; *Parlement of Foules*, 3, 4, 8–9, 10, 12, 68 *n.*; translation of Boethius, 4 *n.*, 115–16; *Troilus and Criseyde*, 13 *n.*
Chrysostom, St., 155–6
Cicero, 60 *n.*, 78–9

243

Index

Colours: of flowers, 68, 69–70; symbolical, 138, 162 ff.
Courtesy, 180, 189–90
Crown, as symbol, 58, 158, 161 ff., 165–69
Cursor Mundi, 27 *n.*, 49

Dante, 4, 6, 33, 84, 96, 106 *n.*, 117, 118, 138, 168, 169, 180 *n.*, 185; on Earthly Paradise, 91, 92, 103–4; imagery, 59, 65–6, 167; Maiden Guides, 120–32; River of Jewels, 107–8, 109, 110–11; pearls, 144, 150; technique compared to that of *Pearl*-poet, 208–10, 222–4
Daunger, 16–17, 186
De Die Judicii, 43–4, 47
Destiny, 176–7, 186, 237 ff.
Dew, 139, 142–4, 146
Decameron, 95
Destruction of Troy, 104 *n.*
Donne, John, 74, 78, 159
Douglas, Gavin, 61
Dreams, nature of, 28–30
Duke Huon of Burdeux, 101, 107, 115
Dunbar, William, 58, 81, 84
Dreamer: his rebellious will, 27, 30, 41, 177–8, 203; as a near-personification, 119–20, 134 ff., 198; in the landscape description, 96–7; his *iter ad paradisum*, 97–8; his sleep, 27, 29–30: his involvement in what he sees, 111; his relationship to the Pearl-Maiden, 118–19, 133; to the poet, 119–20, 134–6; to the symbolism, 157; his grief, 21, 233 ff.; his exclusion from heaven, 130, 206–7, 210–11; his awakening, 220 ff., 227 ff.

Earthly Paradise, 55, 84, 91 ff., 121, 158, 162, 176, 203, 205, 218

Ephraem St., the Syrian, 56, 141 *n.*, 147, 150, 151–2, 154 *n.*, 156, 157 *n.*, 166
Epiphanius, 151
Epistle to Diognetus, 35–6
Erber, 15–16, 31, 34–5, 52; *see also* Garden

Flower and Leaf, 15
Flower: imagery of, 58–9, 150, 161, 167; unfading, 62 ff., 149; violet, lily, and rose, 69; crocus, 69 *n.*; colours of, 33, 68, 69–70; golden, 171; of the virtues, 68 ff., 149; *see also* Rose

Garden: as *topos*, 31 ff.; biblical, 16 ff., 35 ff.; in relation to treasure, 54–9; Seasons of the Year in, 46–51; Garden of Love, 32, 34, 89–90, 93, 94, 113; *see also* Earthly Paradise, *Erber*
Gilgamesh, the Epic of, 100
Gold: as symbol, 161 ff., 171–2; as setting for pearls, 9–10; in alchemy, 145, 164, 165; in colour scheme of poem, 145, 162
Gregory of Tours, 111
Gregory, St., of Nyssa, 36, 43, 47, 68–9, 79
Gregory, St., the Great, 43, 63–4, 79, 82 *n.*, 149, 150, 154 *n.*, 233–4

Herbert, George, 58, 64, 82–3
Herrick, Robert, 67–8, 149 *n.*, 154
Hilton, Walter, 57, 76, 196 *n.*
Hugh of St. Victor, 149
Hymn of the Soul, Gnostic, 147, 166

'In a tabernacle of a toure', 17 *n.*
'In a valey of þis restles mind', 94
In rosa vernat lilium, 146

Jerome, St., 150
Jerusalem: Earthly, 184, 204, 206; Heavenly, 7, 54, 84, 91, 149,

244

Index

Index